Aircraft
Spotter's Guide

Aircraft
Spotter's Guide

VINTAGE WARBIRDS TO MODERN AIRLINERS

Robert Jackson

THUNDER BAY
P · R · E · S · S

San Diego, California

THUNDER BAY
P · R · E · S · S

Thunder Bay Press
An imprint of the Advantage Publishers Group
5880 Oberlin Drive, San Diego, CA 92121-4794
www.thunderbaybooks.com

Library of Congress Cataloging-in-Publication Data available upon request.

ISBN 1-59223-343-0

Editorial and design by
Amber Books Ltd
Bradley's Close
74–77 White Lion Street
London N1 9PF
United Kingdom
www.amberbooks.co.uk

Project Editor: James Bennett

Designer: Colin Hawes

Picture Research: James Hollingworth

Printed in Korea

1 2 3 4 5 09 08 07 06 05

Contents

Introduction

It is a fact that, after national sports such as soccer, it is the air display that draws the biggest crowds in the world's developed countries. Air shows have a magic all of their own, as crowds thrill to the thunder of modern combat jets like the F-15, F-16, Tornado and Harrier, and marvel at the vintage aircraft of a bygone era. Yet, without the benefit of a programme and a running commentary on the flying display, many air show enthusiasts who might easily identify a Harrier or an F-15 as it carries out its display in front of them might be hard put to identify such aircraft flying overhead outside of the air show context.

Such is the nature of modern aerodynamics that most aircraft designed to perform the same task end up looking alike. The differences between a Eurofighter Typhoon, France's Dassault Rafale and Sweden's Saab Gripen are subtle, and almost indistinguishable to the untrained eye; yet with even the minimum of recognition training the differences stand out immediately.

Proficiency in aircraft recognition comes only with regular, concentrated study – in other words, with experience. To start with, the secret is to see an individual aircraft type as a complete entity, adding on the subtle details once the whole aircraft is firmly fixed in the mind. For example, does the aircraft have a swept wing, a delta wing or a straight wing? What kind of engines, how many, and where are they positioned?

ABOVE: *A pair of Northrop Grumman A-10 Thunderbolt II attack aircraft. The A-10's large twin engines, seemingly 'bolted on' to the fuselage, are a key recognition feature.*

ABOVE: *A Boeing 777, the largest twin-jet airliner in service. Although civil airliners are a common sight, distinguishing different types is not always easy.*

The trick is not to try to assimilate too much detail at once. Choose a dozen or so aircraft which you think you are most likely to see and make yourself thoroughly familiar with them through the photos and silhouettes in this book. Then, once you know what to look for, and have the details firmly imprinted on your mind, move on to other types, and start to build your expertise. Gradually, you will find yourself making automatic comparisons between individual types as you become familiar with the characteristics of a growing number of aircraft.

Many readers, of course, will never see some of the aircraft featured in this guide. It all depends where you are, and when. But don't be taken by surprise. Nowadays, for example, Russian types are frequent visitors to western countries, so the F-15 Eagle you think you've just seen might turn out to be a Sukhoi Su-27 Flanker.

ABOVE: *A Sukhoi Su-27 Flanker of the Russian Knights display team.*

Robert Jackson

Aermacchi MB.326

One of the most important light attack and training aircraft to emerge during the Cold War era, the Aermacchi MB.326 first flew on 10 December 1957. Several variants have been produced during the aircraft's lengthy career, depending on the customer's requirements. The most noteworthy version was the MB.326K single-seater of 1970, which, although designed as an operational trainer, could also be used in a tactical support role. In its various guises the MB.326 has been used by the air forces of Argentina, Australia, Brazil, Dubai, Ghana, South Africa, Tunisia, Zaire and Zambia. In South African service the aircraft was known as the Impala, while the EMBRAER version was called the AT-26 Xavante.

ABOVE: *The South African-built MB.326 was known as the Impala.*

Specification

Crew: 2 **Powerplant:** *one 1814kg (4000lb) thrust Rolls-Royce Viper 632-42 turbojet* **Max speed:** *890km/h (553mph)* **Service ceiling:** *12,500m (41,000ft)* **Max range:** *1090km (680 miles)* **Wing span:** *10.85m (35ft 7in)* **Length:** *10.67m (35ft)* **Height:** *3.72m (12ft 2in)* **Weight:** *5895kg (13,000lb) loaded* **Armament:** *two 30mm (1.18in) DEFA cannon; up to 1814kg (4000lb) of external ordnance*

MAJOR VARIANTS
MB.326B: two-seat trainer
MB.326F: two-seat trainer
MB.326K: single-seat attack and training aircraft
EMB.326GB: two-seat light attack aircraft

RECOGNITION FEATURES
Low-mounted straight wing with tip tanks; single engine; wing root air intakes; square-cut tailfin with tailplane mounted on upper rear fuselage

Aermacchi MB.339

ABOVE: *The Aermacchi MB.339, a development of the MB.336.*

Specification (MB.339K)

Crew: *1* **Powerplant:** *one 2018kg (4450lb) thrust Piaggio-built RR Viper 680-43 turbojet* **Max speed:** *815km/h (508mph)* **Service ceiling:** *14,240m (46,700ft)* **Combat radius:** *371km (230 miles)* **Wing span:** *11.22m (36ft 10in)* **Length:** *11.24m (36ft 1in)* **Height:** *3.99m (13ft 1in)* **Weight:** *6350kg (14,000lb)* **Armament:** *two 30mm (1.18in) cannon; up to 1814kg (4000lb) of external ordnance*

MAJOR VARIANTS
MB.339A: trainer and close-support aircraft
MB.339AM: specialist anti-ship variant for Malaysia
MB.339CD: (FD) full digital version; fighter trainer

RECOGNITION FEATURES
Similar to MB.326, but with sharper nose section and raised rear seat in the trainer variants

The Aermacchi MB.339 was developed from the MB.326 to replace this aircraft and the Fiat G.91T in the advanced jet training and close-support roles, the new aircraft being produced in single-seat (MB.339K) and two-seat (MB.339A/B/C) configurations, like its predecessor. Customers for the two-seat trainer-attack version have included Argentina, Dubai, Eritrea, Ghana, Italy, Malaysia, Nigeria, Peru and the United Arab Emirates.

Aermacchi/Aeritalia/Embraer AMX

The AMX multi-role combat aircraft is the product of collaboration between the Italian companies Aeritalia and Aermacchi on the one hand, and the Brazilian EMBRAER company on the other, and is the result of a joint requirement formulated by both countries for a new lightweight tactical fighter-bomber. The first prototype AMX flew in May 1984. The aircraft entered service with the Italian Air Force in 1990, and deliveries to the Brazilian Air Force began a year later.

ABOVE: *The AMX was a joint venture between Italy and Brazil.*

Specification

Crew: *1* **Powerplant:** *one 5003kg (11,030lb) thrust Rolls-Royce Spey Mk 807 turbofan* **Max speed:** *1047km/h (651mph)* **Ceiling:** *13,000m (42,650ft)* **Combat radius:** *556km (345 miles)* **Wing span:** *8.87m (29ft 1in)* **Length:** *13.23m (43ft 5in)* **Height:** *4.55m (14ft 11in)* **Armament:** *one 20mm (0.79in) M61A1 cannon or two 30mm (1.18in) DEFA cannon; up to 3800kg (8377lb) of external ordnance; wingtip rails for AAMs*

MAJOR VARIANTS
AMX: single-seat fighter-bomber variant
AMX-T: two-seat trainer variant

RECOGNITION FEATURES
High-mounted swept wing; shoulder air intakes; swept tail surfaces; rather tubby appearance overall

Aerospatiale (Fouga) CM.170 Magister

ABOVE: *The last of 921 examples of the Magister was built in 1969.*

Specification (CM.170)

Crew: *2* **Powerplant:** *two 400kg (880lb) thrust Turboméca Marboré turbojets* **Max speed:** *650km/h (403mph)* **Service ceiling:** *11,000m (36,090ft)* **Max range:** *925km (575 miles)* **Wing span:** *11.40m (37ft 5in)* **Length:** *10.06m (33ft)* **Height:** *4.38m (14ft 4in)* **Weight:** *3200kg (7055lb) loaded* **Armament:** *two 7.5mm (0.29in) or 7.62mm (0.3in) machine guns; rocket projectiles or wire-guided missiles*

Famous as the former mount of the French Patrouille de France and the Belgian Diables Rouges aerobatic teams, the Aerospatiale (Fouga) CM.170 Magister first flew in 1951 and was one of the most successful jet trainers ever developed, seeing widespread service with the French and several other air forces. It was the first jet trainer to enter service anywhere in the world. In the light ground-attack role, the Magister distinguished itself in the Arab–Israeli war of 1967, carrying out devastating rocket attacks against Egyptian armour in Sinai. The CM.175 Zephyr was a version for the French Navy. The Magister remains operational with several minor air arms, and many are in private ownership.

MAJOR VARIANTS
CM.170 Magister: primary jet trainer
CM.175 Zephyr: navalized version
CM.170-3 Super Magister: light attack version

RECOGNITION FEATURES
'Butterfly' type tail; long wing with swept leading edges and straight trailing edges; tip tanks; long tandem cockpit; engine nacelles along sides of fuselage

Aero Vodochody L-29 Delfin

A two-seat basic and advanced trainer, capable of operating from grass, sand or waterlogged strips, the Aero L-29 Delfin (Dolphin) first flew in April 1959 and in 1961 was selected as standard training equipment for the Soviet Air Force, which took delivery of over 2000 units of the 3600 aircraft built. The type subsequently served with all the Warsaw Pact air forces and with many other air arms within the Soviet sphere of influence. The type first entered service in 1963 and remained in production for 11 years. In Soviet service, the L-29 had the NATO reporting name 'Maya'.

ABOVE: *An Aero Vodochody L-29 of the Slovak Air Force.*

Specification (L-29)

Crew: 2 **Powerplant:***one 890kg (1960lb) thrust Motorlet M701 VC-150 turbojet* **Max speed:** *655km/h (407mph)* **Service ceiling:** *11,000m (36,100ft)* **Range:** *640km (397 miles)* **Wing span:** *10.29m (33ft 8in)* **Length:** *10.81m (35ft 5in)* **Height:** *3.13m (10ft 3in)* **Weight:** *3280kg (7231lb) loaded* **Armament:** *none*

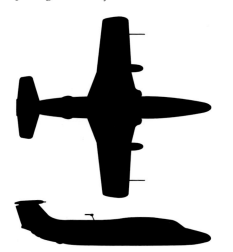

MAJOR VARIANTS
L-29: basic two-seat trainer version
L-29R: reconnaissance variant, fitted with wingtip tanks

RECOGNITION FEATURES
Mid-mounted straight wing, cranked at trailing-edge wing root; T-tail; tandem two-seat cockpit

Aero Volochody L-39 Albatros

ABOVE: *The L-39 Albatros has been modernized over the years.*

Specification (L-39C)

Crew: *2* **Powerplant:** *one 1720kg (3793lb) thrust Ivchenko AI-25TL turbofan* **Max speed:** *630km/h (391mph)* **Service ceiling:** *9000m (16,404ft)* **Max range:** *1750km (1087 miles)* **Wing span:** *9.46m (31ft)* **Length:** *12.32m (40ft 5in)* **Height:** *4.72m (15ft 5.5in)* **Weight:** *5270kg (11,618lb) loaded* **Armament:** *one 23mm (0.906in) twin-barrel cannon; four hardpoints for underwing stores*

Designed to succeed the L-29 as the standard jet trainer in service with the former Warsaw Pact, the L-39 Albatros first flew in November 1968 and evolved into the L-39C, the standard trainer variant. The fuselage is of semi-monocoque construction, built in two main portions. The front portion houses electrical and radio equipment in the nose and a pressurized crew compartment. The rear section, aft of the crew seats, contains the fuel tanks and engine bay, and can be quickly removed for rapid servicing. Fitted with a turbofan, the L-39 is much more powerful than its predecessor, permitting its use as a light attack aircraft. Both versions of the aircraft are in service with some 20 air arms.

MAJOR VARIANTS
L-39C: basic two-seat trainer
L-39ZO: single-seat light attack aircraft
L-39ZA: two-seat light attack aircraft
L-59: uprated two-seat version with longer pointed nose and uprated engine

RECOGNITION FEATURES
Low, straight wing with narrow tip tanks; single engine; shoulder-type intakes aft of cockpit; swept tailfin

AIDC Ching-Kuo

The Ching-Kuo, Taiwan's indigenous air defence fighter, was developed with much assistance from a number of US companies, including General Dynamics, and resembles a heavily modified F-16. The prototype flew for the first time on 28 May 1989 and was damaged in a landing accident some months later; the second prototype crashed in July 1989, killing its pilot. Despite these mishaps the programme went ahead and the first Ching-Kuo was delivered to the Chinese Nationalist Air Force in 1994, although the lifting of restrictions on the sale of US military aircraft to Taiwan (which was why the Ching-Kuo was developed in the first instance) resulted in the original requirement for 250 aircraft being reduced to 130.

ABOVE: *The AIDC Ching-Kuo resembles a heavily modified F-16.*

Specification

Crew: 1 **Powerplant:** *two 4291kg (9460lb) thrust ITEC TFE1042-70 turbofans* **Max speed:** *1275km/h (792mph)* **Service ceiling:** *16,760m (55,000ft)* **Max range:** *classified* **Wing span:** *9.00m (29ft 6in)* **Length:** *14.48m (47ft 6in)* **Height:** *4.70m (15ft 5in)* **Weight:** *9072kg (20,000lb) loaded* **Armament:** *one 20mm (0.79in) M61A1 Vulcan six-barrel rotary cannon; six external pylons for AAMs, AASMs, and various combinations of rocket or gun pods*

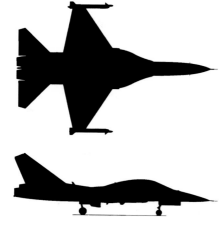

MAJOR VARIANTS
F-CK-1A: single-seat variant
F-CK-1B: two-seat variant

RECOGNITION FEATURES
Similar to F-16, but has twin engines and broader rear fuselage; oval air intakes

AIDC AT-3A Tzu Chung

ABOVE: *A pair of AIDC AT-3 trainers in flight.*

Specification (AT-3A)

Crew: *2* **Powerplant:** *two 1588kg (3500lb) thrust Garrett TFE731-1-2L turbofans* **Max speed:** *904km/h (562mph)* **Service ceiling:** *14,650m (48,065ft)* **Max range:** *2280km (1417 miles)* **Wing span:** *10.46m (34ft 3in)* **Length:** *12.90m (42ft 4in)* **Height:** *4.36m (14ft 3in)* **Weight:** *7940kg (17,505lb)* **Armament:** *provision for two 12.7mm (0.5in) guns in ventral pack; wingtip rails for AAMs; up to 2720kg (5998lb) of stores*

> MAJOR VARIANTS
> **AT-3A:** two-seat operational trainer; basic production version
> **AT-3B:** proposed close-support version

> RECOGNITION FEATURES
> Broad, low-mounted straight wing; twin engines close to fuselage centre-line; square intakes abreast of rear cockpit

The AT-3A twin-turbofan military trainer was developed by the Taiwanese Aero Industry Development Center in collaboration with Northrop. The first prototype flew in September 1980 and 60 production aircraft were built. The aircraft proved to be a very effective advanced trainer, being exceptionally agile and able to carry a wide variety of ordnance. A single-seat light attack version was built and flown in prototype form, but received no orders. A dedicated two-seat attack version has also been tested.

Atlas Cheetah

Resembling Israel's IAI Kfir, the Atlas Cheetah was a direct result of the UN arms embargo imposed on South Africa in 1977. Anxious to upgrade its fleet of ageing Mirage III aircraft, the SAAF embarked on a major modification programme that involved the rebuilding of some 50 per cent of the original Mirage airframe, incorporating modifications that included the addition of intake-mounted canards and dogtooth leading edges. Named Cheetah, the modified aircraft also featured new navigation and weapon systems. The first aircraft, modified from a Mirage IIID2, was declared operational in July 1987, and 30 aircraft were eventually returned to service in their new guise. Both single- and two-seat Mirages were modified. Many Cheetahs were retired and placed in storage when No 5 Squadron SAAF disbanded in 1992. All the remaining aircraft serve with No 2 Squadron. Although budget restrictions limit purchasing power,

ABOVE: *The Atlas Cheetah was a rebuilt version of the Mirage III.*

Specification

Crew: *1–2* **Powerplant:** *one 7200kg (15,873lb) thrust SNECMA Atar 9K-50 turbojet* **Max speed:** *2337km (1452mph)* **Service ceiling:** *17,000m (55,775ft)* **Combat radius:** *1200km (745 miles)* **Wing span:** *8.22m (26ft 11in)* **Length:** *15.40m (50ft 6in)* **Height:** *4.25m (13ft 11in)* **Weight:** *13,700kg (30,200lb) loaded* **Armament:** *two 30mm (1.18in) DEFA cannon; external stores*

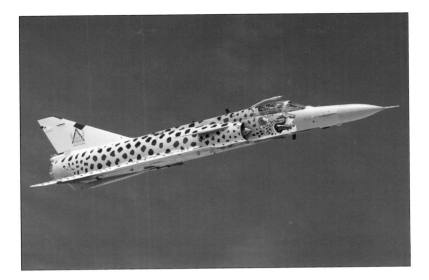

ABOVE: *A Cheetah decorated to celebrate the 75th anniversary of the South African Air Force.*

the SAAF wishes to buy 28 Saab J-39 Gripens and 24 British Aerospace Hawk 100 aircraft, the latter for use in the light attack role. Although the Cheetah will gradually give way to the Gripen, the two aircraft are likely to serve side-by-side for some years.

MAJOR VARIANTS
Cheetah C: single-seat strike aircraft
Cheetah D: trainer, pathfinder and all-weather attack aircraft
Cheetah E: single-seat strike aircraft

RECOGNITION FEATURES
Tailless delta; small canards (winglets) forward of main wing; air intakes below cockpit; nose forward of cockpit has 'drooped' appearance

Avioane IAR-93/SOKO J-22

The IAR-93A/J-22 strike fighter was developed by a joint Romanian–Yugoslav team. After 30 pre-series prototypes were built (15 in each country), series production began in Romania (with IAv Craiova, now Avioane) in 1979 and with Soko in Yugoslavia in 1980. Romanian IAR-93s and Yugoslav Oraos are generally similar. Romanian production models comprised the initial non-afterburning single- and two-seat IAR-93A (26 single-seat and 10 two-seaters built), and the single- and two-seat IAR-93B with afterburning engines (165 built). Soko built 75 J-22s at Mostar in Bosnia until 1992 when the factory was abandoned and the J-22 jigs were transferred to UTVA within the new Yugoslav state.

ABOVE: *The Avioane IAR-93/ SOKO J-22.*

Specification (IAR-93A)

Crew: *1* **Powerplant:** *two 2268kg (5000lb) thrust Turbomecanica (RR Viper) turbojets* **Max speed:** *1160km (721mph)* **Service ceiling:** *12,500m (41,000ft)* **Combat radius:** *530km (329 miles)* **Wing span:** *9.62m (31ft 6.75in)* **Length:** *14.90m (48ft)* **Height:** *4.45m (14ft 7.25in)* **Weight:** *10,100kg (22,267lb) loaded* **Armament:** *two 23mm (0.9in) cannon; up to 2800kg (6173lb) of external stores*

MAJOR VARIANTS
Orao 1: non-afterburning; relegated to reconnaissance duties as the IJ-22
NJ-22: production two-seat reconnaissance variant
J-22: production single-seater

RECOGNITION FEATURES
High-mounted swept wing with leading-edge extension at wing root; swept tail surfaces; air intakes situated just under cockpit

Boeing (Douglas) A-4 Skyhawk

ABOVE: *A Skyhawk armed with Bullpup air-to-surface missiles.*

Specification (A-4E)

Crew: *1* **Powerplant:** *one 3855kg (8500lb) thrust Pratt & Whitney J52-P-6 turbojet* **Max speed:** *1102km/h (685mph)* **Service ceiling:** *14,935m (49,000ft)* **Max range:** *1480km (920 miles)* **Wing span:** *8.38m (27ft 6in)* **Length:** *12.21m (40ft 1in)* **Height:** *4.62m (15ft 2in)* **Weight:** *11,113kg (24,500lb) loaded* **Armament:** *two 20mm (0.79in) cannon; 3719kg (8200lb) of external ordnance*

In 1950, the Douglas Aircraft Company began design studies of a turbojet-powered shipboard attack aircraft capable of delivering nuclear weapons and performing a wide variety of conventional attack missions. The result was the XA4D-1 Skyhawk, whose prototype flew on 22 June 1954. The first of 165 production A4D-1 Skyhawks were delivered to Attack Squadron VA-27 on 27 September 1956 and were replaced on the production line by the A4D-2, production of which ran to 542 examples. Plans had been made to re-engine the Skyhawk with the Pratt & Whitney J52-P-2 turbojet as the A4D-3, but this variant was cancelled and the next Skyhawk to appear was the A4D-2N, which had a lengthened nose to accommodate terrain-clearance radar. The variant also featured a rocket-boosted low-level ejection seat. Deliveries to the USN began in 1959 and ended in 1962 after 638 aircraft had been built. The 1000th production Skyhawk was delivered in February 1961, and in July that year another variant, the A4D-5 (later redesignated A-4E) made its appearance, with an uprated engine, greater offensive load and a 27 per cent range increase. Five hundred were built. The next variant, the A-4F, was an

Boeing (Douglas) A-4 Skyhawk (continued)

attack bomber with a J52-P-8A turbojet, heavily armoured cockpit and updated avionics housed in a 'hump' aft of the cockpit. Production was completed in 1968 after 146 machines had been built. The TA-4F was a tandem two-seat trainer, and the A-4G and TA-4G were similar aircraft supplied to the Royal Australian Navy. The A-4H was a variant supplied to Israel, the TA-4J was a simplified version of the TA-4F, the A-4K was a variant for the RNZAF, and the A-4M was developed for the USMC. During the 1960s the Skyhawk equipped some 40 USN and USMC squadrons, and saw extensive action during the Vietnam War. About 40 per cent of Israel's Skyhawks were lost during the Yom Kippur war of 1973, but this attrition was made good by the delivery of A-4N Skyhawk IIs, a light attack version. The A-4Y was an updated A-4M for the USMC. The 2900th Skyhawk was delivered in 1977. Skyhawks were supplied to Singapore and Argentina, which used them during the Falklands War of 1982.

ABOVE: *An A-4E Skyhawk of the US Navy being prepared for launch from a carrier deck.*

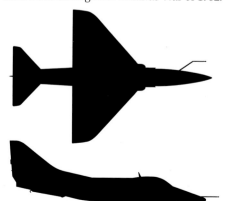

MAJOR VARIANTS
A4D-2: initial production version
A4D-2N: lengthened nose with terrain-clearance radar
A4D-5 (A-4E): uprated engine, increased offensive load
A-4F: attack bomber with armoured cockpit, improved avionics
A-4M: USMC version, later updated to **A-4Y**
A-4N Skyhawk II: light attack version

RECOGNITION FEATURES
Small aircraft of delta-wing configuration with tail; dorsal hump; single engine; air intakes above wing

Boeing B-52H Stratofortress

ABOVE: *A Boeing B-52 shows its raw power on take-off.*

Specification (B-52H)

Crew: *6* **Powerplant:** *eight 9231kg (17,000lb) thrust Pratt & Whitney TF-33P-3 turbofans* **Max speed:** *1014km/h (630mph)* **Service ceiling:** *(with normal load) 16,765m (55,000ft.)* **Max range:** *13,680km (8500 miles)* **Wing span:** *56.40m (185ft)* **Length:** *48.00m (157ft 7in)* **Height:** *14.75m (48ft 3in)* **Weight:** *empty 77,200kg (171,000lb); maximum take-off 204,120kg (450,000lb)* **Armament:** *maximum offensive payload 22,675kg (50,000lb); in the nuclear mission mode, can carry the Common Strategic Rotary Launcher (CSRL) in the aft bomb bay which can accommodate up to eight B83 or B61 nuclear weapons or eight AGM-86B or AGM-129A cruise missiles*

During the dangerous years of the 1960s, the mighty Boeing B-52 was the symbol of America's awesome striking power. Few could have imagined that it would still be in first-line service half a century after the prototype first flew. It has remained at the core of the West's airborne strategic bomber forces ever since it entered service with the USAF Strategic Air Command in 1955, its operational career spanning almost all of the Cold War era. In addition, the B-52 has experienced the full range of technical and operational changes that have proven necessary to enable the strategic bomber to survive in an intensely hostile environment, particularly one dominated by sophisticated surface-to-air missiles.

The B-52 was the product of a USAAF requirement, issued in April 1946, for a new jet heavy bomber to replace the Convair B-36 in Strategic Air Command. Two prototypes were ordered in September 1949, the YB-52 flying for the first time on 15 April 1952 powered by eight Pratt & Whitney J57-P-3 turbojets. On 2 October 1952 the XB-52 also made its first flight, both aircraft having the same powerplant. The two B-52 prototypes were followed by three B-52As, the first of which flew on 5 August 1954. The production B-52B

Boeing B-52H Stratofortress (continued)

was followed by the B-52C, 35 of which were built, and by the B-52D, the first of which flew on 14 May 1956; 170 were eventually built. Following the B-52E (100 built) and the B-52F (89) came the major production variant, the B-52G. The last version was the B-52H, which had been intended to carry the cancelled Skybolt air-launched

IRBM but was modified to carry four Hound Dogs instead. The B-52 was the mainstay of the West's airborne nuclear deterrent forces for three decades, but it was in a conventional role that it went to war, first over Vietnam, then in the Gulf War of 1991, and more latterly in support of operations in the former Yugoslavia, Afghanistan and again in Iraq. Aircraft remaining in service are the B-52H model.

ABOVE: *The Boeing B-52H has not been used in the nuclear role for which it was intended.*

MAJOR VARIANTS
B-52A: first production variant
B-52B: first operational variant; improved reconnaissance, navigation and bombing systems
B-52C: larger fuel capacity
B-52D: large-scale production version; dedicated bomber
B-52E: internal improvements; upgraded bombing and navigation avionics
B-52F: uprated engines
B-52G: most numerous type; reduced structural weight; new AN/ASG-15 fire-control system for gun turret; increased fuel capacity; improved range and avionics
B-52H: current variant; see main text

RECOGNITION FEATURES
High-mounted, swept wing; eight turbofan engines in paired under-wing pods; sensor blisters under nose; fuel tanks under outboard wing panels

Boeing (McDonnell Douglas)/BAe AV-8B Harrier II

ABOVE: *AV-8B Harrier IIs of the United States Marine Corps.*

Specification (AV-8B)

Crew: *1* **Powerplant:** *one 9866kg (21,750lb) thrust Rolls-Royce Mk 105 Pegasus vectored-thrust turbofan* **Max speed:** *1065km/h (661mph)* **Service ceiling:** *15,240m (50,000ft)* **Combat radius:** *277km (172 miles)* **Wing span:** *9.25m (30ft 4in)* **Length:** *14.36m (47ft 1in)* **Height:** *3.55m (11ft 7in)* **Weight:** *14,061kg (31,000lb) loaded* **Armament:** *two 25mm (0.98in) Aden cannon; external hardpoints with provision for up to 4082kg (9000lb) of stores (short take-off) or 3175kg (7000lb) of stores (vertical take-off); stores include AAMs, ASMs, free-fall or guided bombs, cluster bombs, dispenser weapons, napalm tanks, rocket launchers and ECM pods*

The V/STOL Harrier II traces its lineage back to 1957, when Hawker Siddeley Aircraft Ltd launched the concept of the P.1127 V/STOL aircraft. The P.1127 was designed around the Bristol BE.53 vectored-thrust engine, the forerunner of the Rolls-Royce Pegasus. A development of the P.1127, the Kestrel, was evaluated in 1965 by pilots of the RAF, US Air Force, US Navy, US Army and the Federal German Luftwaffe. The aircraft was selected by the RAF and, named Harrier GR.1, entered service on 1 April 1969. This, the world's first operational V/STOL aircraft, was followed by the GR.1A and GR.3, the latter having a nose-mounted laser rangefinder and and uprated Pegasus Mk 103 engine. In 1966 six Kestrels were sent to the USA for tri-service trials on land and sea under the designation XV-6A, and in 1969 the US Marine Corps received approval to buy the first of 102 aircraft, with the designation AV-8A. American funding had played a key role in the development of the Harrier, and it was Vietnam, a land war requiring timely, fixed-wing close air support, that finally influenced the purchase decision. However,

Boeing (McDonnell Douglas)/BAe AV-8B Harrier II (continued)

although the AV-8A Harrier was conceptually correct, the Marines needed an aircraft with more capacity. As a result, the AV-8B Harrier II programme was launched. Design leadership of the advanced Harrier rested with McDonnell Douglas, but it soon developed into a joint effort between that company and British

Aerospace, and it was to become the biggest Anglo-American collaborative aircraft programme ever. In RAF service, the Harrier II is designated GR.5 or GR.7, the latter having a night-attack capability; the GR.9 is an updated version with improved avionics. The AV-8B also serves with the naval air arms of Spain and Italy. The BAe Sea Harrier, developed specifically for the Royal Navy, first flew in December 1978 and the Sea Harrier FRS.1 played a significant part in the Falklands War four years later. It was followed into service by the FRS.2, with improved radar. The Sea Harrier is in service with the Indian Navy.

ABOVE: *The Harrier II is able to carry a significant weapons load, and has proved a valuable asset to US peacekeeping forces.*

MAJOR VARIANTS
GR.1: first service variant
GR.3: nose-mounted laser ranger finder; uprated Pegasus Mk 103 engine
AV-8A: first service version for USMC
AV-8B Harrier II: increased lift from new wing-nozzle-flap arrangement; general performance and combat improvements over AV-8A; in RAF service known as **GR.5**, **GR.7** or **GR.9**

RECOGNITION FEATURES
Shoulder-mounted swept wing with marked anhedral; cockpit mounted well forward on nose; very large air intakes; outrigger wheels protruding past wing trailing edge; fairing under extreme rear fuselage; anhedral on tailplane

Boeing (McDonnell Douglas) F-4 Phantom II

ABOVE: *An F-4 Phantom II of the Japanese Air Self-Defense Force.*

Specification (F-4E)

Crew: *2* **Powerplant:** *two 8119kg (17,900lb) thrust General Electric J79-GE-17 turbojets* **Max speed:** *2390km/h (1485mph)* **Service ceiling:** *18,900m (62,000ft)* **Max range:** *2817km (1750 miles)* **Wing span:** *11.70m (38ft 5in)* **Length:** *17.76m (58ft 3in)* **Height:** *4.96m (16ft 3in)* **Weight:** *26,308kg (58,000lb) loaded* **Armament:** *one 20mm (0.79in) M61A1 Vulcan cannon and four AIM-7 Sparrow AAMs; up to 5888kg (12,980lb) of ordnance on underwing pylons*

One of the most potent and versatile combat aircraft ever built, the McDonnell (later McDonnell Douglas) F-4 Phantom II stemmed from a 1954 project for an advanced naval fighter. The XF4H-1 prototype flew for the first time on 27 May 1958. Twenty-three development aircraft were procured, followed by 45 production machines for the US Navy. These were originally designated F4H-1F, but this was later changed to F-4A. A production order was quickly placed for a USAF variant; this was originally designated F-110A, but later changed to F-4C. Deliveries to the USAF began in 1963, 583 aircraft being built. The RF-4B and RF-4C were unarmed reconnaissance variants for the USMC and USAF, while the F-4D was basically an F-4C with improved systems and redesigned radome. The major production version was the F-4E, 913 of which were delivered to the USAF between October 1967 and December 1976. F-4E export orders totalled 558. The RF-4E was the tactical reconnaissance version. The F-4F (175 built) was a version for the Luftwaffe, intended

25

Boeing (McDonnell Douglas) F-4 Phantom II (continued)

primarily for the air superiority role but retaining multi-role capability, while the F-4G Wild Weasel was the F-4E modified for the suppression of enemy defence systems. The successor to the F-4B in USN/USMC service was the F-4J, which possessed greater ground-attack capability; the first of 522 production aircraft was delivered in June 1976. Versions for the Royal Navy and the RAF were designated F-4K and F-4M respectively. Israel received over 200 F-4Es between 1969 and 1976, many of these aircraft seeing considerable action during the Yom Kippur War of 1973. The Japanese Air Self-Defence Force equipped five squadrons with 140 Phantom F-4EJs, most of which were built under licence, and the RAAF leased 24 F-4Es in 1970. Phantoms were delivered to Spain, Greece and Turkey, so that by the mid-1970s several key NATO air forces were standardized on the type. Many remain in service.

ABOVE: *The F-4 Phantom II saw much action with the US Navy and Air Force during the Vietnam War.*

MAJOR VARIANTS
F-4C: first major USAF production version
RF-4B/C: unarmed reconnaissance versions
F-4D: improved systems and redesigned radome
F-4E: uprated engines; leading-edge wing slats; 20mm (0.79in) cannon
F-4F: air-superiority version for Luftwaffe
F-4G: 'Wild Weasel' anti-SAM variant

RECOGNITION FEATURES
Broad low-mounted swept wing with dihedral outer panels; marked anhedral on tailplane; tandem cockpit

Boeing (McDonnell Douglas) F-15 Eagle

ABOVE: *First flown in 1972, the F-15 Eagle was still the USAF's premier air superiority fighter three decades later.*

Specification (F-15E)

Crew: *2* **Powerplant:** *two 10,885kg (23,810lb) thrust Pratt & Whitney F100-PW-220 turbofans* **Max speed:** *2655km/h (1650mph)* **Service ceiling:** *30,500m (100,000ft)* **Max range:** *5745km (3570 miles) with conformal fuel tanks* **Wing span:** *13.05m (42ft 9in)* **Length:** *19.43m (63ft 9in)* **Height:** *5.63m (18ft 5in)* **Weight:** *36,741kg (81,000lb) loaded* **Armament:** *one 20mm (0.79in) M61A1 cannon; four AIM-7 or AIM-120 and four AIM-9 AAMs; many combinations of underwing ordnance*

In 1965 the United States Air Force and various aircraft companies in the USA began discussions on the feasibility of an aircraft and associated systems to replace the F-4 Phantom, and four years later it was announced that McDonnell Douglas had been selected as prime airframe contractor for the new aircraft, then designated FX. As the F-15A Eagle, it flew for the first time on 27 July 1972, and first deliveries of operational aircraft were made to the USAF in 1975. The tandem-seat F-15B was developed alongside the F-15A, and the main production version was the F-15C. The latter was built under licence in Japan as the F-15J. The F-15E Strike Eagle is a dedicated strike/attack variant and, while the F-15C established and maintained air superiority, the F-15E was at the forefront of precision bombing operations in the 1991 Gulf War. The F-15E was supplied to Israel as the F-15I and to Saudi Arabia as the F-15S. In all, the USAF took delivery of 1286 F-15s (all versions), Japan 171, Saudi Arabia 98 and Israel 56. F-15s saw much action in the 1991 Gulf War, and Israeli aircraft were in combat against the Syrian Air Force over the

Boeing (McDonnell Douglas) F-15 Eagle (continued)

Bekaa Valley in the 1980s. The F-15E Strike Eagle carries a two-man crew: the pilot and a back-seat weapons and defensive systems operator. The avionics suite is substantial, and to accommodate it one of the fuselage tanks has been reduced. More powerful engines have been fitted without the need for extensive airframe modifications. Strengthened airframe and landing gear allow a greater weapons load.

ABOVE: *USAF F-15C Eagles of the 57th Fighter Wing pictured at Nellis AFB, Nevada.*

MAJOR VARIANTS
F-15A: initial production version
F-15B: tandem-seat trainer
F-15C: main production version; single-seat air-superiority fighter
F-15D: two-seat version of F-15C
F-15E Strike Eagle: strike/attack variant

RECOGNITION FEATURES
High-mounted, broad swept wing; twin vertical fins; low-mounted broad tailplanes with twin jet pipes in between; raised cockpit canopy; sharply angled air intakes forward of wing leading edge

Boeing (McDonnell Douglas) F/A-18 Hornet

ABOVE: *An F/A-18 Hornet of Carrier Air Wing 9 operating from the USS* Nimitz.

Specification (F/A-18A)

Crew: *1* **Powerplant:** *two 7264kg (16,000lb) thrust General Electric F404-GE-400 turbofans* **Max speed:** *1912km/h (1183mph)* **Service ceiling:** *15,240m (50,000ft)* **Combat radius:** *1065km (662 miles)* **Wing span:** *11.43m (37ft 6in)* **Length:** *17.07m (56ft)* **Height:** *4.66m (15ft 3in)* **Weight:** *25,401kg (56,000lb) loaded* **Armament:** *one 20mm (0.79in) M61A1 Vulcan cannon; external hardpoints with provision for up to 7711kg (17,000lb) of stores*

While the F-14 replaced the Phantom in the naval air superiority role, the aircraft that replaced it in the tactical role (with both the USN and USMC) was the McDonnell Douglas F-18 Hornet. First flown on 18 November 1978, the prototype Hornet was followed by 11 development aircraft. The first production versions were the fighter/attack F/A-18A and the two-seat F/A-18B operational trainer; subsequent variants are the F/A-18C and F/A-18D, which have provision for AIM-120 AAMs and Maverick infra-red missiles, as well as an airborne self-protection jamming system. The aircraft also serves with the Canadian Armed Forces as the CF-188 (138 aircraft) and with six other foreign air forces: Australia, Finland, Kuwait, Malaysia, Spain and Switzerland. It is also the mount of the Blue Angels, the US Navy Aerobatic Team. The F/A-18 demonstrated its capabilities and versatility during Operation Desert Storm, shooting down enemy fighters and subsequently bombing enemy targets with the same aircraft on the same mission, and breaking all records for tactical aircraft in availability, reliability and maintainability. The newest models, the E and F Super Hornets, were rolled out at McDonnell Douglas on 17 September 1995.

Boeing (McDonnell Douglas) F/A-18 Hornet (continued)

The E is a single-seat while the F is a two-seater. The Super Hornet is highly capable across the full mission spectrum: air superiority, fighter escort, reconnaissance, aerial refuelling, close air support, air defence suppression and day/night precision strike. Compared to the original F/A-18 A–D models, Super Hornet has longer range, increased survivability/lethality and improved carrier suitability. The first operational cruise of the F/A-18E Super Hornet was with VFA-115 on board the USS *Abraham Lincoln* (CVN 72) on 24 July 2002, the aircraft seeing combat for the first time on 6 November that year when they participated in a strike on hostile targets in the 'no-fly' zone in Iraq.

ABOVE: *The F/A-18E Super Hornet, pictured here, is a greatly improved version first deployed operationally in 2002.*

MAJOR VARIANTS
F/A-18A: fighter/attack version
F/A-18B: two-seat operational trainer
F/A-18C and D: upgraded single-seat (C) and two-seat (D) variants, with improved avionics and weapons systems
F/A-18E and D Super Hornet: advanced single-seat (E) and two-seat (D) variants; improved range, manoeuvrability and combat performance

RECOGNITION FEATURES
High-mounted wing with sweep on leading edge only; leading-edge 'dog-tooth'; leading-edge wing root extensions; square intakes under wing; twin tailfins

Boeing (Rockwell) B-1B Lancer

ABOVE: *The B-1B has a formidable offensive capability.*

Specification (B-1B)

Crew: *4* **Powerplant:** *four 13,962kg (30,786lb) thrust General Electric F101-GE-102 turbofans*
Max speed: *1328km/h (825mph)*
Service ceiling: *15,240m (50,000ft)*
Max range: *12,000km (7455 miles)*
Wing span: *41.00m (136ft 8in)* spread **Length:** *44.81m (147ft)*
Height: *10.36m (34ft)* **Weight:** *216,634kg (477,000lb) loaded*
Armament: *up to 38,320kg (84,500lb) of Mk 82 or 10,974kg (24,200lb) of Mk 84 iron bombs in the conventional role; 24 SRAMs, 12 B-28 and B-43 or 24 B-61 and B-83 free-fall nuclear bombs; eight ALCMs*

Designed to replace the B-52 and FB-111 in the low-level penetration role, the variable-geometry B-1 prototype flew on 23 December 1974, and subsequent flight trials and evaluations progressed rapidly. On 21 April 1975 a SAC KC-135 tanker crew of the 22nd ARS conducted the first flight-refuelling trials with the new bomber, and on 19 September it was flown for the first time by an SAC pilot, Major George W. Larson of the 4200th Test and Evaluation Squadron at Edwards AFB. Major Larson handled the controls for about one-third of the six-and-a-half-hour flight. Trials continued throughout the following year, but in 1977 President Jimmy Carter cancelled the project. It was resurrected by President Ronald Reagan's administration in 1981 and trials quickly resumed. The operational designation of the supersonic bomber, 100 of which were to be built for SAC, was to be B-1B, the prototypes already built now being known as B-1As.

The first B-1B flew in October 1984 and was well ahead of schedule, deliveries to Strategic Air Command reaching a tempo of four per month in 1986. In April an aircraft from the 96th Bomb Wing completed a 21 hr 40 min

Boeing (Rockwell) B-1B Lancer (continued)

mission that involved five in-flight refuellings to maintain a high all-up weight, the aircraft flying at about 741km/h (460mph) and covering 15,148km (9407 miles). A good deal of so-called 'stealth' technology has been built into the B-1B, greatly enhancing its prospects of penetrating the most advanced enemy defences, and the type has seen action in recent conflicts.

ABOVE: *A B-1B Lancer with wings fully swept. The bomber can penetrate the most advanced air defences.*

MAJOR VARIANTS
B-1A: initial version; never saw production
B-1B: sole production version

RECOGNITION FEATURES
Variable geometry wings; four turbofan engines in podded pairs; long, slender fuselage, small canards under cockpit

BAe (English Electric/BAC) Canberra

ABOVE: *Canberra B (I) 58s of the Indian Air Force.*

The first prototype Canberra B.1 flew on 13 May 1949, and, after the nose was redesigned with a visual bombing station, the aircraft became the B.2, which entered service with No 101 Squadron of RAF Bomber Command in May 1951. A photo-reconnaissance version, the PR.3, was issued to No 540 Squadron in 1953; the PR.7 and PR.9 were two subsequent reconnaissance variants, and it is the PR.9 which is still flying today with the Royal Air Force. The Canberra was built under licence in the USA as the Martin B.57, and in Australia as the B.20 and T.21. India was a major export customer, while other Canberras were sold to Argentina, Chile, Ecuador, France, Peru, Rhodesia/Zimbabwe, South Africa, Sweden, Venezuela and West Germany.

Specification (Canberra PR.9)

Crew: 2 **Powerplant:** *two 4763kg (10,500lb) thrust Rolls-Royce Avon 206 turbojets* **Max speed:** *917km/h (570mph)* **Service ceiling:** *14,630m (48,000ft)* **Max range:** *4274km (2656 miles)* **Wing span:** *19.49m (63ft 11in)* **Length:** *20.32m (66ft 8in)* **Height:** *4.78m (15ft 8in)* **Weight:** *24,925kg (54,950lb) loaded* **Armament:** *none*

MAJOR VARIANTS
B.2: initial production version
PR.3: photo-reconnaissance version
PR.7: improved reconnaissance variant
PR.9: reconnaissance aircraft; has a different wing configuration
Martin B-57: licence-built US version

RECOGNITION FEATURES
Mid-mounted, broad, straight wing, outer panels tapered; twin turbojet engines; dihedral tailplane; cockpit offset to port

BAe (Hawker Siddeley) Hawk

LEFT: *Three BAe Hawks in formation, with an aircraft of the Red Arrows display team at the top and two tactical weapons trainers below.*

Designed as a Gnat and Hunter replacement in the advanced training and strike roles, the Hawker Siddeley Hawk prototype flew in August 1974. The Hawk Series 60 and Series 100 are two-seat export versions, while the Hawk 200 is a single-seat dedicated ground-attack variant. Hawks have been exported to some 20 countries, and a modified variant serves with the US Navy as the T-45A Goshawk. Hawks in RAF service also provide target facilities for front-line fighter units, having replaced the venerable Canberra in that role.

Specification (Hawk T.1A)

Crew: 2 **Powerplant:** *one 2359kg (5200lb) thrust Rolls-Royce/Turbomeca Adour Mk 151 turbofan* **Max speed:** *1038km/h (645mph)* **Service ceiling:** *15,240m (50,000ft)* **Endurance:** *4 hrs* **Wing span:** *9.39m (30ft 9in)* **Length:** *11.17m (36ft 7in)* **Height:** *3.99m (13ft 1in);* **Weight:** *empty 3647kg (8040lb); maximum take-off 7750kg (17,085lb)* **Armament:** *under-fuselage/wing hardpoints for up to 2567kg (5660lb) of stores*

MAJOR VARIANTS
Hawk T.Mk 1: original advanced jet trainer variant
Hawk T.Mk 1A: variant with provision for Sidewinder air-to-air missiles and other stores
Hawk 50/60/100: two-seat version with ground-attack capability
Hawk 200: single-seat ground-attack variant

RECOGNITION FEATURES
Hawk T.Mk 1A: low-mounted, swept wing; tandem cockpit; single engine with air intakes under cockpit; underwing hardpoints for stores

BAe/Boeing T-45 Goshawk

ABOVE: *A T-45 Goshawk on the flight deck of a US aircraft carrier.*

Specification (T-45A)

Crew: 2 **Powerplant:** *one 2507kg (5527lb) thrust Rolls-Royce F405-RR-401 turbofan* **Max speed:** *1038km/h (645mph)* **Service ceiling:** *12,962m (42,500ft)* **Max range:** *1288km (805 miles)* **Wing span:** *9.39m (30ft 10in)* **Length:** *11.98m (39ft 4in)* **Height:** *4.11m (13ft 6in)* **Weight:** *6075kg (13,500lb) loaded* **Armament:** *none*

The T-45A Goshawk, the US Navy version of the British Aerospace Hawk, first flew in April 1988 and is used for intermediate and advanced portions of the Navy/Marine Corps pilot training programme for jet carrier aviation and tactical strike missions. The T-45A replaced the T-2 Buckeye and TA-4 Skyhawk trainers with an integrated training system that includes operations and instrument fighter simulators, academics and training integration system. The T-45A, which became operational in 1991, contains an analogue design cockpit, while the new T-45C, first delivered in December 1997, is built around a new digital 'glass cockpit' design. Known as Cockpit 21, this is equipped with two monochrome 127mm (5in) multifunction displays, which provide navigation, weapons delivery, aircraft performance and communications data. Martin Baker Mk 14 NACES ejection seats are fitted. Primary contractor for the Goshawk in the USA is Boeing.

MAJOR VARIANTS
T-45A Goshawk: original trainer version
T-45C: new variant with digital cockpit

RECOGNITION FEATURES
Low-mounted swept wing; tandem cockpit; air intakes forward of wing root; fairing and arrester hook under rear fuselage

CAC J-7/F-7

Derived from the Soviet MiG-21, the Chengdu Aircraft Company (CAC) J-7/F-7 fighter has been constantly upgraded since it first flew in 1966, to the extent that it can be considered a different aircraft. It is expected to remain in service for the next 10–15 years until the next-generation light-weight multi-role fighter, the J-10, is deployed in significant numbers. To enhance the aircraft's operational capability a J-7FS version is being developed, which introduces beyond-visual-range (BVR) air combat capability to the J-7 family for the first time. A new fire-control radar is housed in a chin radome similar to that built into the Vought F-8 Cusader.

ABOVE: *The CAC J-7 was originally derived from the MiG-21.*

Specification (J-7I)

Crew: *1* **Powerplant:** *one 7507kg (16,535lb) thrust Chengdu Wopen-7BM turbojet* **Max speed:** *2229km/h (1385mph)* **Service ceiling:** *17,500m (57,400ft)* **Max range:** *1160km (721 miles) on internal fuel* **Wing span:** *7.15m (23ft 5in)* **Length:** *13.90m (45ft 9in)* **Height:** *4.10m (13ft 5in)* **Weight:** *10,400kg (22,925lb) loaded* **Armament:** *one 30mm (1.18in) cannon; four under-wing pylons with provision for 1500kg (3307lb) of stores*

MAJOR VARIANTS
J-7E: reduced sweep on the outer wing panels and an increased span
FF-7: two-seat operational trainer

RECOGNITION FEATURES
Small, mid-mounted delta wing; swept tail surfaces; nose intake with shock cone

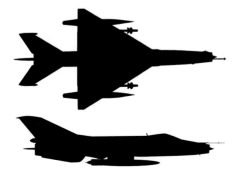

CASA C-101 Aviojet

ABOVE: *A C-101 Aviojet in service with the Spanish Air Force.*

Specification (C-101)

Crew: *2* **Powerplant:** *one 1588kg (3500lb) thrust Garrett AiResearch TFE731 turbofan* **Max speed:** *806km/h (501mph)* **Service ceiling:** *12,800m (42,000ft)* **Endurance:** *7 hrs* **Wing span:** *10.60m (34ft 9in)* **Length:** *12.50m (41ft)* **Height:** *4.25m (13ft 11in)* **Weight:** *4850kg (10,692lb)* **Armament:** *one 30mm (1.18in) DEFA cannon; up to 2000kg (4410lb) of external stores*

The C-101 was developed by the Spanish CASA company as a replacement for the Hispano HA.200 jet trainer. The type made its first flight in June 1977, and deliveries of the 92 production aircraft on order for the Spanish Air Force began in 1980. The C-101's weapons system was upgraded in the 1990s and the improved aircraft was the subject of limited export orders from Chile, Honduras and Jordan.

MAJOR VARIANTS
C-101: variant for Spanish Air Force
C-101BB: version for Chile and Honduras
C-101CC: variant for Chile (also known as **A/T-36**) and Jordan

RECOGNITION FEATURES
Low-mounted, straight wing; single engine with short tailpipe, exhausting under tailfin; air intakes below rear cockpit

Cessna A-37B Dragonfly

The Cessna A-37B light attack aircraft was developed from the T-37, the USAF's first purpose-built jet trainer, which appeared in 1954. The war in Vietnam produced a requirement for an attack version, and 39 T-37s were converted as A-37As in 1966, being fitted with eight underwing hardpoints, wingtip fuel tanks and more powerful engines. The A-37B version had a reinforced structure, increased fuel capacity and provision for in-flight refuelling. Over a 10-year period from 1967 577 A-37Bs were built, many being exported to Latin American countries.

ABOVE: *A veteran of the Vietnam war, the Cessna A-37B still serves with some Latin American air forces.*

Specification (A-37B)

Crew: *1* **Powerplant:** *two 1293kg (2850lb) General Electric J85-GE-17A turbojets* **Max speed:** *816km/h (507mph)* **Service ceiling:** *12,730m (41,765ft)* **Max range:** *740km (460 miles)* **Wing span:** *10.93m (35ft 10in)* **Length:** *8.62m (28ft 3in)* **Height:** *2.70m (8ft 10in)* **Weight:** *6350kg (14,000lb)* **Armament:** *one 7.62mm (0.3in) GAU-2 Minigun six-barrel machine gun; 2268kg (5000lb) of stores*

MAJOR VARIANTS
T-37: two-seat trainer
A-37: single-seat light attack aircraft

RECOGNITION FEATURES
Mid-mounted straight wing; fuselage broad at the nose, tapering towards the tail; engine air intakes in wing leading edge, exhaust pipes in trailing-edge root; square-cut tail with fairing between fin and upper fuselage

Dassault Super Etendard

ABOVE: *The Super Etendard, now approaching the end of its service.*

Specification

Crew: *1* **Powerplant:** *one 5000kg (11,023lb) thrust SNECMA Atar 8K-50 turbojet* **Max speed:** *1180km/h (733mph)* **Service ceiling:** *13,700m (44,950ft)* **Combat radius:** *850km (528 miles)* **Wing span:** *9.60m (31ft 6in)* **Length:** *14.31m (46ft 11in)* **Height:** *3.86m (12ft 8in)* **Weight:** *12,000kg (26,455lb) loaded* **Armament:** *two 30mm (1.18in) DEFA cannon; provision for up to 2100kg (4630lb) of external stores; two Exocet ASMs; MATRA Magic AAMs*

The Dassault Super Etendard, which first flew on 3 October 1975, was fitted with a SNECMA Atar 8K-50 turbojet and was intended for the low-level attack role, primarily against shipping. Fourteen Super Etendards were supplied to Argentina from 1981, and the five that had been delivered at the time of the Falklands War of May–June 1982, armed with the Exocet ASM, proved highly effective against British vessels, sinking the Type 42 destroyer HMS *Sheffield* and the container ship *Atlantic Conveyor*. French Navy Super Etendards serving on the carriers *Charles de Gaulle*, *Foch* and *Clemenceau* were to be replaced by the Dassault Rafale by 2010.

MAJOR VARIANTS
Super Etendard: low-level attack air-craft; anti-ship aircraft

---

RECOGNITION FEATURES
Mid-mounted swept wing; single engine with intakes below cockpit; swept tailfin, very broad at base

Dassault Mirage III

The Mirage III made its first flight on 17 November 1956. Small numbers of Mirage IIIAs and Bs were followed by the first major production version, the Mirage IIIC, in 1960. As the Mirage IIICJ, this variant was supplied to the Israeli Air Force and saw much action during the subsequent Arab–Israeli wars. Sixteen more aircraft of the IIIC series went to South Africa as the Mirage IIICZ. Over the next decade, these were supplemented by deliveries of Mirage IIIEZs, IIIDZs, IIID2Zs and IIIRZs. The SAAF also took three Mirage IIIBZ two-seaters. The Mirage IIIE was a long-range tactical strike variant. A version of the IIIE, the IIIO, was manufactured under licence in Australia. The Mirage IIIEE (the second E denoting *Espagne*) came on to the Spanish Air Force's inventory in 1970, while the Mirage IIIP version for Pakistan saw action in the 1971 conflict with India. Another version of the Mirage IIIE was the IIIS, delivered to the Swiss Air Force. In Argentine service, Mirages saw combat during the Falklands War in 1982.

ABOVE: *A Mirage III of the South African Air Force.*

Specification (Mirage IIIE)

Crew: *1* **Powerplant:** *one 6200kg (13,668lb) thrust SNECMA Atar 9C turbojet* **Max speed:** *1390km/h (883mph)* **Service ceiling:** *17,000m (55,755ft)* **Combat radius:** *1200km (745 miles)* **Wing span:** *8.22m (26ft 11in)* **Length:** *16.50m (56ft)* **Height:** *4.50m (14ft 9in)* **Weight:** *13,500kg (27,760lb) loaded* **Armament:** *two 30mm (1.18in) DEFA cannon; provision for up to 3000kg (6612lb) of external stores*

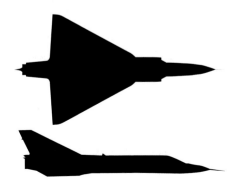

MAJOR VARIANTS
IIIB: two-seat operational trainer
IIIC: one-seat fighter bomber
IIID: two-seat trainer for IIIE
IIIE: one-seat long-range fighter bomber; uprated engine; improved radar and avionics
IIIR: one-seat reconnaissance version

RECOGNITION FEATURES
Tailless delta; Swiss and Brazilian variants have canards aft of air intakes

Dassault Mirage 5/50

ABOVE: *The Dassault Mirage 5/50 was developed for export.*

Specification (Mirage 5)

Crew: *1* **Powerplant:** *one 6200kg (13,668lb) thrust SNECMA Atar 9C turbojet* **Max speed:** *1912km/h (1188mph)* **Service ceiling:** *17,000m (55,773ft)* **Combat radius:** *650km (404 miles)* **Wing span:** *8.22m (26ft 11in)* **Length:** *15.55m (51ft)* **Height:** *4.50m (14ft 9in)* **Weight:** *13,700kg (30,203lb)* **Armament:** *two 30mm (1.18in) cannon; up to 4000kg (8818lb) of stores*

MAJOR VARIANTS
5A: single-seat attack aircraft
5D: two-seat trainer
5R: reconnaissance version
50: uprated engine; improved avionics
Kfir: subvariant built by Israel Aircraft Industries

RECOGNITION FEATURES
Tailless delta; swept tailfin; long nose; air intakes on fuselage sides at rear of cockpit; **Mirage 50** retains nose radome

The Mirage 5 and 50 were the final developments in the III series, and were mainly for export. The Mirage 5 was a fair-weather attack development of the Mirage III, with no all-weather capability, the reduction of electronic equipment permitting more fuel to be carried and reducing unit cost. It was sold to Abu Dhabi, Belgium, Colombia, Egypt, Gabon, Libya, Pakistan, Peru, Venezuela and Zaire. Israel also ordered the Mirage 5, but when France refused to deliver the aircraft it built a copy of it, the Kfir. Some were sold on to Argentina. The Mirage 50 has the higher-powered Atar 9K-50 engine. About 30 were completed, most of them conversions of earlier models, but the only countries to purchase this variant were Chile and Venezuela.

Dassault Mirage F.1

The Mirage F.1 single-seat strike fighter was developed as a private venture. Powered by a SNECMA Atar 09K, the prototype flew for the first time on 23 December 1966. The Mirage F.1 was the subject of large overseas export orders, notably to countries in the Middle East. Export Mirage F.1s were distinguished by a suffix letter, for example the F.1CK for Kuwait. The Mirage F.1AZ was a version for South Africa, which took delivery of both the attack-dedicated F.1AZ and the radar-equipped F.1CZ fighter. Both variants were involved in offensive actions in Angola and in anti-guerrilla strikes in the administered territory of South-West Africa before it gained independence as Namibia in 1989.

ABOVE: *A Mirage F.1 of the French* Armée de l'Air.

Specification (Dassault Mirage F.1AZ)

Crew: *1* **Powerplant:** *one 7200kg (15,873lb) thrust SNECMA Atar 9K-50 turbojet* **Max speed:** *2350km/h (1460mph)* **Service ceiling:** *20,000m (65,615ft)* **Max range:** *900km (560 miles)* **Wing span:** *8.40m (27ft 6in)* **Length:** *15.00m (49ft 2in)* **Height:** *4.50m (14ft 9in)* **Weight:** *15,200kg (33,510lb) loaded* **Armament:** *two 30mm (1.18in) 553 DEFA cannon; up to 6300kg (13,889lb) of ordnance*

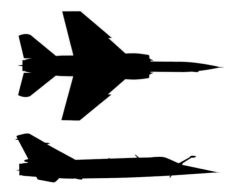

> **MAJOR VARIANTS**
> **F.1B:** two-seat trainer for F.1C
> **F.1C:** all-weather interceptor
> **F.1CR:** reconnaissance variant
> **F.1D:** two-seat trainer for F.1E
> **F.1E:** strike/attack variant

> **RECOGNITION FEATURES**
> High-mounted, broad swept wing; two fins under rear fuselage; tailplane mounted at base of fin; fixed refuelling probe forward of cockpit

Dassault Mirage 2000

The 2000C is the last of the Mirage line.

Specification (Dassault Mirage 2000C)

Crew: *1* **Powerplant:** *one 9700kg (21,384lb) thrust SNECMA M53-P2 turbofan* **Max speed:** *2338km/h (1453mph)* **Service ceiling:** *18,000m (59,055ft)* **Max range:** *1480km (920 miles)* **Wing span:** *9.13m (29ft 11in)* **Length:** *14.36m (47ft 1in)* **Height:** *5.20m (17ft)* **Weight:** *17,000kg (37,480lb) loaded* **Armament:** *two 30mm (1.18in) DEFA 554 cannon; provision for up to 6300kg (13,885lb) of external stores*

The Mirage 2000, the first of the Mirage family to take advantage of 'fly-by-wire' technology, was designed as an interceptor to replace the Mirage F.1. Five prototypes were built, of which four single-seat multirole models were funded by the French government and one two-seater by the manufacturers. The first single-seater flew for the first time at Istres on 10 March 1978, only 27 months after the programme was launched in December 1975. The second flew on 18 September 1978, the third on 26 April 1979 and the fourth on 12 May 1980. The two-seat version, the Mirage 2000B (the fifth prototype) flew on 11 October 1980, and like its single-seat counterparts achieved supersonic speed (between Mach 1.3 and 1.5) on its first flight.

The first production Mirage 2000C-1 made its first flight on schedule on 20 November 1982, and the first production two-seat Mirage 2000B flew on 7 October 1983. The first unit to become operational with the Mirage 2000C-1 was Escadre de Chasse 1/2 'Cigognes' at Dijon on 2 July 1984. The

Dassault Mirage 2000 (continued)

Mirage 2000N, first flown on 2 February 1983, was developed as a replacement for the Mirage IIIE and is armed with the ASMP medium-range nuclear missile. This version is strengthened for operations at 1110km/h (690mph) at 60m (200ft). Seventy-five production aircraft were delivered from 1987. Like its predecessors, the Mirage 2000 has been the subject of substantial export orders from Abu Dhabi, Egypt, Greece, India and Peru. In Indian Air Force service the aircraft, designated Mirage 2000H, is known as the Vajra (Thunderstreak).

ABOVE: *The Mirage 2000N is the nuclear-capable version of the fighter-bomber, carrying the ASMP medium-range missile.*

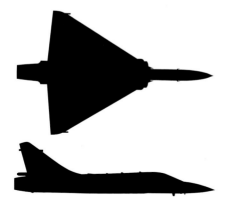

MAJOR VARIANTS
2000B: two-seat trainer
2000C: single-seat interceptor
2000-5: multi-role variant
2000N: attack version capable of delivering ASMP tactical nuclear missile

RECOGNITION FEATURES
Tailless delta configuration; small canards fitted aft of engine intakes; fixed flight refuelling probe forward of cockpit; two-seater variants have longer fuselage

Dassault Rafale

ABOVE: *The navalized Rafale-M is seen here during carrier trials.*

Specification (Rafale-C)

Crew: *1* **Powerplant:** *two 7450kg (16,424lb) thrust SNECMA M88-2 turbofans* **Max speed:** *2130km/h (1324mph)* **Service ceiling:** *classified* **Combat radius:** *1854km (1152 miles)* **Wing span:** *10.90m (35ft 9in)* **Length:** *15.30m (50ft 2in)* **Height:** *5.34m (17ft 6in)* **Weight:** *19,500kg (42,990lb) loaded* **Armament:** *one 30mm (1.18in) DEFA 791B cannon, up to 6000kg (13,228lb) of external stores*

France, originally a member of the European consortium that was set up to develop Eurofighter, decided to withdraw at an early stage and develop her own agile combat aircraft for the 21st century. The result was the Dassault Rafale (Squall). Known originally as the ACX (*Avion de Combat Experimental*), the main characteristics of the prototype were revealed in 1983, at which time it was announced that the type would replace the SEPECAT Jaguar in French Air Force service sometime in the 1990s, and that as the ACM (*Avion de Combat Marine*) it would form a major component of the air groups to be formed for deployment on the French Navy's new generation of nuclear-powered aircraft carriers.

Rafale is produced in three versions, the Rafale-C single-seat multi-role aircraft for the French Air Force, the two-seat Rafale-D, and the navalized Rafale-M. It incorporates digital fly-by-wire, relaxed stability and electronic cockpit with voice command. The fly-by-wire system embodies automatic self-protection functions to prevent the aircraft from exceeding its limits at all times. Functional re-configuration of the system in case of failure is also embodied, and provision

Dassault Rafale (continued)

has been made for the introduction of fibre optics to
enhance nuclear hardening.
Wide use of composites and
aluminium-lithium have resulted in a seven to eight per cent
weight saving.

In the strike role, Rafale can
carry one stand-off nuclear
bomb; in the interception role,
armament is up to eight AAMs
with either IR or active homing
and in the air-to-ground role, a typical load is
16 227kg (500lb) bombs, two AAMs and two
external fuel tanks. The aircraft is compatible
with the full NATO arsenal of air-to-air and
air-to-ground weaponry. Built-in armament
comprises one 30mm (1.18in) DEFA cannon in
the side of the starboard engine duct. The aircraft has a maximum level speed of 2.0M at
altitude and 1390km/h (864mph) at low level.
France, which has plans to have 140 Rafales in
air force service by 2015 (in 2002 orders stood
at 60 aircraft for the Air Force and 24 Rafale M
for the Navy) sees the aircraft as vital to the
defence of her territory.

ABOVE: *A single-seat Rafale-C in company with a two-seat Rafale-D, both in service with the Armée de l'Air.*

MAJOR VARIANTS
Rafale B: fully operational trainer
Rafale C: single-seat multi-role fighter
Rafale M: carrier-capable version for the French Navy

RECOGNITION FEATURES
Tailless delta configuration; moving canards on upper forward fuselage; twin engines with air intakes adjacent to lower fuselage below wing leading edge

Dassault/Dornier Alpha Jet

ABOVE: *The successful Alpha Jet has been widely exported.*

Specification (Alpha Jet A)

Crew: *1* **Powerplant:** *two 1350kg (2976lb) thrust Turbomeca Larzac 04 turbofans* **Max speed:** *927km/h (576mph)* **Service ceiling:** *14,000m (45,930ft)* **Max range:** *2780km (1727 miles)* **Wing span:** *9.11m (29ft 10in)* **Length:** *13.23m (43ft 5in)* **Height:** *4.19m (13ft 9in)* **Weight:** *8000kg (17,637lb) loaded* **Armament:** *one 27mm (1.06in) IWKA Mauser cannon; five hardpoints with provision for up to 2500kg (5511lb) of stores*

In 1968, France and Germany, both of whom had projects for an advanced jet trainer under study, decided to pool their resources and expertise. The result was the excellent Alpha Jet, which, like its rival the British Aerospace Hawk, offered near fighter performance and attack capability at a significant fraction of the cost of a full-spec combat aircraft. Early in the joint development programme, the Germans decided that they had no requirement for a training version of the Alpha Jet, but a need was identified for a light attack aircraft to replace the Fiat G-91R fleet. In February 1972 two prototypes each were ordered by France and Germany, and the type (the French-built version) flew for the first time on 26 October 1973. The first German-built Alpha Jet flew for the first time on 12 April 1978. As designated, the two principal versions were Alpha Jet A (A for *Appui*, or support) light attack aircraft, and the Alpha Jet E (E for *École*, or School) basic and advanced trainer. The E model, which also has a light attack capability, was produced for the French Air Force and a number

Dassault/Dornier Alpha Jet (continued)

of foreign customers, while deliveries of the A model to the Federal German Luftwaffe began in 1979, 175 being delivered between then and 1983. The German Alpha Jets were withdrawn from the combat role, and the last trainers were retired in 1997. The French Air Force took delivery of 176 aircraft between 1978 and 1985, and export customers included

ABOVE: *Alpha Jets of the Patrouille de France display team.*

Belgium, Cameroon, Cote d'Ivoire, Egypt, Morocco, Portugal, Qatar, Thailand and Togo. Some ex-Luftwaffe examples were acquired by the UK test agency, DERA. Dassault marketed advanced Alpha Jets under various names, such as the Alpha Jet NGEA (*Nouvelle Generation École et Attaque*) or Alpha Jet 2. Incorporating -C20 engines, a nose-mounted laser rangefinder and upgraded avionics and weapons capability, the NGEA found no customers as such, although the MS2s bought by Egypt and Cameroon were similar.

MAJOR VARIANTS
Alpha Jet A: light attack aircraft
Alpha Jet E: basic and advanced trainer
Alpha Jet NGEA: advanced version upgraded avionics and weapons systems

RECOGNITION FEATURES
High-mounted, swept wing with 'dogtooth' leading edges; twin engines with long nacelles positioned under wing; slender fuselage with very pointed nose

Eurofighter Typhoon

ABOVE: *An early prototype of the much delayed Eurofighter.*

Specification

Crew: *1/2* **Powerplant:** *two 9185kg (20,250lb) thrust Eurojet EJ.200 turbofans* **Max speed:** *2125km/h (1321mph)* **Service ceiling:** *18,300m (60,000ft)* **Combat radius:** *1389km (862 miles)* **Wing span:** *10.50m (34ft 5in)* **Length:** *14.50m (47ft 4in)* **Height:** *4.00m (13ft 1in)* **Weight:** *21,000kg (46,297lb) loaded* **Armament:** *one 23mm (0.9in) Mauser cannon; 13 fuselage hardpoints for a wide variety of ordnance including AMRAAM, ASRAAM, ASMs, anti-radar missiles, guided and unguided bombs*

In October 1981 the Royal Air Force Operational Requirements Branch began planning for a next-generation fighter to replace the F-4 Phantom in the air defence role, and the Jaguar in the offensive support role. The need crystallized in Air Staff Requirement (Air) 414, which specified a short-range highly agile air defence/offensive support aircraft. The European Fighter Aircraft programme was the project that met this requirement. An outline staff target for a common European fighter aircraft was issued in December 1983 by the air chiefs of staff of France, Germany, Italy, Spain and the UK; the initial feasibility study was completed in July 1984, but France withdrew from the project a year later. A definitive European Staff Requirement (Development), giving operational requirements in greater detail, was issued in September 1987, and the main engine and weapon system development contracts were signed in November 1988. To prove the necessary technology for EFA, a contract was awarded in May 1983 to British Aerospace for the development of an agile demonstrator –

Eurofighter Typhoon (continued)

not a prototype – under the heading Experimental Aircraft Programme, or EAP.

In December 1992, the project was re-launched as Eurofighter 2000, the planned in-service entry having now been delayed by three years. The first two Eurofighter proto- types flew in 1994, followed by several more. The original customer requirement was 250 each for the UK and Germany, 165 for Italy and 100 for Spain. The latter country announced a firm requirement for 87 in January 1994, while Germany and Italy revised their respective needs to 180 and 121, the German order to include at least 40 exam- ples of the fighter-bomber version. The UK's order was 232, with options on a further 65. Deliveries to the air forces of all four coun- tries were scheduled to begin in 2001, but not for the first time the schedule slipped. The RAF received its first aircraft on 30 June 2003. Eurofighter has broken into the export mar- ket with an Austrian order for 35 aircraft.

ABOVE: *The Eurofighter Typhoon can carry a substantial amount of air-to-air weaponry.*

RECOGNITION FEATURES
Tailless delta; movable canards on forward fuselage; square, ventral engine intakes; swept fin

MAJOR VARIANTS
Single-/two-seat instrumented production aircraft (IPA).

IAI Kfir

ABOVE: *The Kfir can be identified by its prominent canard foreplanes.*

Specification (Kfir C2)

Crew: *1* **Powerplant:** *one 8119kg (17,900lb) thrust General Electric J79-J1E turbojet* **Max speed:** *2445km/h (1520mph)* **Service ceiling:** *17,680m (58,000ft)* **Combat radius:** *346km (215 miles)* **Wing span:** *8.22m (26ft 11in)* **Length:** *15.65m (51ft 4in)* **Height:** *4.55m (14ft 11in)* **Weight:** *16,200kg (35,715lb) loaded* **Armament:** *one 30mm (1.81in) cannon; up to 5775kg (12,732lb) of ordnance*

The Israeli Aircraft Industries Kfir (Lion Cub) was developed after France imposed an embargo on the sale of combat aircraft to Israel, and was basically a Dassault Mirage III airframe married with a General Electric J79 turbojet. IAI produced 27 Kfir C1s, which equipped two squadrons of the Israeli Air Force; after replacement by the improved C2, all but two were leased to the US Navy for aggressor training as the F-21A. The Kfir C2, which appeared in 1976, was the major production version, 185 being delivered. Most C2s were upgraded to C7 standard between 1983 and 1985. The Kfir was exported to Colombia and Sri Lanka.

MAJOR VARIANTS
C1: first production version
C2: improved aerodynamics and upgraded avionics
TC2: trainer; lengthened nose
C7: uprated engine; avionics

RECOGNITION FEATURES
Tailless delta; prominent canards mounted on forward engine nacelles; square-cut fairing extending forward of swept tailfin; **C.2** has smaller canards

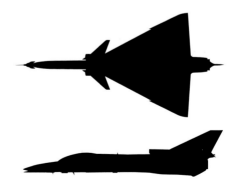

Kawasaki T-4

First flown in 1985, the Kawasaki T-4 was designed to replace the elderly Lockheed T-33 and Fuji T-1 as the Japanese Air Self-Defence Force's principal advanced jet trainer. It entered service with the JASDF in 1988, and since 1994 it has formed the equipment of the Blue Impulse, Japan's national aerobatic team. A total of 208 production T-4s have been built. The JASDF has no further requirement for new T-4s at present. Upgrades are planned, including fitting at least some T-4s with a modern 'glass cockpit' to provide training for the Mitsubishi F-2, and a full-authority digital engine control (FADEC) for the F3-IHI-30 turbofans.

ABOVE: *The T-4 has been in service with the JASDF since 1988.*

Specification

Crew: *2* **Powerplant:** *two 1660kg (3660lb) thrust Ishikawajima-Harima F3-IHI-30 turbofans* **Max speed:** *1038km/h (645mph)* **Service ceiling:** *10,980m (36,000ft)* **Max range:** *1668km (900 miles)* **Wing span:** *9.90m (32ft 7in)* **Length:** *13.00m (42ft 8in)* **Height:** *4.60m (15ft 1in)* **Weight:** *7500kg (16,535lb)* **Armament:** *practice bombs, rockets*

MAJOR VARIANTS
T-4: basic two-seat trainer

RECOGNITION FEATURES
Bears a strong resemblance to the Alpha Jet, but has a more robust appearance; high-mounted, swept wing; twin engines; rounded nose

Lockheed T-33

ABOVE: *A Lockheed T-33 of the Spanish Air Force.*

Specification (T-33)

Crew: *2* **Powerplant:** *one 2449kg (5400lb) thrust Allison J33-A-35 turbojet* **Max speed:** *879km/h (546mph)* **Service ceiling:** *14,630m (48,000ft)* **Endurance:** *3 hrs 7 mins* **Wing span:** *11.85m (38ft 10in)* **Length:** *11.51m (37ft 10in)* **Height:** *3.56m (11ft 8in)* **Weight:** *6551kg (14,442lb) loaded* **Armament:** *two 12.7mm (0.5in) machine guns*

The most widely used advanced trainer in the world, the Lockheed T-33 first flew in 1948 and was developed from the F-80C Shooting Star airframe. It is estimated that some 90 per cent of the West's military jet pilots, and also friendly foreign pilots from other nations, trained on the T-33 during the 1950s and 1960s. T-33 production totalled 5691 in the USA alone, and many others were built under licence in Canada and Japan. A version adapted to carry underwing offensive stores was offered to small air arms in the counter-insurgency role, and surprising numbers are in service with third world air arms. The Lockheed T-1A SeaStar was a modified version of the T-33 for the US Navy, featuring a raised instructor's seat and a larger canopy.

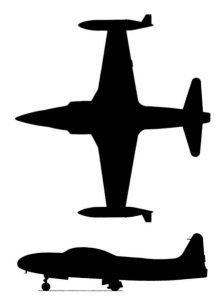

MAJOR VARIANTS
T-33: two-seat fighter
T-1A SeaStar: version for US Navy

RECOGNITION FEATURES
Low-mounted straight wing with large tip tanks; cheek intakes; tailplane mounted at base of fin; long-tandem clear-vision cockpit

Lockheed Martin F-16 Fighting Falcon

The F-16, designed and built by General Dynamics, had its origin in a USAF requirement of 1972 for a lightweight fighter and first flew on 2 February 1974. In service with many air arms other than the USAF, it carries an advanced GEC-Marconi HUDWACS (Head-Up Display and Weapon Aiming Computer System) in which target designation cues are shown on the head-up display as well as flight symbols. The HUDWAC computer is used to direct the weapons to the target, as designated on the HUD. The F-16 HUDWAC shows horizontal and vertical speed, altitude, heading, climb and roll bars and range-to-go information for flight reference. There are five ground-attack modes and four air-combat modes. In air combat, the 'snapshoot' mode lets the pilot aim at crossing targets by drawing a continuously computed impact line (CCIL) on the HUD. The lead-computing off sight (LCOS) mode follows a designated target; the dogfight mode combines snapshoot and LCOS, and there is also an air-to-air missile mode. The F-16's underwing hardpoints are stressed for manoeuvres up to 9g, enabling the F-16 to dogfight while still carrying

ABOVE: *A Lockheed Martin F-16D in flight.*

Specification (F-16C)

Crew: *1* **Powerplant:** *either one 10,800kg (23,770lb) Pratt & Whitney F100-PW-200 or one 13,150kg (28,984lb) thrust General Electric F110-GE-100 turbofan* **Max speed:** *2142km/h (1320mph)* **Service ceiling:** *15,240m (50,000ft)* **Combat radius:** *925km (525 miles)* **Wing span:** *9.45m (31ft)* **Length:** *15.09m (49ft 6in)* **Height:** *5.09m (16ft 8in)* **Weight:** *16,057kg (35,400lb)* **Armament:** *one 20mm (0.79in) General Electric M61A1 multi-barrelled cannon; seven external hardpoints for up to 9276kg (20,450lb) of ordnance*

ABOVE: *An F-16C of the USAF 52nd Fighter Wing, Spangdahlem Air Base, Germany.*

weaponry. The F-16B and -D are two-seat versions, while the F-16C, delivered from 1988, featured numerous improvements in avionics and was available with a choice of engine. F-16s have seen action in the Lebanon (with the Israeli Air Force), in the Gulf War and the Balkans. A typical stores load might include two wingtip-mounted Sidewinders, with four more on the outer underwing stations; a podded GPU-5/A 30mm (1.18in) cannon on the centreline; drop tanks on the inboard underwing and fuselage stations; a Pave Penny laser spot tracker pod along the starboard side of the nacelle; and bombs, ASMs and flare pods on the four inner underwing stations. The aircraft can carry advanced beyond-visual-range missiles, Maverick ASMs, HARM and Shrike anti-radar missiles, and a weapons dispenser carrying various types of sub-munitions including runway denial bombs, shaped-charge bomblets, anti-tank and area-denial mines. The F-16 has been constantly upgraded to extend its life well into the 21st century.

MAJOR VARIANTS
F-16A: single-seat fighter
F-16B: two-seat trainer
F-16C: upgraded variant featuring improved avionics, cockpit systems and fire-control
F-16D: two-seat version of F-16C

RECOGNITION FEATURES
Mid-mounted small delta wing; single engine; ventral air intake; slender nose with raised cockpit; two ventral fins under rear fuselage

Lockheed Martin F-117A Night Hawk

The amazing F-117A 'Stealth' aircraft began life in 1973 as a project called 'Have Blue', launched to study the feasibility of producing a combat aircraft with little or no radar and infrared signature. Two Experimental Stealth Tactical (XST) Have Blue research aircraft were built and flown in 1977 at Groom Lake, Nevada (Area 51). One was destroyed in an accident, but the other went on to complete the test programme successfully in 1979. The evaluation of the two Have Blue aircraft led to an order for 65 production F-117As. F-117As played a prominent part in the Gulf Wars of 1991 and 2003, making first strikes on high-priority targets; they were also used used in the Balkans and Afghanistan. The last of 59 F-117As was delivered in July 1990. Along with the Northrop Grumman B-2 Spirit 'stealth bomber', the Night Hawk is the USAF's primary attack weapon, the F-117 force being able to exert an influence on an air campaign that far outweighs its meagre size.

ABOVE: *The unmistakable shape of the F-117A Night Hawk.*

Specification

Crew: *1* **Powerplant:** *two 4899kg (10,800lb) thrust General Electric F404-GE-F1D2 turbofans* **Max speed:** *1100km/h (683mph)* **Service ceiling:** *20,000m (65,617ft)* **Max range:** *3080km (1913 miles)* **Wing span:** *13.20m (43ft 4in)* **Length:** *20.08m (65ft 11in)* **Height:** *3.78m (12ft 5in)* **Weight:** *23,814kg (52,500lb) loaded* **Armament:** *2268kg (5000lb) of stores on internal rotary dispenser, including AGM-88 HARM anti-radiation missile, AGM-65 Maverick ASM, BLU-109 laser-guided bombs; B61 free-fall nuclear bomb*

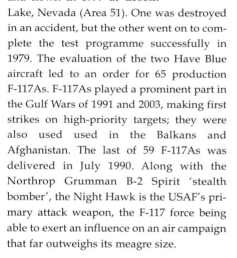

MAJOR VARIANTS
F-117A: production version

RECOGNITION FEATURES
Angular, many-faceted design; sharply swept low wing blended with fuselage; 'butterfly' tail; box-like air intakes above wing

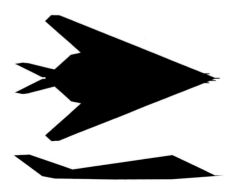

Lockheed Martin F-22 Raptor

ABOVE: *The distinctive profile of the Lockheed Martin F-22 Raptor.*

Specification

Crew: 1 **Powerplant:** *two 15,872kg (35,000lb) thrust Pratt & Whitney F119-P-100 turbofans* **Max speed:** *2335km/h (1450mph)* **Service ceiling:** *19,812m (65,000ft)* **Combat radius:** *1285km (800 miles)* **Wing span:** *13.10m (43ft)* **Length:** *19.55m (64ft 2in)* **Height:** *5.39m (17ft 8in)* **Weight:** *27,216kg (60,000lb) loaded* **Armament:** *AIM-9X and AMRAAM AAMS; GBU-32 Joint Direct Attack Munition and other advanced weapons*

The F-22 was developed in the 1980s and 90s to meet a specific threat, which at that time was presented by large numbers of highly agile Soviet combat aircraft. Its task was to engage them in their own airspace with beyond visual range weaponry. The aircraft thus combines many stealth features. Its air-to-air weapons, for example, are stored internally; three internal bays house advanced short-range, medium-range and beyond visual range air-to-air missiles. Following a combat assessment in 1993, it was decided to add a ground-attack capability, and the internal weapons bay can also accommodate 454kg (1000lb) GBU-32 precision guided missiles. The F-22 is designed for a high sortie rate, with a turn-around time of less than 20 minutes, and its avionics are highly integrated to provide rapid reaction, much of its survivability depending on the pilot's ability to locate a target early and kill it with a first shot. The USAF requirement is for 438 aircraft.

MAJOR VARIANTS
F-22A: production version

RECOGNITION FEATURES
Mid-mounted diamond-shaped wing with sharply swept leading edges; twin tails, angled outwards; box-type air intakes; raised single-seat cockpit; stealth features

Lockheed Martin X-35A/B

The X-35A Joint Strike Fighter project orig- inated in a 1980s requirement by the US Marine Corps and the Royal Navy for a replacement for the Sea Harrier and AV-8B by early in the 21st century. Various research studies were undertaken on both sides of the Atlantic into advanced short take-off, vertical landing (STOVL) concepts, the most promis- ing of which appeared to involve the use of a dedicated lift-fan located behind the cockpit. In November 1996 Boeing and Lockheed Martin were each awarded contracts to build

ABOVE: *The X-35 is a far from attractive aircraft, as is evident from this image of the demonstra- tion aircraft in flight.*

MAJOR VARIANTS
X-35A: CTOL version
X-35B: STVOL version
X-35C: carrier-capable version

LEFT: *Both versions of the X-35 are characterized by a deep, bulky fuselage and twin tailfins.*

RECOGNITION FEATURES
Deep, bulky fuselage; short wing with swept leading edge; large box- type air intakes angled forward and outward from fuselage; twin tailfins

ABOVE: *The X-35B has a dedicated lift fan behind the cockpit.*

Specification (X-35B)

Crew: *1* **Powerplant:** *one 19,026kg (42,000lb) thrust Pratt & Whitney F119-PW-611S turbofan and one 8154kg (18,000lb) thrust Rolls-Royce lift fan* **Max speed:** *Mach 1.4+* **Service ceiling:** *15,240m+ (50,000ft+)* **Combat radius:** *1000km (621 miles)* **Wing span:** *10.05m (33ft)* **Length:** *15.52m (50ft 11in)* **Height:** *not known* **Weight:** *22,680kg (50,000lb) loaded* **Armament:** *six AIM-120C AMRAAM or two AIM-120C AMRAAM and two 907kg (2000lb) JDAM in internal fusleage bay; provision for one 20mm (0.79in) M61A2 rotary cannon with 400 rounds in starboard wing root (USAF CTOL variant); provision for four underwing pylons with 2268kg (5000lb) of stores each*

two Concept Demonstrator Aircraft (CDA) – one conventional take-off and landing (CTOL) version and one short take-off, vertical landing (STOVL) version. The Boeing design received the designation X-32 and the Lockheed Martin design the designation X-35. For the two CDA aircraft, the designation X-35A was allocated to the CTOL version and X-35B to the STOVL version. The Lockheed Martin X-35A made its first flight on 24 October 2000 and the X-35B on 16 July 2001.

Lockheed Martin (General Dynamics) F-111C

Although the aircraft that once formed the very core of NATO's tactical nuclear strike force is now retired from USAF service, it continues to fly with the Royal Australian Air Force, and will continue to do so for some time. The prototype F-111A variable geometry interdictor/strike aircraft flew for the first time on 21 December 1964, the initial variant being followed into service by the F-111E, which featured modified air intakes to improve performance above 2.2M, and the F-111F, a fighter-bomber variant combining the best features of the F-111E and the FB-111A (the strategic bomber version) and fitted with the more powerful TF30-F-100 engines. The F-111C (24 built) was the strike version for the RAAF.

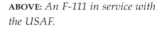

ABOVE: *An F-111 in service with the USAF.*

Specification (F-111C)

Crew: *2* **Powerplant:** *two 11,385kg (25,100lb) thrust Pratt & Whitney TF-30-P100 turbofans* **Max speed:** *2655km/h (1650mph)* **Service ceiling:** *17,985m (59,000ft)* **Max range:** *4707km (2925 miles)* **Wing span:** *19.20m (63ft) spread; 9.74m (32ft 11in) swept* **Length:** *22.40m (73ft 6in)* **Height:** *5.22m (17ft 1in)* **Weight:** *45,359kg (100,000lb) loaded* **Armament:** *one 20mm (0.79in) M61A-1 cannon; 14,290kg (31,000lb) ordnance*

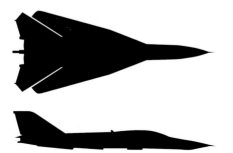

MAJOR VARIANTS
F-111A: initial production variant
F-111E: improved performance version
F-111F: fighter/bomber variant

RECOGNITION FEATURES
High-mounted, variable-geometry wing; broad tailfin and tailplanes; long, pointed nose; side-by-side cockpit

Mitsubishi F.1

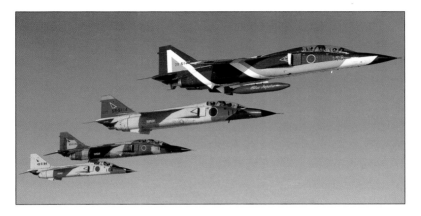

ABOVE: *A quartet of Mitsubishi F.1 strike fighters.*

Specification

Crew: *1* **Powerplant:** *two 3315kg (7308lb) thrust Ishikawajima-Harima TF40 IHI-801A turbojets* **Max speed:** *1708km/h (1061mph)* **Service ceiling:** *15,240m (50,000ft)* **Combat radius:** *350km (218 miles)* **Wing span:** *7.88m (25ft 10in)* **Length:** *17.86m (58ft 7in)* **Height:** *4.39m (14ft 4in)* **Weight:** *13,700kg (30,203lb) loaded* **Armament:** *one 20mm (0.79in) JM61 cannon; up to 2722kg (6000lb) of external stores*

MAJOR VARIANTS
F.1: single-seat attack aircraft

RECOGNITION FEATURES
Small, high-mounted swept wing; long fuselage with engine nacelles extending below the wing; dorsal hump behind cockpit; anhedral tailplane

Designed to replace the F-86 Sabre in the Japanese Air Self-Defence Force, the F.1 strike fighter was developed from the T.2 supersonic trainer. The second and third production T.2s were converted as prototypes, and the first of 77 F.1s was delivered in September 1977, the last delivery being made in March 1987. The Mitsubishi F.1, which flew for the first time in November 1976, was the first postwar jet combat aircraft designed in Japan.

Mitsubishi F.2

First flown in 1995, the Mitsubishi F.2 is a much modified version of the F-16 Falcon. It has a greater wing span than the Falcon, and more hardpoints, as well as a three-piece canopy. The requirement is for 83 single-seater and 47 two-seater aircraft. The F.2A is the single-seat version and the F.2B is the two-seat version. Flight trials of the prototypes were successfully completed by 1997, and the aircraft entered production in 1998. The first production aircraft was delivered to the Japanese Defence Agency in September 2000, and by the end of March 2001, 18 F.2 fighters had been delivered.

ABOVE: *The two-seat prototype Mitsubishi F.2 in flight.*

Specification (F.2A)

Crew: *1* **Powerplant:** *one 22,200kg (48,928lb) thrust General Electric F110-GE-129 turbofan* **Max speed:** *2142km/h (1320mph)* **Service ceiling:** *15,240m (50,000ft)* **Combat radius:** *925km (525 miles)* **Wing span:** *11.10m (36ft 6in)* **Length:** *15.50m (50ft 11in)* **Height:** *4.90m (16ft 3in)* **Weight:** *22,100kg (48,708lb) loaded* **Armament:** *one 20mm (0.79in) M61A1 cannon; 13 hardpoints for underwing stores, AAMs etc*

MAJOR VARIANTS
F.2A: single-seat version
F.2B: two-seat version

RECOGNITION FEATURES
Similar in appearance to F-16, but larger with three-piece canopy; air intake under fuselage; twin fins under rear fuselage

Nanchang Q-5 Fantan

ABOVE: *The Q-5 Fantan is a modified version of the MiG-19.*

Specification

Crew: *1* **Max speed:** *1190km/h (739mph)* **Service ceiling:** *16,000m (52,500ft)* **Combat radius:** *400km (249 miles)* **Wing span:** *9.68m (31ft 9in)* **Length:** *15.65m (51ft 4.25in)* **Height:** *4.33m (14ft 2.75in)* **Weight:** *11,830kg (26,080lb) loaded* **Armament:** *two 23mm (0.9in) cannon; up to 2000kg (4409lb) of external stores*

MAJOR VARIANTS
Q-5: single-seat attack aircraft
Q-5A: modified to carry nuclear weapons
Q-5B: doppler radar in nose; maritime mission capable
Q-5I: internal bomb bay removed to provide extra fuel storage; extra hardpoints; improved landing gear
Q-5IA: improved weapon sighting systems
Q-5K: advanced avionics version

RECOGNITION FEATURES
Mid-mounted, sharply swept wing; sharp nose; twin engines with intakes on fuselage sides; swept tail surfaces

---

The basic design of the Fantan close-support fighter was derived from the MiG-19, the Chinese type retaining the same wing and rear fuselage configuration as the Russian aircraft. The Fantan's two turbojets are mounted side-by-side in the fuselage, with an attack radar mounted in the nose. Service deliveries began in 1970, and by 1980 approximately 100 were in service. The Fantan has been exported to Pakistan, Bangladesh, Myanmar (Burma) and North Korea. The Nanchang factory, based in Kiangsi province, has also developed a modernized version of the basic model, equipped with an Alenia FIAR Pointer 2500 ranging radar for export, this variant being designated A-5M.

Northrop Grumman B-2 Spirit

Development of the Northrop Grumman B-2 was begun in 1978 and the USAF originally wanted 133 examples, but by 1991 successive budget cuts had reduced this to 21 aircraft. The prototype flew on 17 July 1989 and the first production B-2 was delivered to the 393rd Bomb Squadron of the 509th Bomb Wing at Whiteman AFB, Missouri, on 17 December 1993.

In designing the Advanced Technology Bomber (ATB), as the B-2 project was originally known, the Northrop Company decided on an all-wing configuration from the outset. The all-wing approach was selected because it promised to result in an exceptionally clean configuration for minimizing radar cross-section, including the elimination of vertical tail surfaces, with added benefits such as span-loading structural efficiency and high lift/drag ratio for efficient cruise. Outboard wing panels were added for longitudinal balance, to increase lift/drag ratio and to provide sufficient span for pitch, roll and yaw control. Leading-edge sweep was selected for balance and trans-sonic aerodynamics, while the overall planform was designed to have neutral longitudinal (pitch) static stability. The wing leading edge is so designed that air is channelled into the engine intakes from all

ABOVE: *A Northrop Grumman B-2 Spirit accompanied by two Lockheed Martin F-117 Night Hawk attack aircraft.*

Specification

Crew: *4* **Powerplant:** *four 8618kg (19,000lb) thrust General Electric F118-GE-110 turbofans* **Max speed:** *764km/h (475mph)* **Service ceiling:** *15,240m (50,000ft)* **Max range:** *11,675km (7255 miles)* **Wing span:** *52.43m (172ft)* **Length:** *21.03m (69ft)* **Height:** *5.18m (17ft)* **Weight:** *181,437kg (400,000lb) loaded* **Armament:** *16 AGM-129 Advanced Cruise Missiles, or various combinations of nuclear or conventional weapons*

ABOVE: *The B-2 is the culmination of Northrop's many years of experience with flying wing designs, dating back to World War II.*

directions, allowing the engines to operate at high power and zero airspeed. In trans-sonic cruise, air is slowed from supersonic speed before it enters the hidden compressor faces of the GE F118 engines. The B-2 lifts off at 260km/h (161mph), the speed independent of take-off weight. Normal operating speed is in the high subsonic range and maximum altitude around 15,240m (50,000ft). The aircraft is highly manoeuvrable, with fighter-like handling characteristics.

A stores management processor handles the B-2's 22,730kg (50,120lb) weapons load. A separate processor controls the Hughes APQ-181 synthetic-aperture radar and its input to the display processor. The Ku-band radar has 21 operational modes, including high-resolution ground mapping.

MAJOR VARIANTS
B-2: multi-role stealth bomber

RECOGNITION FEATURES
Tailless flying wing with a double-W trailing edge and numerous stealth features

Northrop Grumman EA-6B Prowler

The EA-6B Prowler electronic-warfare aircraft is a derivative of the A-6 Intruder carrier-based attack bomber, the last example being delivered to the US Navy in December 1969 (488 built). The last basic attack variant of the Intruder was the A-6E, which first flew in February 1970. Other conversions of the A-6A were the A-6C, with enhanced night attack capability, and the KA-6D flight refuelling tanker. The Intruder is no longer in service, but the Prowler has been upgraded and is expected to remain active until 2007.

ABOVE: *The EA-6B is a formidable electronic warfare aircraft.*

Specification

Crew: 4 **Powerplant:** *two 5074kg (11,200lb) thrust Pratt & Whitney J52-P-408 turbojets* **Max speed:** *1043km/h (648mph)* **Service ceiling:** *14,480m (47,500ft)* **Max range:** *1627km (1011 miles)* **Wing span:** *16.15m (53ft)* **Length:** *16.64m (64ft 7in)* **Height:** *4.93m (16ft 2in)* **Weight:** *27,397kg (60,400lb) loaded* **Armament:** *five external hardpoints for ECM pods*

MAJOR VARIANTS
EA-6A: ECM aircraft based on A-6 Intruder
EA-6B: upgraded avionics and ECM equipment

RECOGNITION FEATURES
Mid-mounted, broad swept wing; bulbous cockpit area; low-mounted tailplane; ECM fairing on top of tailfin; air intakes on lower forward fuselage

Northrop Grumman F-5 Tiger

ABOVE: *An F-5 armed with two Sidewinder air-to-air missiles.*

Specification (F-5A)

Crew: *1* **Powerplant:** *two 1850kg (4080lb) thrust General Electric J85-GE-13 turbojets* **Max speed:** *1487km/h (924mph)* **Service ceiling:** *15,390m (50,500ft)* **Combat radius:** *314km (195 miles)* **Wing span:** *7.70m (25ft 3in)* **Length:** *14.38m (47ft 2in)* **Height:** *4.01m (13ft 2in)* **Weight:** *9374kg (20,667lb) loaded* **Armament:** *two 20mm (0.79in) M39 cannon; up to 1996kg (4400lb) of external stores*

After nearly three years of intensive evaluation, it was announced on 25 April 1962 that the Northrop N156, which had first flown in 1959, had been selected as the new all-purpose fighter for supply to friendly nations under the Mutual Aid Pact, and the aircraft entered production as the F-5A Freedom Fighter, the first example flying in October 1963. The F-5A entered service with USAF Tactical Air Command in April 1964. An improved version, the F-5E Tiger II, was selected in November 1970 as a successor to the F-5A series. The RF-5E is a reconnaissance version, and the F-5B/F are two-seat trainers. The F-5 has had great export success and continues to serve with many air forces.

MAJOR VARIANTS
F-5A: single-seat fighter
F-5B: two-seat trainer
F-5E Tiger II: export version with improved performance and STOL capability

---

RECOGNITION FEATURES
Low-mounted stubby wing with swept leading edges; long nose; low cockpit; twin engines; single fin, low tailplane

Northrop Grumman F-14 Tomcat

Although its development history was beset by problems, the variable-geometry F-14 Tomcat emerged from them all to become one of the most formidable interceptors of all time, designed from the outset to establish complete air superiority in the vicinity of a carrier task force and also to attack tactical objectives as a secondary role. The prototype F-14A flew for the first time on 21 December 1970 and was followed by 11 development aircraft. The fighter completed carrier trials in the summer of 1972 and deliveries to the US Navy began in October that year, the Tomcat forming the interceptor element of a carrier air wing. The Tomcat can carry a mixture of ordnance up to a maximum of 6568kg (14,500lb), and is fitted with a variety of ECM equipment.

Development of the production F-14A was hampered by the loss of the prototype in December 1970, but 478 aircraft were supplied to the US Navy in total, and 80 more F-14As were exported to Iran in the later 1970s. The F-14B, a proposed version with Pratt & Whitney F401-P-400 turbofans, was

ABOVE: *The Tomcat continues to provide the US Navy with a powerful fleet defence capability.*

Specification (F-14A)

Crew: 2 **Powerplant:** *two 9480kg (20,900lb) thrust Pratt & Whitney TF30-P-412A turbofans* **Max speed:** *2517km/h (1564mph)* **Service ceiling:** *17,070m (56,000ft)* **Max range:** *1994km (1239 miles) with full weapons load* **Wing span:** *19.55m (64ft 1in) spread, 11.65m (38ft 2in) swept* **Length:** *19.10m (62ft 8in)* **Height:** *4.88m (16ft)* **Weight:** *empty 18,191kg (40,104lb); maximum take-off 33,724kg (74,349lb)* **Armament:** *one 20mm (0.79in) M61A1 Vulcan rotary cannon, plus a combination of AIM-7 Sparrow medium-range AAMs, AIM-9 short-range AAMs, and AIM-54 Phoenix long-range AAMs*

ABOVE: The variable-geometry F-14 Tomcat, with wings in fully swept configuration, displays its weapons load.

cancelled, but 32 F-14As were fitted with the General Electric F110-GE-400 and redesignated F-14B. The F-14D is an improved version with more powerful radar, enhanced avionics, a redesigned cockpit and a tactical jamming system; 37 aircraft were built from new and 18 converted from F-14As.

During the Gulf War of 1991 the type shared the air combat patrol task with the McDonnell Douglas F-15 Eagle. Since then the type has seen active service in the Balkans and Afghanistan, and for a second time in Iraq.

MAJOR VARIANTS
F-14A: initial production interceptor
F-14B: upgraded F-14A
F-14C: as F-14B but with ground-attack capability
F-14D: improved digital avionics; redesigned cockpit

RECOGNITION FEATURES
High-mounted, variable-geometry wing (gives the aircraft a delta appearance when fully swept); twin engines; twin tailfins; tandem cockpit

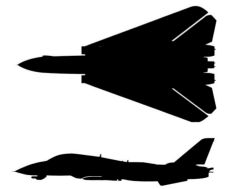

Northrop Grumman (Fairchild) A-10 Thunderbolt II

In December 1970 Fairchild Republic and Northrop were each selected to build a prototype of a new close-support aircraft for evaluation under the USAF's A-X programme, and in January 1973 it was announced that Fairchild Republic's contender, the YA-10, had been chosen. The aircraft made its first flight on

10 May 1972. The A-10 was designed to operate from short, unprepared strips less than 457m (1500ft) long. Deliveries began in March 1977 to the 354th Tactical Fighter Wing at Myrtle Beach, South Carolina. The tactics developed for use against Soviet armour were used to deadly effect in the 1991 Gulf War. The A-10 is expected to remain in service until 2028.

ABOVE: *The A-10 was one of NATO's key Cold War assets.*

Specification

Crew: *1* **Powerplant:** *two 4112kg (9065lb) thrust General Electric TF34-GE-100 turbofans* **Max speed:** *706km/h (438mph)* **Service ceiling:** *7625m (25,000ft)* **Combat radius:** *463km (250 miles)* **Wing span:** *17.53m (57ft 6in)* **Length:** *16.26m (53ft 4in)* **Height:** *4.47m (14ft 8in)* **Weight:** *22,680kg (50,000lb) loaded* **Armament:** *one 30mm (1.18in) GAU-8/A rotary cannon; 11 hardpoints for up to 7528kg (16,000lb) of ordnance*

MAJOR VARIANTS
A-10A: production ground-attack aircraft
A-10B: two-seat fully operational trainer

RECOGNITION FEATURES
Low-mounted, straight wing; twin turbofans mounted on upper rear fuselage; twin tailfins

Northrop Grumman (Vought) A-7 Corsair II

ABOVE: *A-7 Corsairs of the Portuguese Air Force.*

Specification (A-7H)

Crew: *1* **Powerplant:** *one 6465kg (14,250lb) thrust Allison TF41-1 (Rolls-Royce Spey) turbofan* **Max speed:** *1123km/h (698mph)* **Service ceiling:** *15,545m (51,000ft)* **Max range:** *1127km (700 miles)* **Wing span:** *11.80m (38ft 9in)* **Length:** *14.06m (46ft 1in)* **Height:** *4.90m (16ft)* **Weight:** *19,050kg (42,000lb) loaded* **Armament:** *one 20mm (0.79in) M61 Vulcan cannon; up to 6804kg (15,000lb) of external stores*

The prototype A-7 flew for the first time on 27 September 1965, and several versions were subsequently produced for the US Navy and USAF by the Vought Corporation, a subsidiary of Ling-Temco-Vought. The first attack variant was the A-7A, 199 A-7As being delivered before production switched to the A-7B, which had an uprated engine. The next variant was the A-7D tactical fighter for the USAF, which went into action in Vietnam in October 1972; 459 were built, many being allocated to Air National Guard units. The final major Corsair variant, the two-seat A-7K, served only with the ANG. The A-7 continues to serve as an attack aircraft with the Hellenic Air Force.

> MAJOR VARIANTS
> **A-7A:** first production aircraft
> **A-7B:** improved attack capability with uprated engine
> **A-7C:** improved avionics; Vulcan cannon
> **A-7D:** USAF tactical fighter-bomber
> **A-7E:** Improved US Navy variant; upgraded engine and FLIR

> RECOGNITION FEATURES
> High-mounted swept wing with anhedral; deep tubby fuselage with chin air intake, small radome above; cockpit in extreme nose; low-mounted tailplane, single fin

PAC/NAMC K-8 Karakorum

First flown in November 1990, the K-8 Karakorum is a joint venture between the China Nanchang Aircraft Manufacturing Company (CNAMC) and the Pakistan Aeronautical Complex (PAC) to develop a basic jet trainer with light attack capabilities. Originally identified as the Nanchang L-8, the name was changed to the K-8 Karakorum in reference to the mountain range straddling the Chinese–Pakistani border. Full-scale development began in 1987. Current Chinese procurement plans are unclear, but Pakistan reportedly plans to acquire 75 to 100 units.

ABOVE: *The K-8 Karakorum demonstrator aircraft.*

Specification

Crew: *2* **Powerplant:** *one 1630kg (3600lb) thrust Garrett TFE731-2A-2A turbofan* **Max speed:** *800km/h (497mph)* **Service ceiling:** *13,000m (42,640ft)* **Max range:** *1400km (870 miles)* **Wing span:** *9.60m (31ft 7in)* **Length:** *11.60m (38ft)* **Height:** *4.20m (13ft 9in)* **Weight:** *3630kg (8000lb)* **Armament:** *one ventral 23mm (0.9in) cannon; 943kg (2080lb) of stores on four underwing pylons*

MAJOR VARIANTS
K-8: two-seat trainer; light attack capable

RECOGNITION FEATURES
Low-mounted straight wing; tandem cockpit; single turbofan with intakes below rear of cockpit; low tailplane; ventral cannon

Panavia Tornado

ABOVE: *An electronic counter-measures (ECM) version of the Panavia Tornado in service with the German Luftwaffe.*

Specification (ADV)

Crew: 2 **Powerplant:** *two 7493kg (31,970lb) thrust Turbo-Union RB.199-34R Mk 104 turbofans* **Max speed:** *2337km/h (1452mph)* **Service ceiling:** *21,335m (70,000ft)* **Intercept radius:** *about 1853km (1000 miles)* **Wing span:** *13.91m (45ft 7in) spread; 8.60m (28ft 2in) swept* **Length:** *18.68m (61ft 3in)* **Height:** *5.95m (19ft 6in)* **Weight:** *27,987kg (61,700lb) loaded* **Armament:** *two 27mm (1.06in) IWKA-Mauser cannon; six external hardpoints with provision for up to 5806kg (12,800lb) of stores, including short- and medium-range AAMs, and drop tanks*

The first of nine Tornado IDS (Interdictor/Strike) prototypes flew in Germany on 14 August 1974, aircrews of the participating nations having been trained at RAF Cottesmore in the UK, which received the first Tornado GR.1s in July 1980. The RAF took delivery of 229 GR.1 strike aircraft, the Luftwaffe 212, the German Naval Air Arm 112, and the Italian Air Force 100. RAF and Italian Tornados saw action in the 1991 Gulf War. The Tornado GR.1A is a variant with a centreline reconnaissance pod, deliveries beginning in 1990, while the GR.4, armed with Sea Eagle anti-shipping missiles, is an anti-shipping version, the GR.4A being the tactical reconnaissance equivalent. Forty-eight Tornado IDS were delivered to Saudi Arabia.

In 1971, the UK Ministry of Defence issued Air Staff Target 395, which called for a minimum-change, minimum-cost, but effective interceptor to replace the British Aerospace Lightning and the F-4 Phantom in the air defence of the United Kingdom. Primary armament was to be the British Aerospace Dynamics XJ521 Sky Flash medium-range air-to-air missile, and the primary sensor a

Panavia Tornado (continued)

Marconi Avionics pulse-Doppler radar. The result was the Air Defence Variant (ADV) of the Tornado IDS aircraft. Three Tornado ADV prototypes were built. The first squadron, No 29, was formed at RAF Coningsby in May 1987 and was declared operational at the end of November. The aircraft eventually armed seven squadrons in addition to No 229 OCU (which became No 56 Reserve Squadron on 1 July 1992), 18 F.Mk 2s being followed by 155 F.Mk 3s, with improved radar. The Tornado ADV also serves with the air forces of Italy and Saudi Arabia.

ABOVE: *A pair of Tornado F.Mk 3s of the Royal Air Force.*

MAJOR VARIANTS
GR.1: production strike aircraft
GR.1A: centreline reconnaissance pod
GR.4: strike/anti-shipping variant
GR.4A: tactical reconnaissance version of GR.4
F.3: ADV variant

RECOGNITION FEATURES
High-mounted, variable-geometry wing; large tailfin and tailplane; tandem cockpit; twin engines with angled air intakes; **ADV** has longer fuselage than the **IDS**

RAC-MiG (Mikoyan) MiG-21

ABOVE: *The MiG-21 is one of the most successful combat aircraft ever designed.*

Specification
(MiG-21MF Fishbed-J)

Crew: *1* **Powerplant:** *one 7507kg (16,535lb) thrust Tumanskii R-25 turbojet* **Max speed:** *2229km/h (1385mph)* **Service ceiling:** *17,500m (57,400ft)* **Max range:** *1160km (721 miles) on internal fuel* **Wing span:** *7.15m (23ft 5in)* **Length:** *15.76m (51ft 8in)* **Height:** *4.10m (13ft 5in)* **Weight:** *10,400kg (22,925lb) loaded* **Armament:** *one 23mm (0.9in) GSh-23 twin-barrel cannon in pack under fuselage; four underwing pylons with provision for 1500kg (3307lb) of ordnance/stores*

The MiG-21 (NATO reporting name 'Fishbed') was a child of the Korean War, where Soviet air combat experience had identified a need for a light, single-seat target-defence interceptor with high supersonic manoeuvrability. Two prototypes were ordered, both appearing early in 1956; one, codenamed 'Faceplate', featured sharply swept wings and was not developed further. The intial production versions (Fishbed-A and -B) were built only in limited numbers, being short-range day fighters with a comparatively light armament of two 30mm (1.18in) NR-30 cannon, but the next variant, the MiG-21F Fishbed-C, carried two K-13 Atoll infrared homing AAMs, and had an uprated Tumansky R-11 turbojet as well as improved avionics. The MiG-21F was the first major production version; it entered service in 1960 and was progressively modified and updated over the years that followed. In the early 1970s the MiG-21 was virtually redesigned, re-emerging as the MiG-21B (Fishbed-L) multi-role air superiority fighter and ground-attack version. The Fishbed-N,

RAC-MiG (Mikoyan) MiG-21 (continued)

which appeared in 1971, introduced new advanced construction techniques, greater fuel capacity and updated avionics for multi-role air combat and ground attack. In its several versions the MiG-21 became the most widely used jet fighter in the world, being licence built in India, Czechoslovakia and China (where it was designated Shenyang F-8), and equipping some 25 Soviet-aligned air forces. A two-seat version, the MiG-21U, was given the NATO reporting name 'Mongol'.

ABOVE: *A MiG-21 in the colours of the Polish Air Force, a major operator of the type during the Cold War era.*

MAJOR VARIANTS
MiG 21F: first major production version
MiG-21PF: improved engine and radar; all-weather capability
MiG-21PFMA: ground-attack capable variant
MiG-21MF: new engine
MiG-21B (Fishbed-L): improved multi-role attack fighter
MiG-21RF: reconnaissance variant

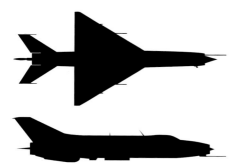

RECOGNITION FEATURES
Mid-mounted, small delta wing; broad, swept tailfin and swept tailplane; nose intake with cone

RAC-MiG (Mikoyan) MiG-23/27

ABOVE: *The multi-role MiG-27 'Flogger'.*

Specification (MiG-23MF)

Crew: *1* **Powerplant:** *one 10,000kg (22,046lb) thrust Tumanskii R-27F2M-300 turbojet* **Max speed:** *2445km/h (1520mph)* **Service ceiling:** *18,290m (60,000ft)* **Combat radius:** *966km (600 miles)* **Wing span:** *13.97m (45ft 10in) spread; 7.78m (25ft 6in) swept* **Length:** *16.71m (54ft 10in)* **Height:** *4.82m (15ft 9in)* **Weight:** *18,145kg (40,000lb)* **Armament:** *one 23mm (0.9in) GSh-23L cannon; AAMs*

The MiG-23 (NATO reporting name 'Flogger') entered service with the Frontal Aviation's attack units of the 16th Air Army in Germany in 1973. It is a variable-geometry fighter-bomber with wings sweeping from 23 to 71 degrees, and was the Soviet Air Force's first true multi-role combat aircraft. The MiG-23M Flogger-B was the first series production version and equipped all the major Warsaw Pact air forces; an export version for Libya and other Middle East air forces was designated MiG-23MS Flogger-E. The MiG-23UB Flogger-C was a two-seat combat-capable trainer, while the MiG-23BN/BM Flogger-F and -H were fighter-bomber versions for export. The MiG-27, which began to enter service in the late 1970s, was a dedicated battlefield support variant known to NATO as Flogger-D; the MiG-27D and -27K Flogger-J were improved versions, while the MiG-23P was a dedicated air defence variant. About 5000 MiG-23/27s were built, and in the 1990s the type was in service with 20 air forces.

MAJOR VARIANTS
MiG-23M: first series production variant
MiG-27D and K: improved battlefield support variants

RECOGNITION FEATURES
High-mounted, variable-geometry wing; air intakes on forward fuselage sides aft of cockpit; deep fairing between fin and fuselage; ventral fin under rear fuselage; broad tailplane

RAC-MiG (Mikoyan) MiG-25

The prototype MiG-25 (NATO reporting name 'Foxbat') was flown as early as 1964 and was apparently designed to counter the projected North American B-70 bomber, with its Mach 3.0 speed and ceiling of 21,350m (70,000ft). The cancellation of the B-70 left the Foxbat in search of a role; it entered service as an interceptor in 1970 with the designation MiG-25P (Foxbat-A), its role to counter all air targets in all weather conditions, by day or by night, and in dense hostile electronic warfare environments. The MiG-25P continues to serve in substantial numbers, and constitutes part of the Russian S-155P missile interceptor system. The aircraft is produced by RAC MiG (formerly MiG-MAPO), which is based in Moscow, and the Sokol Aircraft Manufacturing Plant Joint Stock Company, at Nizhni Novgorod in Russia. Variants of the MiG-25 are also in service in the Ukraine, Kazakhstan, Azerbaijan, India, Iraq, Algeria, Syria and Libya.

ABOVE: *One of the fastest aircraft ever built, the MiG-25 'Foxbat'.*

Specification (MiG-25P)

Crew: *1* **Powerplant:** *two 10,200kg (22,487lb) thrust Tumanskii R-15B-300 turbojets* **Max speed:** *2974km/h (1848mph)* **Service ceiling:** *24,383m (80,000ft)* **Combat radius:** *1130km (702 miles)* **Wing span:** *14.02m (45ft 11in)* **Length:** *23.82m (78ft 1in)* **Height:** *6.10m (20ft)* **Weight:** *37,425kg (82,508lb) loaded* **Armament:** *four underwing pylons for various combinations of air-to-air missile*

MAJOR VARIANTS
MiG-25R, MiG-25RB and MiG-25BM: derivatives of the MiG-25P
MiG-25R: reconnaissance variant
MiG-25RB: high-level bombing capability against area targets

RECOGNITION FEATURES
High-mounted, broad swept wing; twin tails; swept tailpane separated by jet pipes; pointed nose with low cockpit; long, sharply angled air intakes extending forward of wing

RAC-MiG (Mikoyan) MiG-29

ABOVE: *MiG-29 interceptors of the Indian Air Force, which operates the type in substantial numbers.*

Specification (MiG-29M)

Crew: *1* **Powerplant:** *two 9409kg (20,725lb) thrust Sarkisov RD-33K turbofans* **Max speed:** *2300km/h (1430mph)* **Service ceiling:** *17,000m (55,775ft)* **Max range:** *1500km (932 miles)* **Wing span:** *11.36m (37ft 3in)* **Length:** *17.32m (56ft 10in)* **Height:** *7.78m (25ft 6in)* **Weight:** *18,500kg (40,785lb) loaded* **Armament:** *one 30mm (1.18in) GSh-30 cannon; eight external hardpoints with provision for up to 4500kg (9921lb) of stores, including six AAMs rocket pods, bombs etc*

The appearance in the early 1980s of the MiG-29 (NATO reporting name 'Fulcrum'), with its superb agility and its apparent ability to perform combat manoeuvres that could not be matched by any aircraft in the West, came as an unpleasant surprise to NATO. Just as the F-15 was developed to counter the MiG-25 Foxbat and the MiG-23 Flogger, both of which were unveiled in the late 1960s, the MiG-29 Fulcrum and another Russian fighter, the Sukhoi Su-27 Flanker, were designed in response to the F-15 and its naval counterpart, the Grumman F-14 Tomcat. The Fulcrum-A became operational in 1985. The MiG-29K is a navalized version, the MiG-29M is a variant with advanced fly-by-wire systems, and the MiG-29UB is a two-seat operational trainer. The Indian Navy has plans to order 50 MiG-27K fighters to operate from the aircraft carrier *Admiral Gorshkov*, which is being acquired from Russia.

The Russian Air Force has begun upgrading 150 of its MiG-29 fighters, which will be designated MiG-29SMT. The upgrade comprises increased range and payload, a new

RAC-MiG (Mikoyan) MiG-29 (continued)

glass cockpit, new avionics and improved radar. The radar will be the Phazatron Zhuk (Beetle); it will be able to track 10 targets simultaneously out to a range of 245km (152 miles). A two-seater version, the MiG-29M2, has also been demonstrated, as has a super-manoeuvrable variant, the MiG-29OVT, with three-dimensional thrust-vectoring engine nozzles. About 600 MiG-29s serve with the Russian Air Force and the type also serves with 22 other air forces. All MiG-29 variants have the same configuration, combining a wing swept at 40 degrees with highly swept wing root extensions, underslung engines with wedge intakes and twin fins.

ABOVE: *The first prototype of a proposed new generation upgraded version designated MiG-29UBT.*

MAJOR VARIANTS
MiG-29: first production model
MiG-29S: improved fighter
MiG-29K: navalized version
MiG-29M: fly-by-wire systems; upgraded engine; revised tail/wing layout
MiG-SMT: improved performance, cockpit features and avionics
MiG-OVT: three-dimensional thrust-vectoring engine nozzles

RECOGNITION FEATURES
Broad, swept wing; swept wing root extensions; engine nacelles extending under fuselage, with angled air intakes; twin tailfins; swept tailplane separated by twin jet pipe nozzles; raised cockpit on slender forward fuselage

RAC-MiG (Mikoyan) MiG-31

ABOVE: *The MiG-31 was developed from the MiG-25.*

Specification

Crew: *2* **Powerplant:** *two 15,500kg (34,171lb) thrust Soloviev D-30F6 turbofans* **Max speed:** *3000km/h (1865mph)* **Service ceiling:** *20,600m (67,600ft)* **Combat radius:** *1400km (840 miles) with weapons load* **Wing span:** *13.46m (44ft 2in)* **Length:** *22.68m (74ft 5in)* **Height:** *6.15m (20ft 2in)* **Weight:** *46,200kg (101,850lb) loaded* **Armament:** *multiple AAM configurations*

Just as the MiG-29 and the Su-27/37 were developed to take on the air superiority role, the MiG-31 (NATO reporting name 'Foxhound'), a greatly developed version of the MiG-25, was initiated to counter the threat to the former Soviet Union from B-52s and B-1s carrying air-launched cruise missiles. The aircraft is a two-seat, all-weather, all-altitude interceptor designed to be guided automatically to its targets and to engage them under ground control. In a typical mission profile, an interception would be made by a flight of four aircraft, the leader being linked to the AK-RLDN ground radar guidance network and the other three linked to the leader by APD-518 digital datalink.

MAJOR VARIANTS
MiG-31B: upgraded interceptor
MiG-31D: upgraded interceptor/ anti-satellite variant
MiG-31M: heavily improved interceptor; increased weapons capability; ESM pods

---

RECOGNITION FEATURES
Broadly similar to **MiG-29 Foxbat**, but with two-seat cockpit. Jet pipes extend aft of tail unit; small twin fins under rear fuselage

RAC-MiG MFI

The RAC-MiG (formerly MiG-MAPO) Multi-role Front-Line Fighter (MFI – *Mnogofunksionalni Frontovoi Istrebiel*) was unveiled publicly on 12 January 1999. The first prototype was delivered early in 1994. The RAC-MiG enterprise claims the new fighter would be able to outperform the F-22 Raptor, the most advanced US air-superiority fighter. The future of the aircraft is uncertain because of shortage of funds.

ABOVE: *The MFI could be Russia's answer to the F-22 Raptor.*

Specification

Crew: *1* **Powerplant:** *two 17,821kg (39,340lb) thrust Lyulka AL-41F vectored-thrust turbofans* **Max speed:** *2,448km/h+ (1521mph+)* **Service ceiling:** *not known* **Max range:** *not known* **Wing span:** *15.00m (49ft 3in)* **Length:** *19.00m (62ft 4in)* **Height:** *6.00m (19ft 8in)* **Weight:** *19,973kg (44,092lb) loaded (approx)* **Armament:** *not known*

MAJOR VARIANTS
MFI: multi-role frontline fighter

RECOGNITION FEATURES
Delta wing; large canards on forward fuselage; twin tailfins; large square air intake under fuselage

Saab 105

ABOVE: *The Saab 105 has served the Swedish Air Force for decades.*

Specification

Crew: *2* **Powerplant:** *two 743kg (1637lb) thrust Turbomeca Aubisque turbojets* **Max speed:** *750km/h (466mph)* **Service ceiling:** *12,000m (39,360ft)* **Max range:** *1900km (1180 miles)* **Wing span:** *9.50m (31ft 2in)* **Length:** *10.80m (35ft 4in)* **Height:** *2.70m (8ft 9in)* **Weight:** *4050kg (8926lb) loaded* **Armament:** *one podded 30mm (1.18in) Aden gun under each wing, or a total of 12 135mm (5.31in) ground-attack rockets*

The Saab 105 was initiated as a private venture to meet a Swedish Air Force requirement for a jet trainer to replace the de Havilland Vampire T.11 in use during the 1950s. The first prototype flew in 1963 and deliveries began in 1966. Starting in 1970, 46 Sk 60As (the 105's designation) were converted into Sk 60B standard, giving them three hardpoints beneath each wing enabling them to operate in the light attack role. Thirty Sk 60As were also modified to Sk 60C standard. These had the same wing and weapon modifications as on Sk 60B. A reconnaissance camera was also fitted in the nose. The Saab 105 is also used by Austria, the latter operating 40 aircraft with more powerful General Electric J85 engines. Swedish Sk 60s are being upgraded, and are expected to serve until 2015.

> **MAJOR VARIANTS**
> **Sk 60A:** initial production version
> **Sk 60B:** light attack variant
> **Sk 60C:** reconnaissance camera fitted in nose
> **Sk 60D:** trainer

> **RECOGNITION FEATURES**
> High-mounted, slightly swept wing; side-by-side cockpit; T-type tail

Saab J-35 Draken

Designed to intercept transonic bombers at all altitudes, the Draken first flew on 25 October 1955. The initial production version, the J-35A, entered service early in 1960. The major production version of the Draken was the J-35F, which was virtually designed around the Hughes HM-55 Falcon radar-guided air-to-air missile and was fitted with an improved S7B collision-course fire-control system, a high-capacity datalink system integrating the aircraft with the STRIL 60 air defence environment, an infrared sensor under the nose and PS-01A search and ranging radar. The J-35C was a two-seat operational trainer, while the last new-build variant, the J-35J, was a development of the J-35D. The Saab RF-35 was a reconnaissance version. Total Draken production was around 600 aircraft, equipping 17 RSAF squadrons; the type was also exported to Finland and Denmark. The Draken was the first supersonic aircraft in western Europe to be deployed operationally. It continues to serve in the Austrian Air Force.

ABOVE: *The Saab J-35 Draken in Swedish service.*

Specification (J-35J)

Crew: *1* **Powerplant:** *one 7830kg (17,262lb) thrust Svenska Flygmotor RM6C turbojet* **Max speed:** *2125km/h (1320mph)* **Service ceiling:** *19,812m (65,000ft)* **Max range:** *3250km (2020 miles)* **Wing span:** *9.40m (30ft 10in)* **Length:** *15.40m (50ft 4in)* **Height:** *3.90m (12ft 9in)* **Weight:** *16,000kg (35,274lb) loaded* **Armament:** *one 30mm (1.18in) Aden cannon; four AAMs*

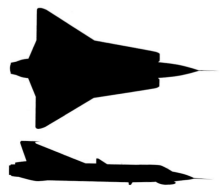

MAJOR VARIANTS
J-35A: initial production version
J-35C: two-seat operational trainer
J-35D: upgraded engine
J-35F: major production version with improved fire-control and radar
RF-35: reconnaissance version

RECOGNITION FEATURES
Mid-mounted, double-delta wing; single engine with oval air intakes; large jet pipe; broad, single fin, no tailplane

Saab SF-37 Viggen

ABOVE: *The Viggen has a unique double-delta configuration.*

Specification (SF-37)

Crew: *1* **Powerplant:** *one 11,799kg (26,015lb) thrust Volvo Flygmotor RM8 turbofan* **Max speed:** *2124km/h (1320mph)* **Service ceiling:** *18,290m (60,000ft)* **Combat radius:** *1000km (621 miles)* **Wing span:** *10.60m (34ft 9in)* **Length:** *16.30m (53ft 5in)* **Height:** *5.60m (18ft 4in)* **Weight:** *20,500kg (45,194lb) loaded* **Armament:** *6000kg (13,228lb) of stores*

The first of seven SF-37 Viggen (Thunderbolt) prototypes flew for the first time on 8 February 1967, followed by the first production AJ-37 single-seat all-weather attack variant in February 1971. Deliveries of the first of 110 AJ-37s to the Royal Swedish Air Force began in June that year. The JA-37 interceptor version of the Viggen, 149 of which were built, replaced the J35F Draken; the SF-37 was a single-seat armed photo-reconnaissance variant; and the SH-37 was an all-weather maritime reconnaissance version, replacing the S-32C Lansen. The SK-37 was a tandem two-seat trainer, retaining a secondary attack role.

MAJOR VARIANTS
AJ-37: all-weather attack fighter
SF-37: armed photo-reconnaissance variant
JA-37: multi-role fighter
SK-37: two-seat operational trainer

RECOGNITION FEATURES
Tandem delta wings; deep fuselage with single fin; no tailplane; air intakes on forward fuselage beside cockpit

Saab JAS-39A Gripen

Despite some teething troubles, Saab's JAS-39 Gripen (Griffon) is proving to be an excellent multi-role combat aircraft, and is competing with Eurofighter and Rafale in the lucrative export market. This lightweight multi-role fighter was conceived in the 1970s as a replacement for the attack, reconnaissance and interceptor versions of the Viggen. The prototype was rolled out on 26 April 1987 and made its first flight on 9 December 1988. The loss of this aircraft in a landing accident on 2 February 1989 led to a revision of the Gripen's advanced fly-by-wire control system. Orders for the Gripen totalled 140 aircraft, all for the Royal Swedish Air Force. The type entered service in 1995. The JAS-39 is a canard delta design with triplex digital fly-by-wire controls, a multi-mode Ericsson pulse-Doppler radar, laser inertial navigation system, wide-angle head-up display and three monochrome head-down displays. The aircraft's Volvo Flygmotor RM.12 turbofan (a licence-built General Electric GE F404) is hardened against birdstrike. Despite the fact that Sweden's impact on the military aircraft export market has not been spectacular, the Gripen has registered one major success; on

ABOVE: *The JAS-39 is the latest combat aircraft from Saab.*

Specification (JAS-39A)

Crew: *1* **Powerplant:** *one 8210kg (18,100lb) thrust Volvo Flygmotor RM.12 turbofan* **Max speed:** *Mach 2 plus* **Service ceiling:** *classified* **Max range:** *3250km (2020 miles)* **Wing span:** *8.00m (26ft 3in)* **Length:** *14.10m (46ft 3in)* **Height:** *4.70m (15ft 5in)* **Weight:** *12,473kg (27,500lb) loaded* **Armament:** *one 27mm (1.06in) Mauser BK27 cannon; six external hardpoints for Sky Flash and Sidewinder AAMs, Maverick ASMs, anti-ship missiles, bombs, cluster bombs, reconnaissance pods, drop tanks, ECM pods etc*

RIGHT: *The JAS-39 Gripen is an extremely agile aircraft. Early problems with its fly-by-wire system have now been overcome.*

3 December 1999 the South African Air Force announced that Saab and British Aerospace would supply 28 Gripens and 24 Hawk 100s, to be delivered between 2005 and 2012. Fourteen Gripens are also to be leased to the Czech Republic, starting in 2005.

MAJOR VARIANTS
JAS-39A: single-seater
JAS-39B: two-seater
JAS-39C: single-seater
JAS-39D: two-seater

RECOGNITION FEATURES
Mid-mounted tailless delta; large movable canards on forward fuselage; single engine, jet pipe extending well aft of wing trailing edge; tailfin has swept leading edge, straight trailing edge

SAIG (Shenyang) J-8 Finback

Although obviously influenced by Russian aircraft, the J-8 was of indigenous design and was the product of an advanced fighter programme that started in China in the late 1960s. Resembling a scaled-up MiG-21 (Shenyang J-7) with two engines, it entered production in 1979, an initial batch of 100 aircraft being built. Design work on an improved version, the J-8-II, began in 1980, with production beginning in the late 1980s. The J-8-II has a completely new forward fuselage with much larger radar and ventral inlets, along with other less obvious improvements. In performance terms, it is comparable to the Sukhoi Su-15 Flagon. The latest version is the J-8-IIM, which flew in March 1996 and which is a joint Chinese–Russian venture.

ABOVE: *The all-weather-capable SAIG J-8 Finback.*

Specification (J-8-II)

Crew: *1* **Powerplant:** *two 6711kg (14,815lb) thrust Liyang (LMC) Wopen 13A-II turbojets* **Max speed:** *2338km/h (1453mph)* **Service ceiling:** *20,200m (66,275ft)* **Combat radius:** *800km (500 miles)* **Wing span:** *9.34m (30ft 8in)* **Length:** *21.59m (70ft 10in)* **Height:** *5.41m (17ft 9in)* **Weight:** *17,800kg (39,242lb)* **Armament:** *six underwing hardpoints for fuel, bombs, rockets or missiles*

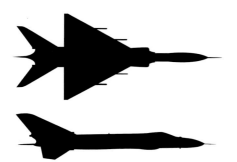

MAJOR VARIANTS
J-8-I: improved fighter with heavier weaponry
J-8-II: new engines; improved radar
J-8-IIM: improved J-8-II for export
J-8D: in-flight refuelling capability

RECOGNITION FEATURES
Mid-mounted delta wing; swept tailplane; large fin under tail

SEPECAT Jaguar

ABOVE: *The SEPECAT Jaguar was licence-built in India.*

Specification (Jaguar GR.Mk 1)

Crew: *2* **Powerplant:** *two 3313kg (7305lb) thrust Rolls-Royce/Turbomeca Adour Mk 102 turbofans* **Max speed:** *1593km/h (990mph)* **Service ceiling:** *14,000m (50,000ft)* **Combat radius:** *557km (357 miles)* **Wing span:** *8.69m (28ft 6in)* **Length:** *16.83m (55ft 2in)* **Height:** *4.89m (16ft)* **Weight:** *15,500kg (34,172lb) loaded* **Armament:** *two 30mm (1.18in) DEFA cannon; external hardpoints for 4536kg (10,000lb) of stores; two AIM-9L Sidewinders*

Developed jointly by the British Aircraft Corporation and Breguet (later Dassault-Breguet) under the banner of SEPECAT (Societe Europeenne de Production de l'Avion Ecole de Combat et Appui Tactique), the Jaguar emerged from development as a much more potent aircraft than originally envisaged. The first French version to fly, in September 1968, was the two-seat E model, 40 being ordered by the French Air Force, followed in March 1969 by the single-seat Jaguar A tactical support aircraft. Service deliveries of the E began in May 1972, the first of 160 Jaguar As following in 1973. The British versions, known as the Jaguar S (strike) and Jaguar B (trainer), flew on 12 October 1969 and 30 August 1971 respectively, being delivered to the RAF as the Jaguar GR.Mk 1 and T.Mk 2.

MAJOR VARIANTS
Jaguar A (France) **GR.1** (British): single-seat attack bomber
Jaguar B (France) **T.2** (British): two-seat operational trainer
Jaguar International: export version

RECOGNITION FEATURES
High-mounted swept wing; long fuselage with distinctive 'cutaway' under tail above jet pipes

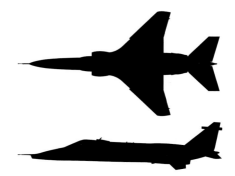

SOKO G-2A Galeb

The SOKO G-2A Galeb (Seagull) jet trainer was the first Yugoslav-designed jet aircraft to go into production, entering service with the Yugoslav Air Force in 1963. Also used as a light attack aircraft, it was operated mainly by the Yugoslav Air Force Air Academy, but was also exported to Libya and Zambia as the G-2AE. During the Yugoslav civil war, the Galeb was used in action by the 105th Fighter-Bomber Regiment of the Serbian Air Force. The G-4 Super Galeb, which first flew in 1980, was a completely new design, with swept flying surfaces and updated systems.

ABOVE: *The SOKO Galeb was one of the former Yugoslavia's aviation success stories.*

Specification (G-2A)

Crew: 2 **Powerplant:** *one 1134kg (2500lb) thrust Rolls-Royce Viper 11 Mk 226 turbojet* **Max speed:** *730km/h (454mph)* **Service ceiling:** *12,000m (39,370ft);* **Max range:** *1240km (771 miles)* **Wing span:** *9.73m (31ft 11in)* **Length:** *10.34m (33ft 11in)* **Height:** *3.28m (10ft 9in)* **Weight:** *4300kg (9480lb) loaded* **Armament:** *two 12.7mm (0.5in) machine guns; underwing racks for bombs, rockets and bomblet containers*

> ### MAJOR VARIANTS
> **G-2:** two-seat version
> **J-1 Jastreb:** single-seat version

> ### RECOGNITION FEATURES
> **G-2A:** low-mounted straight wing with tip tanks; single engine; tandem cockpit

Sukhoi Su-17/22

ABOVE: *A Sukhoi Su-22 of the Slovak Air Force.*

Specification (Su-17M-4 Fitter-K)

Crew: *1* **Powerplant:** *one 11,250kg (24,802lb) thrust Lyulka AL-21F-3 turbojet* **Max speed:** *2220km/h (1380mph)* **Service ceiling:** *15,200m (49,865ft)* **Combat radius:** *675km (419 miles)* **Wing span:** *13.80m (45ft 3in)* **Length:** *18.75m (61ft 6in)* **Height:** *5.00m (16ft 5in)* **Weight:** *19,500kg (42,990lb) loaded* **Armament:** *two 30mm (1.18in) cannon; up to 4250kg (9370lb) of stores*

In the late 1960s the Sukhoi bureau redesigned the original Su-7, giving it a more powerful engine, variable-geometry wings and increased fuel tankage. In this guise it became the Su-17/20 (NATO reporting name 'Fitter-C'), which was unique among combat aircraft in being a variable-geometry derivative of a fixed-wing machine. The development of the Fitter-C was a facet of the Russians' practice of constant development, enabling them to keep one basic design of combat aircraft in service for 30 or 40 years and foster long-term standardization. The Su-22 was an updated version with terrain-avoidance radar and other improved avionics. The Fitter remains in service with several air forces.

MAJOR VARIANTS
Su-17: initial production version
Su-17M: improved ground-attack model
Su-22: new version; improved avionics, engines and weapons systems

RECOGNITION FEATURES
Low-mounted, variable-geometry wing; nose intake with cone; single engine; long fairing behind cockpit

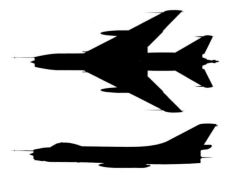

Sukhoi Su-24

LEFT: *The Sukhoi Su-24 'Fencer' presented one of the most serious air threats to NATO in the dangerous years of the Cold War.*

Specification (Su-24M)

Crew: *2* **Powerplant:** *two 11,250kg (24,802lb) thrust Lyulka AL-21F3A turbojets* **Max speed:** *2316km/h (1439mph)* **Service ceiling:** *17,500m (57,415ft)* **Combat radius:** *1050km (650 miles)* **Wing span:** *17.63m (57ft 10in) spread; 10.36m (34ft) swept* **Length:** *24.53m (80ft 5in)* **Height:** *4.97m (16ft)* **Weight:** *39,700kg (87,520lb) loaded* **Armament:** *one 23mm (0.9in) GSh-23-6 six-barrelled cannon; nine external pylons with provision for up to 8000kg (17,635lb) of stores*

The Sukhoi Su-24 (NATO reporting name 'Fencer') was designed from the outset to fly at very low level in order to penetrate increasingly effective air defence systems. It made its first flight in 1970 and deliveries of the first production version, the Fencer-A, began in 1974. Several variants of the Fencer were produced, culminating in the Su-24M Fencer-D, which entered service in 1986. This variant has in-flight refuelling equipment, upgraded nav/attack systems, and laser/TV designators. The Su-24MR is a tactical reconnaissance version.

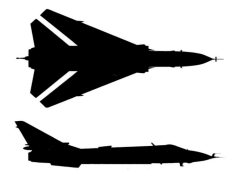

MAJOR VARIANTS
Su-24: primary model
Su-24M: main bomber version featuring improved radar and attack systems
Su-24MR: reconnaissance variant

RECOGNITION FEATURES
High-mounted, variable geometry wing; square intakes on fuselage sides aft of side-by-side cockpit; swept tail surfaces, large low-mounted tailplane

Sukhoi Su-25

ABOVE: *The Su-25 is comparable to the USAF's A-10.*

Specification (Su-25K)

Crew: *1* **Powerplant:** *two 4500kg (9921lb) thrust Tumanskii R-195 turbojets* **Max speed:** *975km/h (606mph)* **Service ceiling:** *7000m (22,965ft)* **Combat radius:** *750km (466 miles)* **Wing span:** *14.36m (47ft 1in)* **Length:** *15.53m (50ft 11in)* **Height:** *4.80m (15ft 9in)* **Weight:** *17,600kg (38,800lb) loaded* **Armament:** *one 30mm (1.18in) GSh-30-2 cannon; up to 4400kg (9700lb) of stores*

MAJOR VARIANTS
Su-25UBK: two-seat export variant
Su-25UBT: navalized version with a strengthened undercarriage and arrester gear
Su-25UT (Su-28): two-seat trainer version

RECOGNITION FEATURES
High-mounted straight wing with tapered leading edge; engine nacelles along fuselage sides; tailfin broad at base, tapering sharply

A Russian requirement for an attack aircraft in the A-10 Thunderbolt II class materialized in the Sukhoi Su-25 (NATO reporting name 'Frogfoot'), which was selected in preference to a rival design, the Ilyushin Il-102. Deployment of the single-seat close-support Su-25K began in 1978, and the aircraft saw considerable operational service during the former Soviet Union's involvement in Afghanistan. As a result of lessons learned during the Afghan conflict an upgraded version known as the Su-25T was produced, with improved defensive systems to counter weapons like the Stinger SAM.

Sukhoi Su-27

The introduction, in the mid-1970s, of the USAF F-15 Eagle and F-16 Fighting Falcon put the then Eastern Bloc fighter pilots at a distinct disadvantage. The deployment of the Su-27 Flanker (NATO reporting name 'Flanker') and MiG-29 ('Fulcrum') in the mid-1980s redressed the situation. Designed as a high-performance fighter with a fly-by-wire control system and the ability to carry up to 10 AAMs, the highly manoeuvrable Su-27 is one of the most imposing fighters ever built. The first 'Flanker-A' prototypes flew on 20 May 1977 and entered service as the 'Flanker-B' in 1984. The development of the Su-27 fighter plane was completed in the early 1980s, and the plane subsequently set more than 40 world records for altitude and take-off speed. It was the forerunner of an entire family of combat types, including the Su-27UB operational trainer, the Su-33 ship-based fighter, the Su-37 multi-mission aircraft and the Su-32FN

ABOVE: *The Sukhoi Su-27 holds a number of world records.*

Specification (Sukhoi Su-27B)

Crew: *1* **Powerplant:** *two 12,500kg (27,557lb) thrust Lyulka AL-31M turbofans* **Max speed:** *2500km (1500mph)* **Service ceiling:** *18,000m (59,055ft)* **Combat radius:** *1500km (930 miles)* **Wing span:** *14.70m (48ft 2in)* **Length:** *21.94m (71ft 11in)* **Height:** *6.36m (20ft 10in)* **Weight:** *30,000kg (66,138lb) loaded* **Armament:** *one 30mm (1.18in) GSh-3101 cannon; AAMs*

ABOVE: *This Su-27 displays a somewhat unusual camouflage pattern on its upper surfaces.*

two-seat specialized version. The Su-27UB is a two-seat training version of Su-27 which first flew in March 1985.

In 1997 Sukhoi signed a contract with Vietnam to supply six Su-27s, two Su-27SKs and four Su-27UBs. By the end of 1997 approval had been given for the licenced production of the Su-27SK in China, and negotiations on the sale of a further 55 Su-27 fighters to China also began.

MAJOR VARIANTS
Su-27P: air defence interceptor
Su-27UB: operational trainer
Su-33: ship-based fighter
Su-37: multi-mission aircraft
Su-27SK: Chinese licence-built variant

RECOGNITION FEATURES
Mid-mounted semi-delta wings with square tips; leading-edge root extensions extend downward and forward of the wing roots; twin turbofan engines with square, diagonally cut air intakes mounted under the wings alongside the fuselage; twin, swept tailfins, tapered with square tips; swept, tapered tailplanes

Sukhoi Su-34

The Su-34 long-range strike aircraft is the approximate equivalent of the USAF's F-15E Strike Eagle and is expected to be in first-line Russian service in 2005. It is planned as a replacement for Su-24 and Su-25 aircraft. The aircraft design retains the basic layout and construction of the Su-27 airframe, with a conventional high-wing configuration and a substantial part of the on-board equipment. The Su-34 has a changed contour of the nose section to hold an advanced multi-mode phased array radar with terrain-following and terrain-avoidance modes. The capacity of the internal fuel tanks has been increased with a resulting increased take-off weight. Changes have been made to the central tail boom for a rear-warning radar.

ABOVE: *The Sukhoi Su-34 is a development of the Su-27 Flanker, and is intended for the long-range strike role.*

Specification

Crew: 2 **Powerplant:** *two 12,500kg (27,557lb) thrust Lyulka AL-31F or AL-35 turbofan engines* **Max speed:** *1900km/h (1180mph)* **Service ceiling:** *14,000m (45,920ft)* **Max range:** *1130km (701 miles)* **Wing span:** *14.70m (48ft 2in)* **Length:** *25.50m (82ft 8in)* **Height:** *6.20m (20ft 4in)* **Weight:** *45,100kg (99,404lb) loaded* **Armament:** *one 30mm (1.18in) gun; up to 8000kg (17,635lb) of external stores*

MAJOR VARIANTS
Su-34FN: maritime strike variant

RECOGNITION FEATURES
Mid-mounted, broad swept wing; side-by-side cockpit; twin fins mounted on wing; under-fuselage air intakes; rear fuselage cone housing RWR; canards

Sukhoi Su-35

ABOVE: *The Su-35 Flanker development has advanced fly-by-wire and radar systems.*

Specification

Crew: *1* **Powerplant:** *two 13,982kg (30,865lb) thrust Lyulka AL-32FM turbofans* **Max speed:** *2500km/h (1500mph)* **Service ceiling:** *18,000m (59,055ft)* **Max range:** *4000km (2484 miles)* **Wing span:** *15.00m (49ft 2in)* **Length:** *22.00m (72ft 2in)* **Height:** *6.00m (19ft 8in)* **Weight:** *34,000kg (74,956lb) loaded* **Armament:** *one 30mm (1.18in) gun; 8000kg (17,635lb) of stores*

The Su-35 all-weather air superiority fighter is derived from the Su-27M Flanker-B. The Su-35, which has a similar powerplant and configuration to the Su-27, is an attempt to provide a second-generation Su-27 with improved agility and operational capability. The programme was seriously delayed because of problems with the radar and digital quadruplex fly-by-wire control systems. A new fire-control system was incorporated to improve the aircraft's ground-attack capability. The status of the Su-35 is uncertain, but an even more advanced version with thrust vectoring, the Su-37, has been developed.

MAJOR VARIANTS
Su-35: production model
Su-37: advanced version with thrust vectoring

RECOGNITION FEATURES
Resembles a single-seat Su-35

Tupolev Tu-16

Production of the Tu-16 (NATO reporting name 'Badger') Badger-A began in 1953 and it began to enter service with the Soviet Air Force's Long-Range Aviation in 1955. The Badger-A was also supplied to Iraq (9) and Egypt (30). The principal sub-variant of the Badger-A was the Tu-16A, configured to carry the USSR's air-deliverable nuclear weapons. In its later incarnations the Tu-16 was used in the anti-shipping, maritime reconnaissance, flight refuelling and electronic jamming roles. The Badger-L was one of the last variants in a long line of electronic intelligence gatherers. The Tu-16 was also licence built in China as the Xian H-6.

ABOVE: *Tupolev Tu-16 Badgers in Egyptian Air Force service.*

Specification (Tu-16PM Badger-L)

Crew: *7* **Powerplant:** *two 9500kg (20,944lb) thrust Mikulin RD-3M turbojets* **Max speed:** *960km/h (597mph)* **Service ceiling:** *15,000m (49,200ft)* **Max range:** *4800km (2983 miles)* **Wing span:** *32.99m (108ft 3in)* **Length:** *34.80m (114ft 2in)* **Height:** *10.36m (34ft 2in)* **Weight:** *75,800kg (167,110lb) loaded* **Armament:** *two 23mm (0.9in) cannon in radar-controlled barbettes*

MAJOR VARIANTS
Tu-16PP: ECM variant
Tu-16R: maritime reconnaissance model
Tu-16T: torpedo-armed naval bomber

RECOGNITION FEATURES
Mid-mounted swept wing; twin turbojets mounted at wing roots; glazed nose; swept tail surfaces; tail gun position

Tupolev Tu-22M

ABOVE: *The highly effective Tu-22M Backfire was designed specifically for long-range anti-shipping operations.*

Specification

Crew: *4* **Powerplant:** *two 20,000kg (44,092lb) thrust Kuznetsov NK-144 turbofans* **Max speed:** *2125km/h (1321mph)* **Service ceiling:** *18,000m (59,055ft)* **Max range:** *4000km (2485 miles)* **Wing span:** *34.30m (112ft 6in) spread; 23.40m (76ft 9in) swept* **Length:** *36.90m (129ft 11in)* **Height:** *10.80m (35ft 5in)* **Weight:** *130,000kg (286,596lb) loaded* **Armament:** *one 23mm (0.9in) GSh-23 twin-barrel cannon in radar-controlled tail barbette; up to 12,000kg (26,455lb) of stores in weapons bay, or one S-4 missile, or three AS-16 missiles*

The Tupolev Tu-22M (NATO reporting name 'Backfire') attack bomber first flew in 1971, reached initial operational capability (IOC) in 1973 and, during the years that followed, replaced the Tu-16 Badger in Soviet service. The mission of the new bomber, peripheral attack or intercontinental attack, became one of the most fiercely contested intelligence debates of the Cold War, and it was a long time before the true nature of the threat it posed – anti-shipping attack – became known. The original design (Backfire-A) underwent major modifications and re-emerged as the Tu-22M2 Backfire-B. About 400 Tu-22Ms were produced, 240 of them M2s/3s. The M3 (Backfire-C) variant had reduced defensive armament and the flight refuelling probe was deleted; a reconnaissance version, the Tu-22MR, entered service in 1985, and the Tu-22ME is the latest of the attack variants. The variable-geometry Tu-22M Backfire's design was based on that of the earlier Tu-22 Blinder, which had many shortcomings and which saw operational service in Afghanistan during the Soviet intervention there.

One of the principal Backfire units, whose aircraft are frequently seen, is the 924th Reconnaissance Air Regiment, Northern Fleet,

Tupolev Tu-22M (continued)

Olenya, Russia. The 924th Reconnaissance Air Regiment is sometimes referred to as the 924th Missile Carrier Regiment. Its role during the Cold War would have been to attack NATO ships in the North Atlantic and North Sea, or any naval unit that was approaching the Russian coast. To do this, large numbers of Backfires would have been deployed to make saturation attacks on NATO naval forces, using the Kh-22M (AS-4 Kitchen) air-to-surface missile.

ABOVE: *The variable-geometry Backfire, seen here with wings fully spread, was a serious threat to NATO task forces.*

MAJOR VARIANTS
Tu-22M2: standard production version
Tu-22M3: reduced defensive armament; no in-flight refueling probe
Tu-22MR: reconnaissance variant
Tu-22P: ECM aircraft
Tu-22U: training aircraft

RECOGNITION FEATURES
Low-mounted variable-geometry wing; twin engines in fuselage with large intakes; swept tail surfaces; large fairing from base of tailfin to upper fuselage

Tupolev Tu-95/Tu-142

ABOVE: *The venerable Tupolev Tu-95/142 Bear in flight.*

Specification (Tu-142)

Crew: *10* **Powerplant:** *four 11,190kW (15,000hp) Kuznetsov NK-12MV turboprop engines* **Max speed:** *805km/h (500mph)* **Service ceiling:** *13,400m (43,962ft)* **Max range:** *12,550km (7800 miles)* **Wing span:** *48.50m (159ft)* **Length:** *47.50 (155ft 10in)* **Height:** *11.78m (38ft 8in)* **Weight:** *154,000kg (340,000lb) loaded* **Armament:** *six 23mm (0.9in) cannon; weapons load of up to 11,340kg (25,000lb)*

The massive Tupolev Tu-95 (NATO reporting name 'Bear') entered service with the Soviet Strategic Air Forces in 1957. The initial Tu-95M Bear-A freefall nuclear bomber was followed by the Tu-95K-20 Bear-B of 1961, this being a maritime attack and reconnaissance version with a large radome under the nose and a Kh-20 (AS-3 Kangaroo) cruise missile. The Tu-95KM Bear-C was a specialized maritime reconnaissance version, as was the similar Bear-D, while the Bear-E and -F were upgraded variants with a new electronics suite. These and later aircraft were designated Tu-142. Eight Tu-142s were supplied to the Indian Navy.

MAJOR VARIANTS
Tu-95M: freefall nuclear bomber
Tu-95K-20: maritime attack and reconnaissance variant
Tu-95KD: in-flight refuelling probe fitted
Tu-95KM: maritime reconnaissance
Tu-142: improved variant; longer fuselage; improved engines

RECOGNITION FEATURES
Mid-mounted swept wing; four turboprop engines, inboard pair with long nacelles; swept tail surfaces; rear gun position

Tupolev Tu-160

The Tu-160 (NATO reporting name 'Blackjack') supersonic variable-geometry bomber first flew on 19 December 1981, but one of the two prototypes was lost in an accident. Comparable to but much larger than the Rockwell B-1B, the type entered series production in 1984 and the first operational examples were deployed in May 1987. Thirty-six aircraft (out of a planned total of 100, the number reduced after the collapse of the Soviet Union) were in service, these being divided between the 184th Air Regiment in the Ukraine and the 121st Air Regiment at Engels Air Base. The Ukraine-based aircraft were eventually returned to Russia, along with 600 air-launched missiles, as part of a deal which involved paying off a commercial debt.

ABOVE: *The Tu-160, the last Soviet strategic bomber.*

Specification

Crew: *4* **Powerplant:** *four 25,000kg (55,115lb) thrust Kutnetsov NK-321 turbofans* **Max speed:** *2000km/h (1243mph)* **Service ceiling:** *18,300m (60,040ft)* **Max range:** *14,000km (8694 miles)* **Wing span:** *55.70m (182ft 9in) spread; 35.60m (116ft 9in) swept* **Length:** *54.10m (177ft 6in)* **Height:** *13.10m (43ft)* **Weight:** *275,000kg (606,261lb) loaded* **Armament:** *provision for up to 16,500kg (36,376lb) of stores in two internal weapons bays and on underwing hardpoints*

MAJOR VARIANTS
Tu-160: production version

RECOGNITION FEATURES
Low-mounted, variable-geometry wing; four paired turbofan engines in ventral position on either side of fuselage; large fairing from base of tailfin to upper fuselage

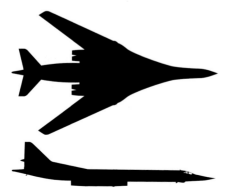

British Aerospace (Hawker Siddeley) Nimrod

ABOVE: *The Nimrod was developed from the Comet airliner.*

Specification (Nimrod MR.2)

Crew: *13* **Powerplant:** *four 5507kg (12,140lb) thrust Rolls-Royce Spey Mk 250 turbofan engines* **Max speed:** *925km/h (575mph)* **Service ceiling:** *12,800m (42,000ft)* **Max range:** *9262km (5755 miles)* **Wing span:** *35.00m (114ft 10in)* **Length:** *39.34m (129ft 1in)* **Height:** *9.08m (29ft 9in)* **Weight:** *87,090kg (192,000lb) loaded* **Armament:** *internal bay with provision for 6123kg (13,500lb) of stores*

The Hawker Siddeley Nimrod was designed to replace the Shackleton as the RAF's standard long-range maritime patrol aircraft. Deliveries of production Nimrod MR.Mk 1 aircraft began in October 1969. The first 38 Nimrods were delivered between 1969 and 1972, equipping five squadrons and No 236 OCU; another eight were delivered in 1975, while three, designated Nimrod R.1, were converted to the electronic intelligence role. From 1979 the Nimrod fleet was significantly upgraded to MR.2 standard, with improved avionics and weapon systems. Flight refuelling equipment was added at the time of the 1982 Falklands War. All Nimrods were scheduled to be rebuilt between 2003 and 2008, retaining only the fuselage shell of existing aircraft. The new aircraft, designated Nimrod MRA.4, has new wings and undercarriage and BMW/Rolls-Royce fuel-efficient engines.

MAJOR VARIANTS
Nimrod MR.Mk 2: maritime reconnaissance/ASW aircraft
Nimrod MR.Mk 4: maritime reconnaissance/ASW aircraft
Nimrod R.1: electronic intelligence aircraft

RECOGNITION FEATURES
Four engines in wing roots; angular tailfin with deep fairing surmounted by sensor pod; extended tail boom housing equipment pod extending forward of each wing leading edge

Beriev A-40 Albatross

The Beriev A-40 Albatross (NATO reporting name 'Mermaid') is the world's largest amphibious aircraft and was designed to replace the Be-12 and Il-38 in maritime patrol and ASW roles. Design work on the Albatross began in 1983, but it was not until 1988 that the type was made publicly known in the West when

the US announced it had taken satellite photographs of a jet-powered amphibian under development in Russia. The Albatross made its first flight in December 1986, while its first public appearance was a fly-by at the 1989 Soviet Aviation Day Display at Tushino, Moscow. As many as 20 A-40 Albatrosses have been ordered for CIS naval service, but the status of this order is unclear.

ABOVE: *The A-40 is the world's largest amphibious aircraft.*

Specification

Crew: *5 flight crew plus 3 observers*
Powerplant: *two 117.7kN (26,455lb) thrust Aviadvigatel D-30KPV turbofans and two 24.5kN (5510lb) thrust RKBM (formerly Klimov) RD-60K booster turbojets*
Max speed: *760km/h (472mph)*
Service ceiling: *9706m (31,825ft)*
Max range: *5500km (3415 miles)*
Wing span: *41.62m (136ft 7in)*
Length: *38.92m (127ft 8in)*
Height: *11.07m (36ft 4in)* **Weight:** *86,000kg (189,595lb)* **Armament:** *torpedoes, mines and depth charges in internal weapons bay*

> MAJOR VARIANTS
> **A-40:** maritime patrol aircraft
> **Be-42:** proposed search-and-rescue variant
> **Be-40P:** proposed airliner version

> RECOGNITION FEATURES
> High-mounted swept wing; twin turbofan engines with boosters; T-type tail; flying boat hull with single step

Beriev Be-12 Chaika

ABOVE: *The Be-12 has given many years of superb service.*

Specification

Crew: *5–6* **Powerplant:** *two 2984kW (4000hp) Ivchenko AI-20D turboprops* **Max speed:** *610km/h (379mph)* **Service ceiling:** *12,185m (40,000ft)* **Max range:** *4000km (2485miles)* **Wing span:** *32.91m (108ft)* **Length:** *29.18m (95ft 9in)* **Height:** *6.68m (21ft 11in)* **Weight:** *29,500kg (65,035lb) loaded* **Armament:** *up to 10,092kg (22,250lb) of bombs and depth charges; no defensive armament*

First seen publicly in 1961, the turboprop-powered Beriev Be-12 (NATO reporting name 'Mail') amphibian first flew in 1960 and service deployment was rapid. It featured a sharply cranked, high-set wing, and the single-step hull had a high length-to-beam ratio and was fitted with two long strakes to keep spray away from the engines on take-off. There was a glazed observation position in the nose, and a 'stinger' tail housed Magnetic Anomaly Detection (MAD) equipment. The Be-12 remains in service with the naval air arms of Russia and the Ukraine.

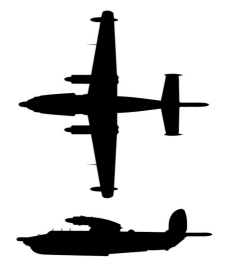

MAJOR VARIANTS
Be-12: production amphibious aircraft

RECOGNITION FEATURES
Sharply cranked, high-set 'gull' wings; twin turboprops mounted on top of wings; twin tailfins; projecting nose-mounted radome; extended tail boom housing MAD equipment

Beriev Be-200

The Be-200 is based on the Be-42 and employs many of the design features and technologies developed for the latter aircraft, but is smaller overall and designed for civil roles, firefighting in particular. The airframe is strengthened to cope with the demands of water operations and fire-

bombing and there is some use of advanced aluminium lithium alloys. In firefighting configuration the aircraft can uplift 12 tonnes (26,460lb) of water, and in ambulance config-uration it can accommodate seven medical attendants and 30 stretcher patients. It can carry 8 tonnes (17,635lb) of freight in cargo configuration. Design work on the Be-200 began in 1989. It is being developed by Betair, a collaboration between Beriev and Irkutsk in central Russia (where the aircraft will be built), and Swiss company ILTA Trade Finance, which is providing marketing and financing support, and other partners.

ABOVE: *The Beriev Be-200 demonstrating its firefighting capabilities.*

Specification

Crew: *3* **Powerplant:** *two 73.6kN (16,550lb) thrust ZMKB Progress D436T turbofans* **Max speed:** *720km/h (447mph)* **Service ceiling:** *11,895m (36,090ft)* **Max range:** *3850km (2390 miles)* **Wing span:** *32.78m (107ft 7in)* **Length:** *32.05m (105ft 2in)* **Height:** *8.90m (29ft 3in)* **Weight:** *37,200kg (79,365lb)* **Payload:** *8 tonnes (17,635lb) of freight in cargo configuration*

MAJOR VARIANTS
Can be configured as freighter, amphibious fire-fighting aircraft or a passenger aircraft **Be-210**.

RECOGNITION FEATURES
Similar to **Be-42 (A-40) Albatross**, but much smaller; twin turbofans mounted above rear fuselage; T-type tail; moderately swept wing

Boeing E-3 Sentry

ABOVE: *Constantly patrolling the skies of the west, the E-3 Sentry now has an important new role in detecting possible airborne terrorist threats.*

Specification (E-3D)

Crew: *up to 19* **Powerplant:** *four 10,872kg (24,000lb) thrust CFM56-2A-3 turbofans* **Max speed:** *853km/h (530mph)* **Service ceiling:** *10,670m (35,000ft)* **Max range:** *9266km (5758 miles)* **Wing span:** *44.98m (147ft 7in)* **Length:** *46.61m (152ft 11in)* **Weight:** *150,820kg (332,500lb) loaded* **Armament:** *none*

The E-3 Sentry is an airborne warning and control system (AWACS) aircraft that provides all-weather surveillance, command, control and communications. The aircraft is a modified Boeing 707/320 commercial airframe with a rotating radar dome. The dome is 9.10m (30ft) in diameter and contains a radar subsystem that permits surveillance from the Earth's surface up into the stratosphere, over land or water. The radar has a range of more than 375km (250 miles) for low-flying targets and further for aerospace vehicles flying at medium to high altitudes. The E-3 is operated by NATO, the USA, Britain, Saudi Arabia and France.

MAJOR VARIANTS
E-3A: initial production version
E-3B: modernized E-3A
E-3C: improved AWACS systems

RECOGNITION FEATURES
Low-mounted swept wing with dihedral; four podded turbofans; swept tail surfaces; large rotating radome above rear fuselage

Dassault (Breguet) Br.1050 Alizé

In 1954, two years after the first flight of the second prototype Br.960 Vultur strike aircraft, the French Navy's requirement altered dramatically, and it was decided that this aircraft would serve as the prototype of a new shipboard anti-submarine aircraft. It flew in this form on 26 March 1955 with the designation Br.965 and was followed by three prototypes of the new anti-submarine aircraft, the Breguet Br.1050 Alizé (Tradewind). The first of these flew on 6 October 1956 and the type was ordered into production, 75 aircraft eventually being delivered for service on France's aircraft carriers and at shore establishments. Twelve aircraft were also supplied to the Indian Navy. Although no longer in first-line service, some Alizés are still flying.

ABOVE: *Some examples of the Alizé are still flying.*

Specification

Crew: *3* **Powerplant:** *one 1566kW (2100hp) Rolls-Royce Dart RDa21 turboprop engine* **Max speed:** *458km/h (285mph)* **Service ceiling:** *6100m (20,000ft)* **Max range:** *2872km (1785 miles)* **Wing span:** *15.60m (51ft 2in)* **Length:** *13.87m (45ft 6in)* **Height:** *4.76m (15ft 7in)* **Weight:** *8199kg (18,100lb) loaded* **Armament:** *three depth charges or one torpedo internally; two depth charges and six RPs or two ASMs underwing*

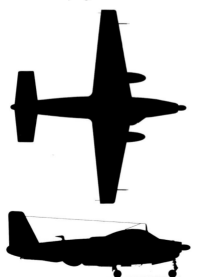

> **MAJOR VARIANTS**
> **Br.1050:** shipboard anti-submarine aircraft

> **RECOGNITION FEATURES**
> Single turboprop engine; distinctive hump-backed appearance; low wing with large nacelles housing main undercarriage

Dassault (Breguet) Br.1150 Atlantic

ABOVE: *The Dassault-Breguet Atlantique NG in service.*

Specification (Atlantique 2)

Crew: *12/16* **Powerplant:** *two 4554kW (6105hp) Rolls-Royce Tyne RTy.20 Mk 21 turboprop engines*
Max speed: *658km/h (409mph)*
Service ceiling: *10,000m (32,800ft)*
Max range: *9000km (5590 miles)*
Wing span: *37.42m (122ft 9in)*
Length: *31.62m (103ft 9in)*
Height: *10.89m (35ft 8in)* **Weight:** *43,500kg (95,900lb) loaded*
Armament: *homing torpedoes; standard NATO bombs, HVAR rockets, underwing ASMs or depth charges*

> MAJOR VARIANTS
> **Atlantic 1:** original ASW/maritime patrol version
> **Atlantique 2:** modified version for the French Navy

> RECOGNITION FEATURES
> Low-mounted, straight wing; two turboprop engines; glazed nose; tail boom housing Magnetic Anomaly Detection (MAD) equipment; deep 'double-hull' fuselage

The Breguet Br.1150 Atlantic was a collaborative production between the United States, France, West Germany, Belgium, the Netherlands and Britain. The aircraft was developed for NATO requirement as a Lockheed P-2 Neptune replacement. First deliveries were made to the French Navy in December 1965. France ordered 40 aircraft, Germany 20, Italy 18 and the Netherlands six. A few are also operated by Pakistan. An upgraded version, the Dassault-Breguet Atlantique Nouvelle Generation (ATL-2), was developed for the French Navy, the first aircraft entering service in October 1989.

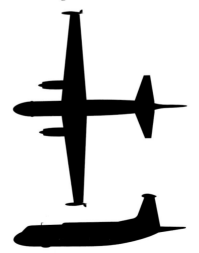

HAMC SH-5

Design of the HAMC SH-5 maritime patrol flying-boat dates back to the early 1960s, but it was not until April 1976 that a prototype made its first flight. The aircraft was intended for a variety of roles, including anti-ship and anti-submarine warfare, minelaying, search and rescue and transport. The SH-5 has a single-step hull and a wide fuselage, enabling the aircraft to carry substantial loads (up to 10,000kg/ 22,045lb of cargo) in three forward compartments. The SH-5 is deployed with the Chinese People's Navy North Sea Fleet at Quingdao. Some examples have been converted as water bombers for firefighting.

ABOVE: *The development of the SH-5 was delayed by China's Cultural Revolution.*

Specification

Crew: *8* **Powerplant:** *four 9415kW (12,620hp) Dongan WJ5A turboprops* **Max speed:** *556km/h (345mph)* **Service ceiling:** *10,250m (33,620ft)* **Max range:** *4750km (2949 miles)* **Wing span:** *36.00m (118ft 1in)* **Length:** *38.90m (127ft 7in)* **Height:** *9.80m (32ft 2in)* **Weight:** *45,000kg (99,208lb)* **Armament:** *missiles, torpedoes, mines, depth charges, bombs*

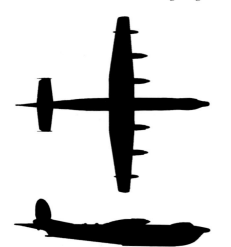

MAJOR VARIANTS
Numerous different configurations
(see main text)

RECOGNITION FEATURES
High-mounted straight wing with
floats close to wingtips; four
turboprop engines; long, narrow,
single-step hull with stinger tail
housing MAD equipment; dihedral
tailplane with twin fins

IAI 707 Phalcon

ABOVE: *The IAI 707 Phalcon is easily identifiable by its bulbous nose radome and fuselage sensors.*

Specification

Crew: *approx 21* **Powerplant:** *four 9520kg (20,982lb) thrust Pratt & Whitney JT3D-3B turbofans* **Max speed:** *973km/h (604mph)* **Service ceiling:** *10,980m (36,000ft)* **Max range:** *6920km (4297 miles)* **Wing span:** *44.40m (145ft 9in)* **Length:** *46.60m (152ft 11in)* **Height:** *12.90m (42ft 6in)* **Weight:** *classified* **Armament:** *none*

Converted from a Boeing 707 by Israel Aircraft Industries, the IAI Phalcon airborne early-warning aircraft system features so many changes that it is an almost completely new aircraft from a recognition point of view. The radar can detect even low-flying objects from distances of hundreds of kilometres, day and night, under all weather conditions. Verification beams sent at specific, individual, newly detected targets eliminate false alarms. Moreover, track initiation is achieved in 2 to 4 seconds as compared to 20 to 40 seconds with a rotodome radar.

MAJOR VARIANTS

Phalcon system can be installed on a variety of platforms, such as the **Boeing 707, Boeing 767, Boeing 747, Airbus** and **C-130**

RECOGNITION FEATURES

Low-mounted swept wing; four podded underwing turbofans; large radar fairings on both sides of forward fuselage; large nose radome

Ilyushin Il-38

The Ilyushin Il-38 (NATO reporting name 'May'), which became operational in 1973, is a long-range maritime patrol development of the Il-18 civil airliner and is the equivalent of the Lockheed P-3 Orion. An extra bay was built into the fuselage and the wings moved forward to counter the extra weight of the weapons bays. Of the 50 or so aircraft produced, 35 were still in service with the Russian Navy in the early 21st century. Eight Il-38s are in service with the Indian Navy, and five of these are undergoing upgrades.

ABOVE: *The Il-38 'May' was developed from the IL-18 airliner.*

Specification

Crew: *12–13* **Powerplant:** *four 2984kW (4000hp) Ivchenko AI-20 turboprops* **Max speed:** *643km/h (400mph)* **Service ceiling:** *8540m (28,000ft)* **Max range:** *7240km (4500 miles)* **Wing span:** *37.48m (122ft 8in)* **Length:** *39.61m (129ft 10in)* **Height:** *10.29m (33ft 9in)* **Weight:** *61,200kg (134,922lb) loaded* **Armament:** *variety of ASW stores*

MAJOR VARIANTS
Il-38: long-range maritime patrol aircraft

RECOGNITION FEATURES
Low-mounted straight wing; four turboprops; 'stinger' tail; long fuselage with radome under the nose

Ilyushin/Beriev A-50

ABOVE: *The A-50 provides an airborne early warning system which, although not as advanced as the E-3 Sentry, is cheaper to operate.*

Specification

Crew: 7 **Powerplant:** *four 12,000kg (26,455lb) thrust Soloviev D-30KP-1 turbofans* **Max speed:** *800km/h (500mph)* **Service ceiling:** *11,285m (37,000ft)* **Max range:** *6400km (4000 miles)* **Wing span:** *50.50m (165ft 8in)* **Length:** *46.59m (152ft 11in)* **Height:** *14.76m (48ft 5in)* **Weight:** *170,000kg (374,785lb) loaded* **Armament:** *none*

Developed by Beriev to replace the Tu-126 Moss in the airborne early warning and detection role, the A-50 (NATO reporting name 'Mainstay') first flew in 1980. The aircraft can remain airborne for four to six hours, extending to 10 hours with flight refuelling. The radar has a detection range of up to 800km (500 miles), and can track 200 targets simultaneously. The Mainstay is not as sophisticated as its western counterpart, the E-3 Sentry, but provides Russian Fighter Regiments with an airborne control capability over both land and water.

MAJOR VARIANTS
A-50: initial production model
A-50M: new radar and improved onboard electronics
A-50U: advanced AEW variant; increased take-off weight and endurance

---

RECOGNITION FEATURES
High-mounted swept wing; four podded turbofans; glazed nose with pronounced bulge underneath; T-type tail; large bulges under fuselage housing undercarriage; saucer-type radome mounted on pylons above rear fuselage

Lockheed Martin P-3 Orion

The P-3 (formerly P3V-1) Orion was Lockheed's winning submission in a 1958 US Navy contest for a new ASW aircraft. The first of two YP3V-1 prototypes flew on 19 August 1958 and deliveries of production P-3As began in August 1962. The WP-3A was a weather reconnaissance version, the next patrol variant being the P-3A. Total P-3A/B production ran to 286 aircraft for the US Navy, plus five for the RNZAF, 10 for the RAAF, and five for Norway. The P-3C, which appeared in 1969, was equipped with a Univac digital computer, the nerve centre of a fully integrated search, analysis and attack system. Further improvements were incorporated in 1974–75, and in addition to the 132 P-3Cs delivered to the USN, 10 aircraft were ordered by the RAAF. Further variants of the Orion include the EP-3A electronic intelligence aircraft, the P-3F, six of which were delivered to Iran in 1975, and the CP-140 Aurora for the Canadian Armed Forces.

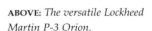

ABOVE: *The versatile Lockheed Martin P-3 Orion.*

Specification (P-3C)

Crew: *10* **Powerplant:** *four 3663kW (4910hp) Allison T56-A-14 turboprops* **Max speed:** *761km/h (473mph)* **Service ceiling:** *8625m (28,300ft)* **Max range:** *3835km (2383 miles)* **Wing span:** *30.37m (99ft 8in)* **Length:** *35.61m (116ft 10in)* **Height:** *10.29m (33ft 8in)* **Weight:** *61,235kg (135,000lb) loaded* **Armament:** *up to 8735kg (19,250lb) of ASW stores*

MAJOR VARIANTS
WP-3A: weather reconnaissance variant
P-3A: production maritime ASW aircraft
P-3B: upgraded weapons and engines
P-3C: upgraded electronics and computer systems

RECOGNITION FEATURES
Long fuselage; low-mounted, relatively short straight wing with four turboprops; straight leading edge and tapered trailing edge; extended 'stinger' tail cone housing MAD equipment

Lockheed Martin S-3A Viking

ABOVE: *An S-3A Viking of the US Navy's VS-29 'Dragonfires'.*

Specification (S-3B)

Crew: *4* **Powerplant:** *two 4207kg (9275lb) General Electric TF34-GE-400B turbofans* **Max speed:** *814km/h (506mph)* **Service ceiling:** *10,670m (35,000ft)* **Max range:** *3705km (2302 miles)* **Wing span:** *20.93m (68ft 8in)* **Length:** *16.26m (53ft 4in)* **Height:** *6.93m (22ft 9in)* **Weight:** *19,278kg (42,500lb) loaded* **Armament:** *internal weapons bay with provision for up to 907kg (2000lb) of ASW stores*

The Lockheed S-3A Viking was designed in response to a 1969 US Navy requirement for a carrier-borne ASW system built around a Univac digital computer. The prototype flew for the first time on 21 January 1972, and 93 production SA-3As had been ordered by the end of 1973, deliveries beginning to VS-41, an operational training unit, in March 1974. The last of 187 Vikings was delivered to the USN in 1978. The Viking fleet was substantially updated to S-3B standard in the early 1990s, some aircraft being converted to the electronic warfare role as ES-3As.

MAJOR VARIANTS
S-3A: initial ASW production model
S-3B: upgraded S-3A; new electronics/avionics
ES-3A: electronic intelligence gathering aircraft

RECOGNITION FEATURES
High-mounted, broad swept wing; stubby fuselage; high, broad swept tailfin; deep cockpit in extreme nose

Lockheed Martin U-2

The Lockheed U-2 high-altitude reconnaissance aircraft first flew in August 1955, an order for 52 production aircraft following quickly. Overflights of the USSR and Warsaw Pact territories began in 1956, and continued until 1 May 1960, when a CIA pilot, Francis G. Powers, was shot down near Sverdlovsk by a Soviet SA-2 missile battery. U-2s were used to overfly Cuba during the missile crisis of 1962, one being shot down, and were also used by the Chinese Nationalists to overfly mainland China, all four aircraft being subsequently lost. U-2s also operated over North Vietnam in 1965–66. The last U-2 variant was the U-2R, but in 1978 the production line was re-opened for the building of 29 TR-1A battlefield surveillance aircraft. All TR-1As were re-designated U-2R in the 1990s.

ABOVE: *A Lockheed U-2 in service with NASA for high-altitude research.*

Specification (U-2R)

Crew: *1* **Powerplant:** *one 7711kg (17,000lb) thrust Pratt & Whitney J75 P-13B turbojet* **Max speed:** *796km/h (495mph)* **Service ceiling:** *27,430m (90,000ft)* **Max range:** *4183km (2600 miles)* **Wing span:** *31.39m (103ft)* **Length:** *19.13m (62ft 9in)* **Height:** *4.88m (16ft)* **Weight:** *18,733kg (41,300lb) loaded* **Armament:** *none*

> MAJOR VARIANTS
> **U-2A:** initial production model
> **U-2C:** improved version; new engine
> **U-2R:** U-2C variant; larger with greater fuel capacity
> **TR-1A:** U-2R variant; improved radar, avionics and ECM equipment

> RECOGNITION FEATURES
> Long, slender fuselage; very long, high-aspect ratio wing; air intakes on fuselage sides aft of single-seat cockpit

Myasishchev M-17/M-55

ABOVE: *The Myasishchev M-55 was the Soviet equivalent of the U-2, and also fulfils a number of research roles.*

Specification (M-55)

Crew: *1* **Powerplant:** *two 9988kg (22,050lb) thrust Aviadvigatel turbofans* **Max speed:** *750km/h (466mph)* **Service ceiling:** *21,350m (70,000ft)* **Max endurance:** *6 hrs 30 mins* **Wing span:** *37.40m (122ft 11in)* **Length:** *22.80m (75ft)* **Height:** *4.70m (15ft 5in)* **Weight:** *19,950kg (44,000lb) loaded* **Armament:** *none*

The Myasishchev M-17 (NATO reporting name 'Mystic') high-altitude aircraft was the Soviet equivalent of the U-2, initially developed to shoot down US reconnaissance balloons/aircraft. Subsequently it was modified as a single-seat reconnaissance and research aircraft. The first two prototypes (Mystic-A) had a single turbojet engine. The subsequent M-55 (Mystic-B), also designated M-17R, is a twin-jet version built by the Molniya Scientific and Industrial Enterprise (which absorbed the Myasishchev Bureau).

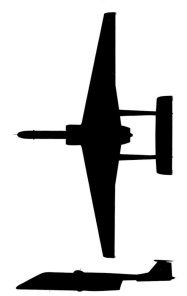

MAJOR VARIANTS
M-17: single engine
M-55: twin engines

RECOGNITION FEATURES
M-55: high-mounted, high-aspect ratio wing; twin turbojets in fuselage nacelle; twin tail booms; twin fins; high-mounted tailplane

Northrop Grumman E-2 Hawkeye

The US Navy's principal electronic surveillance aircraft for many years has been the Grumman E-2 Hawkeye, the prototype of which first flew on 20 October 1960. Sixty-two E-2As were built, including the prototypes, and construction ended early in 1967. The E-2B, which flew in February 1969, had a number of refinements, including an L-304 micro-electronic computer, and all operational E-2As were subsequently updated to E-2B standard. The early model Hawkeyes were equipped with the General Electric APS-96 search and tracking radar, which even in its original form was capable of automatic target detection and tracking over water. A new model, the E-2C, was fitted with an improved radar.

ABOVE: *A Northrop Grumman E-2 Hawkeye in flight.*

Specification (E-2C)

Crew: *5* **Powerplant:** *two 3431kW (4600ehp) Allison T56-A-425 turboprops* **Max speed:** *595km/h (370mph)* **Service ceiling:** *9660m (31,700ft)* **Max range:** *3060km (1900 miles)* **Wing span:** *24.56m (80ft 7in)* **Length:** *17.17m (56ft 4in)* **Height:** *4.88m (18ft 4in)* **Weight:** *22,453kg (49,500lb) loaded* **Armament:** *none*

> **MAJOR VARIANTS**
> **E-2A:** initial production variant
> **E-2B, E-2C:** improved versions
> **TE-2C:** trainer
> **C-2A Greyhound:** carrier on-board delivery transport

> **RECOGNITION FEATURES**
> Large radome mounted on upper fuselage; long, straight wing; twin turboprops; dihedral; tailplane with two large endplate fins and two smaller fins mounted inboard; **C-2A** does not have a radome and has a redesigned fuselage to accommodate freight and a rear loading ramp

Northrop Grumman E-8A J-STARS

ABOVE: *The E-8A J-STARS gives commanders a real-time view of battlefield conditions.*

Specification

Crew: *21* **Powerplant:** *four 8698kg (19,200lb) thrust Pratt & Whitney TF33-102C turbofans* **Max speed:** *945km/h (590mph)* **Service ceiling:** *12,802m (42,000ft)* **Max endurance:** *11 hours unrefuelled* **Wing span:** *44.40m (145ft 8in)* **Length:** *46.60m (152ft 10in)* **Height:** *13m (42ft 8in)* **Weight:** *150,142kg (331,000lb) loaded* **Armament:** *none*

> MAJOR VARIANTS
> **E-8A:** version produced from Boeing 707 airframes
> **E-8B:** new-build airframe model
> **E-8C:** production model

> RECOGNITION FEATURES
> As for Boeing 707, but with a long canoe-shaped radome under the forward fuselage

The J-STARS is a long-range, air-to-ground surveillance aircraft designed to locate, classify and track ground targets in all weather conditions. The prototype E-8A J-STARS was in effect a rebuilt Boeing 707, assembled by Grumman in 1988. Two development E-8As (including the prototype) were produced by Northrop Grumman, both based on Boeing 707 airframes. These two E-8As took part in Operation Desert Storm in 1991, flying 49 combat sorties. The production model is the E-8C, which is a modified Boeing 707-300; it was delivered in June 1996. The E-8 collects data as events occur, and this is relayed to ground stations via a secure, surveillance and control radar link.

Northrop Grumman S-2 Tracker

One of the most important carrier-borne aircraft of the postwar years, the Grumman XS2F-1 Tracker prototype flew for the first time on 4 December 1952. The initial series production S2F-1 (later S-2A) was powered by two 1138kW (1525hp) Wright R-1820-82 engines; 755 were built, first deliveries to the US Navy being made in February 1954. The type was also supplied to Argentina, Japan, Italy, Brazil, Taiwan, Thailand, Uruguay and the Netherlands. Variants were the S-2C, S-2D and S-2E. The majority of Trackers still in service are operated from shore bases. Aircraft used by Argentina and Taiwan have been retrofitted with Garrett turboprop engines.

ABOVE: *An S2-F Tracker of the US Navy in flight.*

Specification (S-2D)

Crew: *4* **Powerplant:** *two 1138kW (1525hp) Wright R-1820-82WA Cyclone 9-cylinder radial engines* **Max speed:** *461km/h (287mph)* **Service ceiling:** *7010m (23,000ft)* **Max range:** *1450km (900 miles)* **Wing span:** *21.23m (69ft 8in)* **Length:** *12.87m (42ft 3in)* **Height:** *4.95m (16ft 3in)* **Weight:** *11,930kg (26,300lb) loaded* **Armament:** *two homing torpedoes, two Mk 101 depth bombs or four depth charges; six 113kg (250lb) bombs, 11.25cm (5in) HVARS or Zuni rockets*

> ### MAJOR VARIANTS
> **S-2A:** first production version
> **S-2C:** increased weapons capacity
> **S-2D:** increased dimensions; four crew
> **RS-2C:** photo-reconnaissance version

> ### RECOGNITION FEATURES
> High-mounted, straight wing; twin piston or turboprop engines; dihedral tailplane; searchlight in starboard wing

Raytheon (Beechcraft) RC-12 Guardrail

ABOVE: *The Raytheon RC-12 Guardrail is readily distinguished from the civil King Air by its many electronic sensors.*

Specification (RC-12D)

Crew: *2* **Powerplant:** *two Pratt & Whitney Canada PT6A-41 turbo-props* **Max speed:** *536km/h (333mph)* **Service ceiling:** *9450m (30,996ft)* **Wing span:** *16.60m (54ft 6in)* **Length:** *13.30m (43ft 9in)* **Height:** *4.50m (15ft)* **Weight:** *5670kg (12,496lb)* **Armament:** *none*

The Raytheon (Beechcraft) RC-12 Guardrail family of electronic intelligence aircraft is based on the Beechcraft King Air twin-engined light transport. The Guardrail comes in several guises, starting with the RC-12D Improved Guardrail V, based on the King Air Model A200CT. This US Army special electronic mission version carries the AN/USD-9 Improved Guardrail remote-controlled communications intercept and direction-finding system. Five RC-12Ds are used by the Israeli Air Force.

MAJOR VARIANTS
The US Army had 13 **RC-12D Improved Guardrail V**s converted from **C-12D**s, with deliveries starting in mid-1983. Other variants, each with its own specialist electronic intelligence task, are the **RC-12G, RC-12H, RC-12K, RC-12N, RC-12P** and **RC-12Q**.

RECOGNITION FEATURES
Low-mounted straight wing with tip tanks; T-type tail; twin turboprops; numerous protruding antennae

Shin Meiwa PS/US-1A

First flown on 5 October 1967 as the PX-S, this long-range STOL amphibian entered service with the Japanese Maritime Self-Defence Force (JMSDF) in 1973 in its PS-1 anti-submarine form, 20 examples being built. Procurement of the PS-1 was halted in 1980. Early in PS-1 production, however, the JMSDF asked Shin Meiwa to develop an amphibious version for search-and-rescue (SAR) duties to replace the service's Grumman UF-1 Albatross flying boats; this emerged as the US-1, which flew in proto-type form on 15 October 1974.

ABOVE: *Although largely replaced by long-range rescue helicopters, the Shin Meiwa US-1A still serves in small numbers.*

Specification (US-1A)

Crew: *9* **Powerplant:** *four 2604kW (3490hp) Ishikawajima-built General Electric T64-1H1-10J turboprops* **Max speed:** *495km/h (310mph)* **Service ceiling:** *8200m (27,000ft)* **Range:** *4200km (2610 miles)* **Wing span:** *33.15m (108ft 9in)* **Length:** *33.46m (109ft 9in)* **Height:** *9.82m (32ft 3in)* **Weight:** *45,000kg (99,200lb) loaded* **Armament:** *none*

MAJOR VARIANTS
PS-1: initial anti-submarine version
US-1: search-and-rescue variant

RECOGNITION FEATURES
High-mounted straight wing; four turboprops; nose radome; single-step hull; T-type tail

Airtech/CASA CN-235

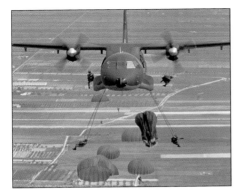

ABOVE: *A CN-235 demonstrating its parachute drop capabilities.*

Specification (CN-235M)

Crew: 4 **Powerplant:** *two 1306kW (1750hp) General Electric CT7-9C3 turboprops* **Max speed:** *460km/h (286mph)* **Service ceiling:** *5485m (17,990ft)* **Max range:** *1300km (800 miles)* **Wing span:** *25.81m (84ft 8in)* **Length:** *21.40m (70ft 2in)* **Height:** *8.17m (26ft 9in)* **Weight:** *16,500kg (36,376lb) loaded* **Payload:** *6000kg (13,227lb); 48 paratroops; 21 stretchers*

MAJOR VARIANTS
CN-235M: military transport
CN-235MP: maritime patrol aircraft

RECOGNITION FEATURES
High wing; twin turboprop engines; tapered leading and trailing edges outboard of engines; large bulges under fuselage housing undercarriage; loading ramp beneath upswept rear fuselage; **CN-235MP** has large ventral radar and carries Harpoon or Exocet missiles

---

Originally developed as a joint venture by CASA of Spain and ITPN of Indonesia and first flown in 1983, the CN-235 is a high-wing, pressurized, twin turboprop aircraft with STOL performance. It was conceived as a tactical military transport and is capable of operating from unpaved runways. The CN-235 can be used to transport up to 48 paratroopers who may exit from either of the two side doors or the rear ramp. The CN-235 is able to carry up to four tons of supplies to forward troops. On medical evacuation missions, the plane can transport up to 21 stretchers, with four attendants. CASA has developed several versions, including a civil airliner variant. Military versions are operated by many nations, including Abu Dhabi, Indonesia, Malaysia, Chile, France, Ireland, Morocco, Oman, Saudi Arabia, South Africa, South Korea and Spain.

Alenia (Aeritalia, Fiat) G.222

A versatile medium transport, the Alenia G.222 flew in prototype form on 18 July 1970. The first of 50 production aircraft was delivered at the end of 1978, replacing the Fairchild C-119 in the Italian Air Force's transport units. The aircraft had some export success, customers including Argentina (3), Dubai (1), Libya (20), Nigeria (4), Somalia (4), USA (10) and Venezuela (8).

ABOVE: *An Alenia G.222 in Italian Air Force service.*

Specification

Crew: *3* **Powerplant:** *two 2536kW (3400hp) General Electric T64-GE-P4D turboprops* **Max speed:** *540km/h (336mph) at 4575m (15,000ft)* **Service ceiling:** *7620m (25,000ft)* **Max range:** *4558km (2832 miles)* **Wing span:** *40.00m (131ft 3in)* **Length:** *32.40m (106ft 3in)* **Height:** *11.65m (38ft 5in)* **Weight:** *16,000kg (35,270lb) loaded*

MAJOR VARIANTS
G.222: basic production version
C-27A (USA): US version

RECOGNITION FEATURES
High-mounted, straight wing; twin turboprops; short fuselage with upswept rear to accommodate loading ramp; low-set tailplane; undercarriage bulges under mid-fuselage

Antonov An-12

ABOVE: *The An-12 was one of the best tactical transports of the Cold War.*

Specification

Crew: *4* **Powerplant:** *four IvchenkoAI-20K turboprops of 2984kW (4000ehp) each* **Cruising speed:** *580km/h (360mph)* **Service ceiling:** *10,200m (33,465ft)* **Max range:** *3200km (2110 miles)* **Wing span:** *38.00m (124ft 8in)* **Length:** *33.10m (108ft 7in)* **Height:** *10.53m (34ft 6in)* **Weight:** *61,000kg (134,482lb) loaded*

The Antonov An-12 (NATO reporting name 'Cub') freighter was developed from the An-10A Ukraina turboprop passenger aircraft, and was intended primarily for military use. Military An-12s were widely exported to 'friendly foreign' countries, including India, which received 41. The An-12 was also produced in China as the Shaanxi Y-8, and is used in a variety of roles, including tanker and intelligence-gatherer. Chinese-built Y-8s have been exported to Myanmar (Burma) and the Sudan, and the type still serves with the Czech Republic, Egypt, Ethiopia, Iraq, Russia, Ukraine and Yemen.

> MAJOR VARIANTS
> **AB-12B:** civilian version
> **AN-12BP:** military transport
> **AN-12BK/PP/PPS:** electronic warfare versions

> RECOGNITION FEATURES
> High-mounted wing with square wingtips; four turboprop engines; upswept rear fuselage to accommodate rear loading ramp; large fairing between fuselage and tailfin; glazed nose with small blister underneath

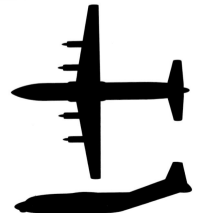

Antonov An-22

First revealed at the Paris Air Show in June 1965, the huge An-22 (NATO reporting name 'Cock') heavy transport entered service with both Aeroflot and the Soviet Air Force, which used it to transport large loads such as dismantled aircraft and missiles on tracked launchers. When it made its debut the An-22 was the heaviest aircraft ever built. Sixty-six aircraft were completed up to 1974, when production ended. The An-22 can be adapted to carry loads 'piggy-back' on top of the fuselage; one example is used by Antonov to ferry wings intended for the An-124.

ABOVE: *When it was first unveiled, the Antonov An-22 was the heaviest aircraft ever built.*

Specification

Crew: *5–6* **Powerplant:** *four 11,190kW (15,000hp) Kuznetsov NK-12MA turboprops* **Max speed:** *740km/h (460mph)* **Service ceiling:** *not known* **Max range:** *10,950km (6800 miles)* **Wing span:** *64.40m (211ft 4in)* **Length:** *57.80m (189ft 7in)* **Height:** *12.53m (41ft 1in)* **Weight:** *250,000kg (551,160lb) loaded* **Payload:** *up to 80,000kg (176,367lb) of cargo*

MAJOR VARIANTS
AN-22: production heavy transport

RECOGNITION FEATURES
High-mounted straight wing, taper-ing towards the tips; four turboprops; long undercarriage bulges on fuse-lage undersides; upswept rear fuse-lage to accommodate loading ramp; twin tailfins; glazed nose

Antonov An-24

ABOVE: *The An-24 went through a protracted development phase, during which the wings were completely redesigned.*

Specification

Crew: *2/3* **Powerplant:** *two 1902kW (2550ehp) Ivchenko AI-24A turboprops* **Max speed:** *450km/h (280mph)* **Service ceiling:** *8500m (27,600ft)* **Max range:** *550km (340miles)* **Wing span:** *29.20m (95ft 7in)* **Length:** *23.50m (77ft 2in)* **Height:** *8.32m (27ft 4in)* **Weight:** *21,000kg (49,300lb) loaded* **Payload:** *48 passengers*

In 1958, Aeroflot produced a requirement for a short-range turboprop-powered aircraft capable of carrying 32–40 passengers, a figure later raised to 44 and then to 48. The design that emerged was the Antonov An-24 (NATO reporting name 'Coke'), a high-wing monoplane with a low-set fuselage comprising two circular arcs, allowing a spacious high-pressure cabin. The airliner went into service with Aeroflot in 1963 and was subsequently supplied to many operators worldwide, being built in China as the Y-7.

MAJOR VARIANTS
An-24V: light tactical transport
Y-7: Chinese version

RECOGNITION FEATURES
High-mounted straight wing with anhedral on the outer panels; twin turboprops; large fairing between tailfin and upper fuselage

Antonov An-26

One version of the An-24 was the An-24RT, which was intended for freight or mixed transport and which had an under-fuselage loading ramp. It was fitted with an RU-19-300 light auxiliary engine in the right-hand engine nacelle, producing more power for aircraft operating from airfields at a high elevation and at high temperatures. Antonov used the An-24TR as the basis for the An-26 (NATO reporting name 'Curl'), a more sophisticated version capable of loading and unloading light, jeep-type vehicles via its under-fuselage ramp, which could be slid forward on tracked rails for direct loading. The aircraft could also be used for air-dropping operations and could be quickly adapted for passenger, paratoop or transport duties.

The An-26, which was flight tested in 1968, serves with many air arms and quasi-civil operators. One of the biggest customers for the An-26 was Yugoslavia, which at one time had 30 aircraft in service, divided between two squadrons at Zagreb and Belgrade. The

ABOVE: *Many of the lessons learned with the An-24 are incorporated in the Antonov An-26, an extremely effective tactical transport.*

MAJOR VARIANTS
An-26: original production version
An-26B: improved version with increased freight handling capability
An-26D: long-range variant
An-26M: ELINT version
An-26P: firefighting variant
An-26RTR: SIGINT version

Specification

Crew: *3* **Powerplant:** *two 2103kW (2820ehp) Ivchenko AI-24T turboprops* **Max speed:** *450km/h (280mph)* **Service ceiling:** *8500m (27,600ft)* **Max range:** *1300km (807 miles)* **Wing span:** *29.20m (95ft 7in)* **Length:** *23.50m (77ft 2in)* **Height:** *8.32m (27ft 4in)* **Weight:** *24,000kg (52,911lb)* **Payload:** *50 passengers*

Polish Air Force's 13th Transport regiment at Krakow/Balice air base also operated a dozen An-26s. Another major customer for the An-26 was Angola, which received at least 30 aircraft; several of these were used in a quasi-military role, flying for both the government and the national airline. Some Angolan An-26s were modified by Antonov to carry bomb racks on the side of the fuselage beneath the wing. In all, An-26s were supplied to around 35 countries. A development of the An-26 is the An-30 Clank, which uses the same basic airframe as the An-26 apart from a new forward fuselage redesigned to accommodate a large glazed nose for the navigator and a darkroom in the main cabin, access between the two being achieved by bodily raising the flight deck. The navigator has special aids to ensure accurate positioning of the aircraft, while the photographic staff have film stores, consoles for controlling the cameras and for processing film.

RECOGNITION FEATURES
High, straight wing with anhedral on outer panels; twin turboprops, rear loading ramp; dihedral tailplane; large fairing from tailfin to upper fuselage

Antonov An-28/An-38

First flown in 1972, the Antonov An-28 is a utility aircraft and light commuter aircraft which was built under licence by PZL Mielec in Poland. The aircraft was intended to replace the versatile Antonov An-2 utility biplane, but a decline in the requirement of utility aircraft in the CIS, and a greatly reduced demand for commuter aircraft, coupled with the fact that many surplus LET 410 Turbolet aircraft were now on the market, brought An-28 production to a virtual standstill. The An-38 is a stretched version, the radial engines of the An-28 being replaced by either Garrett TPE331 or Omsk TVD-20 turboprops. Apart from the type of engines, and the fact that the An-38 is somewhat larger, the two aircraft are similar in overall configuration.

ABOVE: *The Antonov An-28 light transport was designed to replace the versatile An-2 biplane.*

Specification (An-28)

Crew: *1–2* **Powerplant:** *two 701kW (940hp) TVD-10B radials* **Max speed:** *350km/h (217mph)* **Service ceiling:** *6710m (22,000ft)* **Max range:** *1300km (807 miles)* **Wing span:** *22.06m (72ft 4in)* **Length:** *13.00m (42ft 7in)* **Height:** *4.60m (15ft)* **Weight:** *6100kg (13,444lb) loaded* **Payload:** *20 passengers*

MAJOR VARIANTS
An-28: utility/light commuter aircraft
An-38: stretched version of An-28 with new engines

RECOGNITION FEATURES
High-mounted straight wing; two radial engines (**An-38**: turboprops); twin fins

Antonov An-70

ABOVE: *The An-70 is readily identified by its propfan engines.*

Specification

Crew: *3* **Powerplant:** *four Progress D-27 turbine engines driving Aerosila SW-27 counter-rotating propfans* **Max speed:** *800km/h (500mph)* **Service ceiling:** *12,000m (39,360ft)* **Max range:** *7400km (4595 miles)* **Wing span:** *44.10m (144ft 6in)* **Length:** *40.70m (133ft 7in)* **Height:** *16.40m (53ft 9in)* **Weight:** *130,000kg (286,600lb)* **Payload:** *47,000kg (103,615lb)*

The propfan-powered An-70 flew for the first time in December 1994, but in February 1995, on its fourth flight, it collided with an An-72 chase plane and was destroyed. A second prototype was flown for the first time on 24 April 1977, the aircraft making its public debut at the Moscow air show in August. The An-70 is the first aircraft in the world to use propfan engines, in which a gas turbine is used to drive unducted fan engines rather than propellers. It was announced in June 2004 that Russia and the Ukraine would each purchase the An-70.

MAJOR VARIANTS
An-70 proposals include:
An-70: military freighter
An-70-100: two crew
An-77: export version
An-70T: commercial version
An-70TK : twin-propfan convertible passenger/freight aircraft

RECOGNITION FEATURES
High-mounted swept wing; four propfan engines; deep fuselage; low tailplane

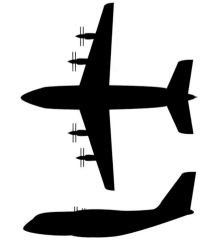

Antonov An-72

First flown in December 1977, the An-72 (NATO reporting name 'Coaler') was designed for short take-off and landing operations from unprepared airfields, which accounts for the rather unusual arrangement of its twin turbofan engines. These are positioned on the leading edge of the wings so that the jet efflux blows over titanium panels in the wing's upper surface, providing extra lift, and also keeps the intakes well clear of surface debris. The An-72 entered service in 1979. The type is operated by Kazakhstan, Peru, Russia, Ukraine and Iran.

ABOVE: *The An-72's high-mounted engines keep the intakes free from debris during operations from unprepared strips.*

Specification (An-72)

Crew: 3 **Powerplant:** *two 6492kg (14,330lb) thrust Lotarev D-36 turbofans* **Max speed:** *760km (472mph)* **Service ceiling:** *8000m (26,246ft)* **Max range:** *3800km (2359 miles)* **Wing span:** *25.83m (84ft 9in)* **Length:** *26.58m (87ft 2in)* **Height:** *8.24m (27ft)* **Weight:** *30,500kg (67,240lb)* **Payload:** *5000kg (11,023lb)*

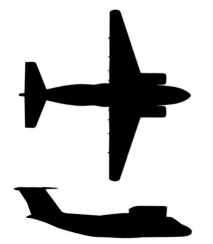

MAJOR VARIANTS
An-72P: maritime patrol variant with bulged observation windows; armament: one 23mm (0.9in) cannon, depth charges, bombs and rockets.
An-74: derivative with improved avionics and increased wing span

---

RECOGNITION FEATURES
High-mounted swept wing with twin turbofans mounted close together on leading edge; undercarriage bulge in fuselage underside; T-type tail

Antonov An-124 Ruslan

ABOVE: *The An-124 gave a huge boost to Aeroflot cargo operations.*

Specification

Crew: *5* **Powerplant:** *four 23,400kg (51,590lb) thrust Lotarev D-18T turbofans* **Max speed:** *865km/h (537mph)* **Service ceiling:** *9760m (32,000ft)* **Max range:** *4500km (2794 miles)* **Wing span:** *73.30m (240ft 4in)* **Length:** *69.50m (227ft 11in)* **Height:** *21.10m (69ft 2in)* **Weight:** *405,000kg (892,620lb) loaded* **Payload:** *up to 451 passengers or 150,000lb (330,700kg) of cargo*

One of the largest aircraft ever built, the mighty An-124 transport (NATO reporting name 'Condor'), designed for very heavy lift, proved a winning design from the outset. The first prototype An-124 flew on 26 December 1982, and the aircraft was making proving flights on Aeroflot's routes by the end of 1985. By 1991 at least 23 An-124s were in service, and the Antonov bureau formed a special company to sell cargo space all over the world. The An-124 was soon used to generate money for Antonov as aircraft were leased out to western air freight companies.

MAJOR VARIANTS
An-124-100: commercial transport
An-124-100M: western avionics fitted
An-124-102: EFIS-equipped flight deck
An-124FFR: firefighter version

RECOGNITION FEATURES
Deep, wide fuselage with high-mounted swept wing; four under-slung podded turbofans

Antonov An-140

Developed by the Antonov Design Bureau as a replacement for the An-24 series, the An-140 medium transport and passenger aircraft entered production in 1999. The An-140 is capable of operating from semi-prepared airfields in a wide range of weather conditions. Export models of the An-140 will be equipped with Pratt & Whitney PW127A turboprop engines, while models for the internal market will have TV3-117VMA-SB2 turboprops. An auxiliary power system, installed in the tail section of the fuselage, allows for autonomous operation of the aircraft from remote airfields.

ABOVE: *Developed to replace the An-24, the Antonov An-140, like most Russian transports, can operate from semi-prepared strips.*

Specification
Crew: 2 **Powerplant:** *two 1865kW (2500hp) TV3-117VMA-SB2 turbo-props* **Max speed:** *575km/h (357mph)* **Service ceiling:** *7200m (23,600ft)* **Max range:** *3700km (2297 miles)* **Wing span:** *25.50m (83ft 7in)* **Length:** *22.60m (74ft 2in)* **Height:** *8.23m (27ft)* **Weight:** *21,500kg (47,407lb)* **Payload:** *52 passengers*

> ### MAJOR VARIANTS
> Proposed roles for the **An-140** include passenger/cargo, ice patrol, fishery protection, and aerial survey. There is also an **An-140-100** project with a stretched fuselage and 68-passenger capacity.

> ### RECOGNITION FEATURES
> High-mounted straight wing with twin turboprops; undercarriage bulges under mid-fuselage

Antonov An-225 Mriya

ABOVE: *There is no mistaking the massive Antonov An-225, originally developed to transport Russia's space shuttle.*

Specification

Crew: *3–4* **Powerplant:** *six 23,370kg (51,590lb) thrust Zaporozhye/Lotarev D18T turbofans* **Max speed:** *700–850km/h (435–528mph)* **Service ceiling:** *n/a* **Max range:** *4500km (2795 miles)* **Wing span:** *88.40m (290ft)* **Length:** *84.00m (275ft 7in)* **Height:** *18.10m (59ft 5in)* **Weight:** *600,000kg (1,322,750lb) loaded* **Payload:** *up to 250,000kg (551,146lb) of cargo*

Trials with a much-modified Myasishchev Mya-4 Bison bomber proved that the 'piggy-back' method of transporting heavy and outsize loads was feasible, carrying components of the Energiya booster used to launch the Russian space shuttle, Buran (Snowstorm). Following these trials, the massive Antonov An-225 Mriya (Dream) made its appearance in 1988. The An-225 was the first aircraft in the world to be flown at a gross weight of 453,000kg (1,000,000lb). It is a fully fly-by-wire design, and each wing is fitted with eight air brakes.

MAJOR VARIANTS
An-225: standard production version

RECOGNITION FEATURES
High-mounted, swept wing, tapering sharply towards the tips; six under-slung podded turbofans; twin tailfins

BAe (BAC) VC-10

Developed by Vickers as a four-jet long-haul airliner, the VC-10 was not a commercial success, being used only by BOAC and East African Airways. Designated VC-10 C.Mk 1, 14 examples were delivered to No 10 Squadron, RAF Air Support Command, between 1966 and 1968. Four standard VC-10s and five Super VC-10s were later converted to flight refuelling tankers and delivered to the RAF in 1984 and 1985 as VC-10 K.Mk 2s and VC-10 K.Mk 3s. A final batch of five ex-British Airways Super VC-10s, converted in the early 1990s, received the designation VC-10 K.Mk 4. In all, 54 VC-10s and Super VC-10s were built.

ABOVE: *An RAF VC-10 trailing its three flight refuelling hoses.*

Specification (VC-10 Mk 3)

Crew: 4 **Powerplant:** *four 9905kg (21,800lb) thrust Rolls-Royce Conway 301 turbofans* **Max speed:** *935km/h (580mph)* **Service ceiling:** *11,600m (38,000ft)* **Max range:** *7600km (4725 miles)* **Wing span:** *55.60m (146ft 3in)* **Length:** *52.30m (171ft 9in)* **Height:** *12.00m (39ft 6in)* **Weight:** *152,000kg (335,000lb) loaded* **Payload:** *18,039kg (39,769lb)*

MAJOR VARIANTS
VC-10: original transport version
VC-10 K.2/3: tanker conversions
Super VC-10: stretched version for greater accommodation and fuel capacity

---

RECOGNITION FEATURES
Low-mounted swept wing; four turbofans mounted in pairs on rear fuselage; swept tail surfaces; T-type tail; hose-and-drogue refuelling points under wings and fuselage

Boeing C-17 Globemaster III

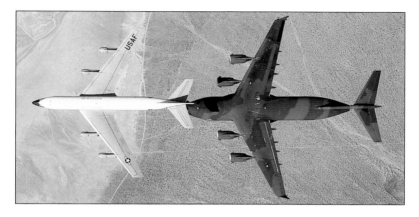

ABOVE: *This picture gives a good idea of the size of the C-17, right, seen here refuelling from a KC-135 tanker aircraft.*

Specification

Crew: *3* **Powerplant:** *four 18,319kg (40,440lb) thrust Pratt & Whitney F117-PW-100 turbofan engines* **Max speed:** *834km/h (518mph)* **Service ceiling:** *13,716m (45,000ft)* **Max range:** *global with flight refuelling* **Wing span:** *51.75m (169ft 10in)* **Length:** *53.00m (174ft)* **Height:** *16.79m (55ft 1in)* **Weight:** *265,352kg (585,000lb) loaded* **Payload:** *102 troops/paratroops; 36 litter and 54 ambulatory patients and attendants; 77,519kg (170,900lb) of cargo*

MAJOR VARIANTS
C-17A: standard production version

Initially developed by McDonnell Douglas, the Boeing C-17 strategic transport made its maiden flight on 15 September 1991, and the first production model was delivered to Charleston Air Force Base, SC, on 14 June 1993. The first squadron of C-17s, the 17th Airlift Squadron, was declared operational on 17 January 1995. The US Air Force originally programmed to buy a total of 120 C-17s, with the last one being delivered in November 2004. The fiscal 2000 budget funded another 14 C-17s for special operations duty. Basing of the original 120 C-17s is at Charleston AFB, SC; McChord AFB, WA (first aircraft arrived in July 1999); Altus AFB, OK; and at an Air National Guard unit in Jackson, MS. Basing of the additional 14 aircraft has not been determined. The aircraft is operated by a crew of three (pilot, co-pilot and load-master), reducing manpower requirements, risk exposure and long-term operating costs. Cargo is loaded onto the C-17 through a large aft door that accommodates military vehicles and palletized cargo. The C-17 can carry virtually all of the Army's air-transportable equipment. The design of the aircraft allows

Boeing C-17 Globemaster III (continued)

it to operate through small, austere airfields. The C-17 can take off and land on runways as short as 914m (3000ft) and only 27m (90ft) wide. Even on such narrow runways, the C-17 can turn around using a three-point star turn and its backing capability. The C-17 is operated by the Air Mobility Command at the 437th Airlift Wing, Charleston AFB, SC; the 62nd Airlift Wing, McChord AFB, WA; and the 315th Airlift Wing (Associate Reserve), Charleston AFB, SC.

ABOVE: *The C-17 has given the US armed forces a new dimension in rapid deployment.*

RECOGNITION FEATURES
High-mounted swept wing with winglets; four podded underwing turbofans; T-type tail; large tailfin becoming broader towards the top

Boeing E-4B

ABOVE: *The Boeing E-4B would carry the US President and his battle staff in the event of a serious war emergency.*

Specification

Crew: *3–10* **Powerplant:** *four 23,556kg (52,500lb) thrust General Electric CF6-50E2 turbofan engines*
Max speed: *940km/h (584mph)*
Service ceiling: *9150m (30,000ft)*
Max range: *9625km (5980 miles)*
Wing span: *59.60m (195ft 8in)*
Length: *70.50m (231ft 4in)*
Height: *19.30m (63ft 5in)* **Weight:** *360,000kg (800,000lb)* **Payload:** *up to 114 (including 94 mission crew)*

A militarized version of the Boeing 747-200, the Boeing E-4B serves as the National Airborne Operations Center for the National Command Authorities. In case of national emergency, the aircraft provides a modern, highly survivable, command, control and communications centre to direct US forces, execute emergency war orders and coordinate actions by civil authorities. The E-4B evolved from the E-4A, which had been in service since late 1974. The first B model was delivered to the US Air Force in January 1980, and by 1985 all aircraft were converted to B models. All four E-4Bs are assigned to the 55th Wing, Offutt Air Force Base, Nebraska.

MAJOR VARIANTS
E-4B: current standard version

RECOGNITION FEATURES
Low-mounted swept wing; four podded turbofans; overall resemblance to Boeing 747, except for dorsal hump behind cockpit and antenna arrays on fuselage upper surface

Boeing KC-135/RC-135

In 1954, the USAF announced its intention to purchase a development of the Boeing 367-80 (the prototype Boeing 707) jet airliner for use as a tanker-transport. The military version flew for the first time on 31 August 1956 with the designation KC-135A and 724 production aircraft were built between then and 1965. In the 1970s the KC-135 fleet was subjected to a major overhaul designed to keep it viable into the 21st century, in parallel with the B-52 force which it had been designed to support in the first place. Because the KC-135A's original Pratt & Whitney TF33-P-S turbofan engines were of 1950s technology, they failed to meet modern standards of increased fuel efficiency, reduced pollution and reduced noise levels. By installing new, CFM56 engines, performance is enhanced and fuel off-load capability has dramatically improved. Related system improvements are incorporated to improve

ABOVE: *The Boeing KC-135 tanker has been constantly upgraded and modernized.*

MAJOR VARIANTS
KC-135A: original tanker variant
KC-135R: updated tanker variant
RC-135S Cobra Ball: ballistic missile reconnaissance aircraft; black radome and large circular windows
RC-135U Rivet Sent: signals intelligence aircraft; air intake under nose to cool electronic equipment; long sensors on either side of forward fuselage and protruding tail boom
RC-135V Rivet Joint: electronic intelligence variant; long sensor blisters on either side of forward fuselage, nose radome and many protruding antennae under fuselage

ABOVE: *An RC-135 refuelling during Operation Desert Storm in 1991.*

Specification (KC-135R)

Crew: *5* **Powerplant:** *four 10,078kg (22,224lb) thrust CFM-International F108-CF-100 turbofans* **Max speed:** *853km/h (530mph)* **Service ceiling:** *12,375m (40,600ft)* **Max range:** *4627km (2875 miles)* **Wing span:** *39.88m (130ft 10in)* **Length:** *41.53m (136ft 3in)* **Height:** *12.70m (41ft 8in)* **Weight:** *146,284kg (322,500lb) loaded* **Payload:** *up to 37,648kg (83,000lb) of fuel*

RECOGNITION FEATURES
KC-135: low-mounted, sharply swept wing with four large turbofan engines in underwing pods; flight refuelling boom under rear fuselage, aft of boom operator's blister
RC-135 variants may be distinguished from the KC-135 by their many external fuselage sensor bulges and slender nose radome

---

the modified airplane's ability to carry out its mission, while decreasing overall maintenance and operation costs. The modified aircraft is designated KC-135R. The modification is so successful that two re-engined KC-135Rs can do the work of three KC-135As. The quieter, more fuel-efficient CFM56 engines are manufactured by CFM International, a company jointly owned by SNECMA of France and General Electric of the United States. The engine is an advanced-technology, high-bypass turbofan; the military designation is F108-CF-100. The KC-135 is also used by France, Singapore and Turkey, while Boeing 707 conversions are operated by several other countries. Other military developments of the Boeing 707 airliner include the RC-135 electronic surveillance and E-3 airborne warning and control aircraft, the latter commonly known as the AWACS.

Boeing (McDonnell Douglas) KC-10

The McDonnell Douglas KC-10 flight refuelling tanker was based on the DC-10 Series 30CF convertible freighter. The KC-10 first flew on 30 October 1980. Although the KC-10's primary mission is aerial refuelling, it can combine the tasks of a tanker and cargo aircraft by refuelling fighters and simultaneously carrying the fighter support personnel and equipment. The KC-10 has provided the USAF with an important 'force multiplier', supporting combat aircraft on long-range deployments.

In addition to the three main DC-10 wing fuel tanks, the KC-10 has three large fuel tanks under the cargo floor, one under the forward lower cargo compartment, one in the centre wing area and one under the rear compartment. Combined, the capacity of the six tanks is more than 160,200kg (356,000lb) of fuel – almost twice that of the KC-135 Stratotanker.

ABOVE: *The versatile KC-10 Extender in flight.*

Specification

Crew: *4* **Powerplant:** *three 23,625kg (52,000lb) thrust General Electric CF6-50C2 turbofans* **Max speed:** *995km/h (619mph)* **Service ceiling:** *12,727m (42,000ft)* **Max range:** *7080km (4400 miles) with cargo* **Wing span:** *50.00m (165ft 4.5in)* **Length:** *54.40m (178ft 6in)* **Height:** *17.40m (58ft 1in)* **Weight:** *265,500kg (590,000lb)* **Payload:** *160,200kg (356,000lb) of fuel*

MAJOR VARIANTS
KC-10A: standard production version

RECOGNITION FEATURES
Low-mounted swept wing with two podded turbofans; third turbofan mounted on tailfin; flight refuelling boom in underside of rear fuselage

de Havilland Canada DHC-4A Caribou

ABOVE: *A DHC-4 Caribou in the insignia of the Ugandan Police.*

Specification

Crew: *2* **Powerplant:** *two 1082kW (1450hp) Pratt & Whitney R-2000-D5 Twin Wasp radials* **Max speed:** *290km/h (180mph)* **Service ceiling:** *8380m (27,500ft)* **Max range:** *2253km (1400 miles)* **Wing span:** *29.15m (95ft 7.5in)* **Length:** *22.12m (72ft 7in)* **Height:** *9.67m (31ft 9in)* **Weight:** *11,793kg (26,000lb) loaded* **Payload:** *30 passengers*

First flown in 1958, the de Havilland Canada Caribou is a short take-off and landing (STOL) utility transport that was designed in conjunction with the Canadian Department of Defence. Its primary use is tactical airlift missions in forward battle areas where only short, improvised airstrips are available. It can carry 26 fully equipped para-troops or more than three tons of equipment. The Caribou's STOL capability makes it particularly suitable for delivering troops, supplies and equipment to isolated outposts.

MAJOR VARIANTS
DHC-4T: variant fitted with twin turboprops

RECOGNITION FEATURES
High mounted, straight wing with tapered trailing edge; twin piston engines; upswept rear fusealge; large, square-cut tailfin; **DHC-4T** has longer engine nacelles

---

de Havilland Canada DHC-5 Buffalo

Developed from the DHC-4 Caribou, the turboprop-powered Buffalo was funded by both the US and Canadian governments. The prototype flew on 9 April 1964. In 1976 the type was substantially updated and a new variant, the DHC-5D, entered production. Hopes for a large production run, however, were dashed when the US Army replaced its fleet of small tactical transports with helicopters. Only 122 were built in two production runs. Production ceased in 1986, but the Buffalo continues to operate with a number of air arms.

ABOVE: *A development of the Caribou, the DHC-5 Buffalo saw service with the USAF in Vietnam.*

Specification (DHC-5D)

Crew: *3* **Powerplant:** *two 2337kW (3133hp) General Electric CT64-820-4 turboprops* **Max speed:** *467km/h (290mph)* **Service ceiling:** *9450m (31,000ft)* **Max range:** *1112km (691 miles)* **Wing span:** *29.26m (96ft)* **Length:** *24.08m (79ft)* **Height:** *8.73m (28ft 8in)* **Weight:** *22,316kg (49,200lb) loaded* **Payload:** *41 passengers or 8164kg (18,000lb) of cargo*

MAJOR VARIANTS
DHC-5A: original production version
DHC-5D: reengined improved variant

RECOGNITION FEATURES
High-mounted straight wing; twin turboprops; T-type tail

Ilyushin Il-76

ABOVE: *The Ilyushin Il-76 has proved adaptable to a number of different roles, including flight refuelling tanker.*

Specification

Crew: *5* **Powerplant:** *four 12,000kg (26,455lb) thrust Soloviev D-30KP-1 turbofans* **Max speed:** *800km/h (500mph)* **Service ceiling:** *15,500m (50,850ft)* **Max range:** *5000km (3100 miles)* **Wing span:** *50.50m (165ft 8in)* **Length:** *46.59m (152ft 11in)* **Height:** *14.76m (48ft 5in)* **Weight:** *170,000kg (374,785lb) loaded* **Payload:** *130 passengers*

The Ilyushin Il-76 (NATO reporting name 'Candid') was the first major project of the Ilyushin Design Bureau in which S.V. Ilyushin himself played no part. The design was directed by G.V. Novozhilov, the work beginning in 1965 to meet an important requirement of both the civil operator Aeroflot and the Soviet military air transport service V-TA for a replacement for the Antonov An-12BP, the most numerous heavy cargo transport. Among the requirements was the ability to carry a 40-tonne (39-ton) cargo for 5000km (3105 miles) in less than six hours. The aircraft also had to be able to operate from short unpaved airstrips, maintain reliability in the extreme climatic conditions of the hot southern steppes and deserts on the one hand and the Arctic wastes of northern Siberia on the other, and be easy to service. The Il-76 first flew on 25 March 1971. During its operational career the Il-76 has had a number of applications other than that of transport. A three-point hose-and-drogue tanker variant, the Il-78 (NATO reporting name 'Midas') became operational in 1987 to replace the Soviet Air Force's age-ing Mya-4 Bison tankers, and the type was

Ilyushin Il-76 (continued)

also converted to the airborne early warning role (NATO reporting name 'Mainstay') to replace the inadequate Tu-126 Moss, which was little more than a stop-gap AEW aircraft. The Il-76M also serves with the Indian Air Force, where it has replaced the Antonov An-12 Cub (as it did in the Soviet Air Force). Another overseas customer was Iraq, which received 19, at least one of which was converted to the AEW role under the name Adnan-1. Two Il-76Ts and two Il-76Ms are operated by Syrianair.

ABOVE: *An Il-76T operated by Aeroflot on final approach.*

MAJOR VARIANTS
Il-76: basic production version
Il-76T: civilian conversion
Il-76K: version for training astronauts
Il-76TD: strengthened wings and fuselage; increased payload and range
Il-76MF: lengthened military variant
Il-76MDP: firefighting conversion

RECOGNITION FEATURES
High-mounted swept wing; four podded turbofans; glazed nose with pronounced bulge underneath; T-type tail; large bulges under fuselage housing undercarriage

Kawasaki C-1A

ABOVE: *The Kawasaki C-1A has a number of distinctive features, including its high-mounted wing, placed well forward.*

Specification

Crew: *5* **Powerplant:** *two 13,159kg (29,000lb) thrust Pratt & Whitney JT8D-9 turbofans* **Max speed:** *815km/h (507mph)* **Service ceiling:** *11,580m (38,000ft)* **Max range:** *3336km (2072 miles)* **Wing span:** *31.00m (101ft 8in)* **Length:** *29.00m (95ft 1in)* **Height:** *10.00m (32ft 9in)* **Weight:** *39,000kg (85,980lb) loaded* **Payload:** *11,900kg (26,235lb)*

In the early 1960s, the Japan Air Self-Defence Force issued Specification C-X for a jet-powered transport to replace the elderly Curtiss C-46 Commando. Two prototypes were built by Kawasaki, the first flying on 12 November 1970, and both aircraft completed their flight test programmes by March 1973. Two pre-production aircraft were built, these being followed by an order for 11 production C-1A transports. The first production C-1A flew in December 1974. By October 1981, a total of 31 C-1As had been delivered. The C-1Kai, featuring a redesigned nose and upgraded avionics, first flew in 1985.

MAJOR VARIANTS
C-1A: basic production transport
C-1Kai: improved variant; upgraded avionics
EC-1: ECM training aircraft fitted with a bulbous nose radome (one example only)

RECOGNITION FEATURES
High-mounted swept wing, placed well forward; twin podded under-wing turbofans; T-type tail

---

Lockheed Martin C-5A Galaxy

The largest transport aircraft in the world at the time of its appearance, the Lockheed C-5A Galaxy was first flown on 30 June 1968. Although the Galaxy has provision for 270 troops on the lower deck and 75 on the upper, the lower deck is intended for freight and can accommodate complete tactical missile systems or M1 Abrams main battle tanks. Despite its large size the Galaxy can operate from rough airstrips. Eighty-one aircraft equipped four MAC squadrons. The C-5B is an improved version, with uprated engines, better avionics and an extended-life wing. Total C-5A/C-5B production was 126 aircraft.

ABOVE: *In service since 1969, the Lockheed Martin C-5A Galaxy is able to operate from unprepared strips.*

Specification (C-5B)

Crew: *5* **Powerplant:** *four 18,642kg (41,000lb) thrust General Electric TF39 turbofans* **Max speed:** *919km/h (571mph)* **Service ceiling:** *10,360m (34,000ft)* **Max range:** *6033km (3749 miles)* **Wing span:** *68.88m (222ft 8in)* **Length:** *75.54m (247ft 10in)* **Height:** *19.85m (65ft 1in)* **Weight:** *348,810kg (769,000lb) loaded* **Payload:** *up to 345 passengers*

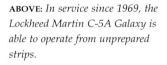

> MAJOR VARIANTS
> **C-5A:** initial production version
> **C-5B:** improved variant

> RECOGNITION FEATURES
> High-mounted swept wing with anhedral; four podded wing-mounted turbofans; swept T-type tail; undercarriage bulges under fuselage

Lockheed Martin C-130 Hercules

ABOVE: *The incredibly versatile Lockheed C-130 Hercules has been in service with air forces around the world for half a century.*

Specification (C-130E)

Crew: *4* **Powerplant:** *four 3021kW (4050hp) Allison T56-A-7 turboprop engines* **Max speed:** *547km/h (340mph)* **Service ceiling:** *10,060m (33,000ft)* **Max range:** *6145km (3820 miles)* **Wing span:** *40.41m (132ft 7in)* **Length:** *29.79m (97ft 9in)* **Height:** *11.68m (38ft 4in)* **Weight:** *70,308kg (155,000lb) loaded* **Payload:** *19,051kg (42,000lb)*

Without doubt the most versatile tactical transport aircraft ever built, the Lockheed C-130 Hercules flew for the first time on 23 August 1954, and many different variants were produced over the next half-century. The initial production versions were the C-130A and -B, of which 461 were built, and these were followed by the major production variant, the C-130E, 510 of which were produced. Other versions include the AC-130E gunship, the WC-130E weather reconnaissance aircraft, the KC-130F assault transport for the USMC, the HC-130H for aerospace rescue and recovery, the C-130K for the RAF, and the LC-130R, which has wheel/ski landing gear. Total production of the Hercules, all variants, was some 2000 aircraft. As well as the US forces and the RAF, the Hercules was supplied to no fewer than 61 air forces around the world. The RAF is the second largest Hercules user, operating 80 aircraft (C.1s, C.3s, C.4s and C.5s). The latest addition to the C-130 fleet is the C-130J, which first flew in 1996 and is replacing the C-130E.

The C-130J incorporates state-of-the-art technology to reduce manpower requirements,

Lockheed Martin C-130 Hercules (continued)

lower operating and support costs, and provide life-cycle cost savings over earlier C-130 models. Compared to older C-130s, the J model climbs faster and higher, flies farther at a higher cruise speed, and takes off and lands in a shorter distance. The C-130J-30 is a stretched version, adding 4.57m (15ft) to the fuselage, increasing the usable space in the cargo compartment. C-130J/J-30 major system improvements include: advanced two-pilot flight station with fully integrated digital avionics; state-of-the-art navigation systems with dual inertial navigation system and global positioning system; fully integrated defensive systems; digital moving map display; new turboprop engines with six-bladed, all-composite propellers; improved fuel, environmental and ice-protection systems; and an enhanced cargo-handling system.

ABOVE: *Operating on behalf of the United Nations, this C-130 is seen dropping supplies during a mercy mission.*

MAJOR VARIANTS
C-130A/B: initial production versions
C-130E: major production variant
AC-130: gunship
C-130K: RAF version
C-130J: major improvements to all systems and performance
C-130J-30: stretched and improved version of C-130J
KC-130J: tanker/transport for USMC

RECOGNITION FEATURES
C-130J: high-mounted straight wing with four turboprops; six-bladed composite propellers with a distinctive scimitar shape; upward-swept rear fuselage

Lockheed Martin C-141 StarLifter

ABOVE: *A C-141 StarLifter pictured over San Francisco Bay.*

Specification

Crew: 4 **Powerplant:** *four 9526kg (21,000b) thrust Pratt & Whitney TF33-7 turbofans* **Max speed:** *912km/h (567mph)* **Service ceiling:** *12,800m (42,000ft)* **Max range:** *10,370km (6445 miles)* **Wing span:** *48.74m (159ft 11in)* **Length:** *51.2m (168ft 3in)* **Height:** *11.96m (39ft 3in)* **Weight:** *155,582kg (343,000lb) loaded* **Payload:** *up to 41,222kg (90,880kg) of cargo*

MAJOR VARIANTS
C-141A: initial production version
C-141B: improved and lengthened version; increased cargo capacity
C-141C: C-141B with glass cockpit

RECOGNITION FEATURES
High-mounted, swept wing with anhedral; four podded underwing turbofans; narrow fuselage of cylindrical cross-section; T-type tail; undercarriage bulges at fuselage mid-point

First flown on 17 December 1963, the C-141A StarLifter heavy-lift strategic transport was designed to provide the USAF Military Air Transport Service with a high-speed global airlift and strategic deployment capability. Deliveries to the USAF began in April 1965 and the aircraft ultimately equipped 13 squadrons of Military Airlift Command, 277 being built. Starting in 1976, all surviving C-141A aircraft were upgraded to C-141B standard, the fuselage being stretched by 7.11m (23ft 4in).

Transall C-160

The Transall C-160 tactical transport was designed and produced as a joint venture between France and Federal Germany, Transall being an abbreviation of the specially formed consortium Transporter Allianz, comprising the companies of MBB, Aerospatiale and VFW-Fokker. The prototype flew for the first time on 25 February 1963, and series production began four years later. The initial variant was the C-160A, consisting of six pre-series aircraft.

ABOVE: *The Transall C-160 was a joint Franco-German venture.*

Specification

Crew: *4* **Powerplant:** *two 4551kW (6100hp) Rolls-Royce Tyne RTy.20 Mk 22 turboprop engines* **Max speed:** *536km/h (333mph)* **Service ceiling:** *8500m (27,900ft)* **Max range:** *4558km (2832 miles)* **Wing span:** *40.00m (131ft 3in)* **Length:** *32.40m (106ft 3in)* **Height:** *11.65m (38ft 5in)* **Weight:** *16,000kg (35,270lb) loaded* **Payload:** *16,000kg (35,275lb)*

MAJOR VARIANTS
C-160A: initial production version
C-160D: Luftwaffe variant
C-160F: export variant for France
C-160T: export variant for Turkey
C-160Z: export variant for South Africa

RECOGNITION FEATURES
High-mounted straight wing; twin turboprops; undercarriage bulges; upswept rear fuselage; long fairing from tailfin to upper fuselage

Aerospatiale/Aeritalia (Alenia) ATR 42/72

ABOVE: *The ATR 42 has proved a highly successful design.*

Specification (ATR 42-300)

Crew: *2* **Powerplant:** *two 1342kW (1800hp) Pratt & Whitney Canada PW120 turboprops* **Max speed:** *560km/h (345mph)* **Service ceiling:** *7620m (25,000ft)* **Max range:** *1950km (1200 miles)* **Wing span:** *24.50m (80ft 7in)* **Length:** *22.60m (74ft 4in)* **Height:** *7.30m (24ft 10in)* **Weight:** *18,600kg (40,920lb) loaded* **Payload:** *42–50 passengers*

The ATR (Avions de Transport Regional) family of twin-engined airliners is the result of a highly successful collaboration between Aerospatiale of France and Italy's Aeritalia (now Alenia). The prototype ATR 42, F-WEGA, flew from Toulouse on 16 August 1984. The ATR family is highly versatile, offering various internal configurations ranging from 42–50 seats in the ATR 42 and

RIGHT: *The ATR 72, seen here, is a larger version of the ATR 42, with an extra twenty seats.*

Aerospatiale/Aeritalia (Alenia) ATR 42/72 (continued)

64–74 in the ATR 72, the 'stretched' version. To these basic passenger options have been added a dedicated freighter (ATR-42F) and a maritime patrol variant, the Petrel. In service the aircraft offers excellent economy on the short-range, rapid turnround sectors that characterize the regional/feeder carriers. The aircraft are tailored to operations from airports with standard facilities. ATR 42/72s are used by some 33 operators worldwide.

ABOVE: *The ATR 42/72 has made inroads into the US market.*

MAJOR VARIANTS
ATR 42-300: the original version
ATR 42-320: identical to the **ATR 42-300**, but with more powerful 1567kW (2100hp) engines
ATR 42-500: uprated version with six-bladed 1790kW (2400hp) PW127E engines
ATR 72-200: offering a standard capacity of 66 seats, the **ATR 72-200** is equipped with two PW124B engines rated at 1790kW (2400shp) each
ATR 72-210: developed to increase hot-and-high and short-field performance capabilities
ATR 72-500: newest member of the ATR family, easily identified by its advanced six-bladed propeller and new cabin interior; airframe changes reduce noise; performance improved with the use of PW127 engines

RECOGNITION FEATURES
Twin turboprop engines; high-mounted wing; under-fuselage bulges housing undercarriage; swept tailfin with high-mounted tailplane

Airbus A300–A380

Specification (Airbus A380-800)

Crew: *2 flight crew* **Powerplant:** *four 302kN (67,890lb) thrust Rolls-Royce Trent 900 or Engine Alliance (General Electric-Pratt & Whitney) GP-7200 turbofans* **Max cruising speed:** *Mach 0.88* **Service ceiling:** *13,115m (43,000ft)* **Max range:** *15,100km (9377 miles)* **Wing span:** *79.80m (261ft 10in)* **Length:** *73.00m (239ft 6in)* **Height:** *24.10m (79ft 1in)* **Weight:** *54?,000kg (1,208,000lb) loaded* **Payload:** *555 passengers*

> ### MAJOR VARIANTS
> **Airbus A300:** medium-haul wide-body airliner
> **Airbus A310:** medium-haul airliner
> **Airbus A320:** short-haul airliner family; **A318** and **A319** are shortened versions, and **A321** a stretched variant
> **Airbus A330:** medium-haul airliner
> **Airbus A340:** long-haul airliner
> **Airbus A380:** long-haul airliner

The first airliner produced by the European Airbus Industries consortium was the 330-passenger A300 in 1972. An improved version, fitted with wingtip fences and upgraded avionics, flew in 1985. The A310, flown in 1982, is shorter than the A300, carrying 280 passengers, and was the first of the family to be fitted with a fly-by-wire control system. The A320 family of short-haul airliners comprises the standard A320, the A319 (a shortened version), the A321, which is a stretched version, and the A318, the latest addition, which was designed to cater for low-density, high-frequency operations. The A330 is a medium-haul airliner capable of carrying 440 passengers, while the A340 is a long-haul four-engined variant. The A380, launched in December 2000, is another four-engined long-haul version and is claimed to be the most advanced, spacious and efficient liner ever conceived. The A380 family starts from a baseline passenger aircraft with a capacity of 555 passengers in three classes, and a range of up to 15,000km (9320 miles). The freighter version, the A380F, will carry a payload of 150 tonnes (330,000lbs) over 10,400km (6463 miles). Stretch, shrink and

Airbus A300–A380 (continued)

extended-range variants of the baseline version will become available as and when the market requires them. The A380 can be powered by Rolls-Royce Trent 900 engines or GP7200 engines from The Engine Alliance (a General Electric and Pratt & Whitney joint venture).

ABOVE: *An A300 of Lufthansa, the first airline to operate the type.*

RECOGNITION FEATURES
Airbus A300 (left): swept wing with twin underwing turbofans; swept tail surfaces
Airbus A310: shorter fuselage than **A300**; low-mounted swept wing with twin underslung turbofans; swept tail surfaces
Airbus A320: narrow, low-mounted, swept wing with twin underslung turbofans; narrower fuselage than **A33/A310**; swept tail surfaces; all variants feature winglets
Airbus A330: narrow low-mounted swept wing, tapering sharply towards the tip; twin underslung turbofans; narrow fuselage; features winglets
Airbus A340: narrow swept wing, tapering sharply towards the tips and fitted with winglets; four underslung turbofan engines; sharply swept tail-fin; narrow fuselage
Airbus A380: narrow swept wing, tapering sharply towards the tips and fitted with winglets; four underslung turbofan engines; sharply swept tail-fin; wide double-deck fuselage.

BAe ATP

ABOVE: *The British Aerospace ATP has not been the hoped-for success, with disappointing sales.*

Specification

Crew: 2 **Powerplant:** *two 1317kW (1765shp) Pratt & Whitney 124A turboprops* **Max speed:** *496km/h (308mph)* **Service ceiling:** *7620m (25,000ft)* **Max range:** *1500km (931 miles)* **Wing span:** *30.60m (100ft 6in)* **Length:** *26.00m (85ft 4in)* **Height:** *7.60m (24ft 11in)* **Weight:** *22930kg (50,560lb) loaded* **Payload:** *68 passengers*

The BAe Advanced Turboprop or ATP is a twin-turboprop airliner that entered commercial service in 1988. A total of 62 ATPs were built before the production ended in 1994. The aircraft is tailored to the needs of short-haul regional operators requiring up to 72 passenger seats and upgrading from previous-generation 30- to 40-seat turboprops. The engine and propeller configuration, which is six-bladed, gives very quiet operating characteristics. Sales have proved disappointing, and the aircraft was modified and named Jetstream 61 to capture some reflected glory.

MAJOR VARIANTS
ATP: standard production version
Jetstream 61: new engine; increased operating weight

RECOGNITION FEATURES
Low-mounted, straight wing; twin turboprops; slightly swept tailfin

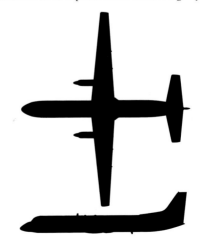

BAe (Avro, Hawker Siddeley) HS.748

Development of the Avro 748, intended to be a replacement for the DC-3 and Vickers Viking, was officially announced on 9 January 1959, when work was already under way at Avro's Chadderton factory near Manchester on the construction of four proto-types, two each for flight trials and static testing. The final configuration chosen was for a low-wing twin-turboprop air-craft with a round section fuse-lage providing accommodation for up to 44 passengers in a pressurized cabin. The pro-totype Avro 748, G-APZV, made its first flight from Woodford on 24 June 1960 and some 600 aircraft were eventually sold to 75 operators worldwide, many still remaining in service.

ABOVE: *The HS.748 has been in service for more than four decades.*

Specification (748 Series 2)

Crew: 2–3 **Powerplant:** *two 1570kW (2105ehp) Rolls-Royce Dart Mk 531 turboprops* **Max speed:** *434km/h (270mph)* **Service ceiling:** *7470m (24,500ft)* **Max range:** *1072km (670 miles)* **Wing span:** *30.02m (98ft 6in)* **Length:** *20.42m (67ft)* **Height:** *7.57m (24ft 10in)* **Weight:** *17,236kg (38,000lb) loaded* **Payload:** *40–52 passengers*

MAJOR VARIANTS
Series 1, 2, 2A and 2B differ only in having progressively uprated versions of the Dart engine.

RECOGNITION FEATURES
Long, straight, fairly narrow wing; twin turboprops; distinctive engine nacelles with large bulge under wing

BAe Jetstream

ABOVE: *The stretched Jetstream 41 variant in service with British Airways Express on its Isle of Man service.*

Specification (Jetstream 31)

Crew: *2* **Powerplant:** *two 671kW (900shp) Garrett TPE331-10 turbo-props* **Max speed:** *490km/h (305mph)* **Service ceiling:** *9630m (31,600ft)* **Max range:** *1250km (780 miles)* **Wing span:** *15.85m (52ft)* **Length:** *14.35m (47ft 2in)* **Height:** *5.30m (17ft 5in)* **Weight:** *7350kg (16,200lb) loaded* **Payload:** *18 passengers*

In January 1966 the British aircraft manufacturer Handley Page announced a new twin-turboprop executive, feeder-liner and military transport, the HP.137 Jetstream. The excellent airframe design was plagued by the poor performance of the Astazou engines. In 1975 the British aviation industry was nationalized, and the newly formed British Aerospace announced plans to produce a Garrett-engined version of the Jetstream, to be built at Prestwick in Scotland and called the Jetstream 31. The prototype flew on 28 March 1980, and production aircraft were offered in airline, executive shuttle or corporate configurations.

MAJOR VARIANTS
Jetstream 41: stretched version with longer fuselage, increased wing span and contra-rotating propellers

RECOGNITION FEATURES
Low-mounted straight wing; twin turboprops; swept tailfin with mid-mounted tailplane

BAe (BAC) One-Eleven

The One-Eleven was the first jetliner designed by the British Aircraft Corporation, formed by the merger of the old firms of Hunting, Vickers, Bristol and English Electric. The prototype BAC One-Eleven flew for the first time on 20 August 1963, 18 months before the aircraft that was to become its main competitor, the Douglas DC-9, and three and a half years before the Boeing 737. Several versions were produced and the airliner was licence built in Romania. The type still serves in some numbers with small airlines.

ABOVE: *The One-Eleven fared badly against the DC-9 and 737.*

Specification (Series 500)

Crew: *3* **Powerplant:** *two 5692kg (12,550lb) Rolls-Royce Spey turbofans* **Max speed:** *871km/h (541mph)* **Service ceiling:** *10,670m (35,000ft)* **Max range:** *2735km (1700 miles)* **Wing span:** *28.50m (93ft 6in)* **Length:** *32.61m (107ft)* **Height:** *7.47m (24ft 6in)* **Weight:** *47,400kg (104,500lb)* **Payload:** *119 passengers*

MAJOR VARIANTS
200 Series: initial production version
300/400 Series: new engines; increased take-off weight and passenger capacity
500 Series: stretched version; 119 passengers

RECOGNITION FEATURES
Low-mounted swept wing; twin turbofans mounted on rear fuselage; swept tailfin with T-type tailplane

BAe Systems (British Aerospace) 146/Avro RJ

Specification (BAe 146-300)

Crew: *2* **Powerplant:** *four 3093kg (6800lb) thrust Avco Lycoming LF502R-3 turbofans* **Max speed:** *776km/h (482mph)* **Service ceiling:** *9455m (31,000ft)* **Max range:** *2180km (1355 miles)* **Wing span:** *26.34m (86ft 5in)* **Length:** *30.10m (101ft 8in)* **Height:** *8.61m (28ft 3in)* **Weight:** *43,091kg (95,000lb)* **Payload:** *112 passengers*

The BAe 146 first flew commercially in 1983, powered by four Honeywell ALF 502 turbofan engines. The aircraft was designed specifically to meet the demanding requirements of the regional air transport market where heavy utilization over short sector lengths coupled with high reliability are paramount requirements. Outstanding airfield performance and whisper-jet noise levels are other attributes of the aircraft, which offers excellent profit potential on low-density routes. A total of 221 BAe 146s were built between 1983 and 1993 when the type was succeeded by the Avro RJ Series. This retains much of the 146's structure, but has new engines and is made by a new manufacturing company. The Avro RJ family of aircraft was built at the BAe Systems Regional Aircraft Centre at the historic Avro Airfield at Woodford in England; 166 aircraft were delivered. The first production aircraft was delivered in 1993 and production ceased in 2002. The last four aircraft built, two RJ85s and two RJ100s, have been leased from BAe

BAe Systems (British Aerospace) 146/Avro RJ (continued)

Regional Aircraft by Blue 1 (formerly Air Botnia) of Finland. The last Avro RJ was delivered in November 2003. The Avro RJ regional jet family extends from 70 to over 100 seats. The three variants of regional jet are RJ70, RJ85 and RJ100, which have different cabin lengths, but complete engineering and operational commonality. One Avro RJ85 is in service with the Bahrain Defence Force, where it is used for transport and other duties.

ABOVE: *Taiwan's Makung Airlines, now known as UNI Airways Corporation, operates a fleet of 146-300s.*

MAJOR VARIANTS
100 Series: 70–84 seats
200 Series: 85–100 seats
300 Series: 100–112 seats
QT: freighter (Quiet Trader)
QC: Quick Change variant
The Statesman: VIP transport
RJ: comes in three variants: the short fuselage **RJ70**, the mid-length fuselage **RJ85** and the stretched **RJ100**

RECOGNITION FEATURES
Shoulder-mounted swept wing; four podded underwing turbofans; T-type tail

Boeing 707

ABOVE: *The Boeing 707 was one of the most prolific airliners ever designed. This example is in the colours of Air Mauritius.*

Specification (Boeing 707-338C)

Crew: *4* **Powerplant:** *four 8620kg (19,000lb) thrust Pratt & Whitney JT3D-7 turbofans* **Max speed:** *972km/h (604mph)* **Service ceiling:** *11,900m (39,000ft)* **Max range:** *9260km (5750 miles)* **Wing span:** *43.33m (142ft 5in)* **Length:** *46.60m (152ft 11in)* **Height:** *12.67m (41ft 7in)* **Weight:** *151,320kg (333,600lb)* **Payload:** *215 passengers*

America entered the age of jet transport on 15 July 1954, when the Boeing 707 prototype, the model 367-80, made its maiden flight from Renton Field, south of Seattle. Forerunner of more than 14,000 Boeing jetliners built since, the prototype, nicknamed the 'Dash 80', served 18 years as a flying test laboratory before it was turned over to the Smithsonian Air and Space Museum in May 1972.

The aircraft made commercial history on 26 October 1958, when Pan American World Airways inaugurated a trans-Atlantic Boeing 707 jet service between New York and Paris. The first commercial 707s, designated the 707-120 series, had a larger cabin and other improvements compared to the prototype. Powered by early Pratt & Whitney turbojet engines, these initial 707s had range capability that was barely sufficient for the Atlantic Ocean. A number of variants were developed for special use, including shorter-bodied aircraft and the 720 series, which was lighter and faster with better runway performance. Boeing quickly developed the larger 707-320 Intercontinental series with a longer fuselage,

Boeing 707 (continued)

bigger wing and higher-powered engines. With these
improvements, which allowed
increased fuel capacity from
68,190 litres (15,000 gallons) to
more than 104,558 litres (23,000
gallons), the 707 had truly
intercontinental range of over
6437km (4000 miles) in a
141-seat (mixed class) seating
configuration. Early in the
1960s, the Pratt & Whitney

JT3D turbofan engines were fitted to provide
lower fuel consumption, reduce noise and
further increase range to about 9660km (6000
miles). When the 707 production line was
closed at the end of May 1991, Boeing had
sold 1010 of all types, not counting military
variants such as the KC-135. Many Boeing
707s are still in commercial service around
the world, and some retired from civil use
have been refurbished as military transports,
tankers and surveillance aircraft.

ABOVE: *A Boeing 707 of Avianca,
the first airline to serve Latin
America and only the second
airline company in the history of
aviation.*

MAJOR VARIANTS
707-120: initial production version
707-220: 707-120 with new engines
707-320: intercontinental variant
707-320C: multi-purpose variant
KC-135: military refuelling aircraft

RECOGNITION FEATURES
Low-mounted swept wing; four podded turbojets or turbofans, narrow
fuselage with swept tail surfaces

Boeing 727

ABOVE: *A Boeing 727 freighter in Federal Express livery.*

Specification (Boeing 727-200)

Crew: *3* **Powerplant:** *three 6575kg (14,500lb) thrust Pratt & Whitney JT8D-9A turbofans* **Max speed:** *920km/h (570mph)* **Service ceiling:** *11,900m (39,000ft)* **Max range:** *4000km (2485 miles)* **Wing span:** *32.90m (108ft)* **Length:** *46.70m (153ft 2in)* **Height:** *10.35m (34ft)* **Weight:** *95,025kg (209,500lb) loaded* **Payload:** *189 passengers*

The versatility and reliability of the Boeing 727 – the first trijet introduced into commercial service – made it the best-selling airliner in the world during the first 30 years of jet transport service. Production of the 727 extended from the early 1960s to August 1984, a remarkable length of time considering the original market forecast was for 250 aircraft. As it turned out, 1831 were delivered. Introduced into service in February 1964, the 727 became an immediate hit with flight crews and passengers alike. With a fuselage width the same as the 707 (and the later 737 and 757), it provided jet luxury on shorter routes. With sophisticated, triple-slotted trailing edge flaps and new leading-edge slats, the 727 had unprecedented low-speed landing and take-off performance for a commercial jet and could be accommodated by smaller airports than the 707 required.

The 727, like all Boeing jetliners, was continually modified to fit the changing market. It began with the 100 series, of which 407 were sold. This was followed by the 100C convertible that featured a main-deck side cargo door, allowing it to carry either cargo

Boeing 727 (continued)

pallets or passengers, or a combination of both, on the main
deck. The 727-200, introduced
in December 1967, had
increased gross weight and a
6m (20ft) longer fuselage that
could accommodate as many
as 189 passengers in an all-
tourist configuration. In all its
variations, 1245 of the 200s

were sold. The last version, the 727-200F, had
a 26,303kg (58,000lb), 11-pallet cargo capability. Fifteen of these were sold to Federal
Express. Structural improvements, a more
powerful engine and greater fuel capacity led
to the Advanced 727-200 in May 1971. This
series had improved payload/range capability, better runway performance and a
completely restyled 'widebody look' as
standard equipment.

ABOVE: *A principal user of the
Boeing 727 was American
Airlines.*

One hundred and one customers purchased
new 727s from Boeing, although dozens
more have placed the aircraft into service as
'second tier' operators. More than 300 727s
built as passenger aircraft have been
converted to freighters, a process that
continues today.

MAJOR VARIANTS
727-100: first production version
727-100C: convertible cargo/
passenger variant
727-200: lengthened version; 189
passengers
727F: freight version

RECOGNITION FEATURES
Low-mounted swept wing, tapering
sharply towards the tips; three tail-
mounted turbofans; T-type tail

Boeing 737

Specification (Boeing 737-400)

Crew: *3* **Powerplant:** *two 7030kg (15,500lb) thrust Pratt & Whitney JT8D-15-17 turbofans* **Max speed:** *925km/h (575mph)* **Service ceiling:** *11,900m (39,000ft)* **Max range:** *4265km (2650 miles)* **Wing span:** *28.35m (93ft)* **Length:** *30.50m (100ft)* **Height:** *11.30m (37ft)* **Weight:** *52,390kg (115,500lb)* **Payload:** *130 passengers*

Although its career has been marred by a number of fatal accidents, the Boeing 737 can be seen as yet another major success story. Development of this famous short-haul jet airliner began in 1964, and within a year Lufthansa had placed an order for 21 aircraft. Production was begun immediately, much time and money being saved by using the same fuselage cross-section as the much larger Boeing 707 and 727. The prototype flew on 9 April 1967.

Sales of the type were steady, but unspectacular, until 1978, when the market erupted. No fewer than 145 sales were recorded. There were a number of reasons for this. Boeing took two large 'one-off' orders from British Airways and Lufthansa, and the US government abolished the rules that had prevented small, but efficient, regional airlines from competing on many routes. The regionals purchased Model 737s to hasten their expansion, and three of them (USAir, Southwest and Frontier) became Boeing's biggest 737 customers, aside from United and Lufthansa. The already phenomenal success of the 737-200, the basic design, achieved renewed vigour with the launch of the 300, 400, 500 and 600 series.

Boeing 737 (continued)

As intended, the advanced model 737 proved attractive to 'Third World' operators, and the airliner became a familiar sight in the Middle and Far East, Africa and Latin America. In Europe, the holiday charter business had matured to the point where airlines could afford brand-new aircraft; the advanced model 737 proved ideal, with 130 seats and plenty of range. In 1980, the Boeing 737 overtook the 727 to become the world's best-selling airliner.

ABOVE: *The Boeing 737 has proved well suited to medium-haul operations all over the world. This aircraft is in the colours of Saudi Arabian Airlines.*

MAJOR VARIANTS
737-100: first production version
737-200: major production variant; 124 passengers
737-300: second generation variant; lengthened fuselage; new engines; 149 passengers
737-400: lengthened 300 series; 168 passengers
737-500: shortened 300 series; 132 passengers
737-600: third generation aircraft
737-700: lengthened 737-600; 149 passengers
737-800: 189 passengers

RECOGNITION FEATURES
Low-mounted swept wing; twin underwing turbofans with long, narrow nacelles; tubby fuselage; swept tail surfaces

Boeing 747

ABOVE: *A Boeing 747 in the striking livery of Virgin Atlantic.*

Specification (747-200)

Crew: *3 (flight deck)* **Powerplant:** *four 22,680kg (50,000lb) thrust Pratt & Whitney JT9D-7FW turbofans* **Max speed:** *940km/h (585mph)* **Service ceiling:** *13,715m (45,000ft)* **Max range:** *9625km (5980 miles)* **Wing span:** *59.65m (195ft 8in)* **Length:** *70.50m (231ft 4in)* **Height:** *19.35m (63ft 6in)* **Weight:** *365,150kg (805,000lb) loaded* **Payload:** *440 passengers*

Popularly known as the 'Jumbo Jet', the Boeing 747 represented a huge breakthrough in commercial air travel. The aircraft flew for the first time on 9 February 1969 and the type entered service with Pan American on the New York–London route on 22 January 1970. The initial version was designated Model 747-100, of which 167 were sold, and on 11 October 1970 Boeing flew the first Model 747-200, which had greater fuel capacity and an increase in gross weight. The basic passenger version is the Model 747-200B, while the Model 747-200F is a dedicated cargo version with no windows and a computerized, powered loading system which enables two loaders to load or unload the aircraft in less than 30 minutes. The Model 747-200B Combi is a mixed-traffic aircraft with a removable bulkhead separating the passenger sections from the cargo area, and the Model 747-200C Convertible can be converted from all-passenger to all-cargo use, and vice versa. The Model 747-100B is an advanced derivative of the 747-100 with strengthened structure, a choice of engines and other modifications; the 747-300 features a stretched upper deck for an extra 37–44

Boeing 747 (continued)

pasengers; the 747-400 is an advanced model with a substantially increased range, extended wings, winglets, two-man cockpit, stretched upper deck and updated avionics; the 747SR is a high-capacity short-range aircraft with structural changes and capacity for 516 passengers; and the 747SP is a special performance long-range model with a short body and enlarged tail. Four 747-200s were bought by the US Air Force to serve as National Emergency Airborne Command Posts under the designation E-4B. The VC-25 is a modified 747-200B; two are available to transport the US President and his staff.

ABOVE: *The Boeing 747 has opened up long-range air travel like no other airliner in aviation history.*

MAJOR VARIANTS
747-100: initial production version
747-200: increased fuel capacity and gross weight; 747-200B is basic passenger variant
747-200F: cargo version
747-200C Convertible: convertible freight/passenger aircraft
747-300: stretched upper deck
747-400: advanced variant; increased range and dimensions; updated avionics

---

RECOGNITION FEATURES
Very large size; low-mounted swept wings; swept tail surfaces; top deck extends to mid-fuselage point; all variants externally similar except long-range **747-400**, which has winglets, and the **747SP**, which is shorter and has a larger tail

Boeing 757

ABOVE: *A Boeing 757-200 in service with British Airways.*

Specification (757-200)

Crew: 2 **Powerplant:** *two Pratt & Whitney PW 2040 or Rolls-Royce RB211-535E turbofans of 18,950kg (41,700lb) and 18,230kg (40,100lb) thrust respectively* **Max speed:** *965km/h (595mph)* **Service ceiling:** *11,900m (39,000ft)* **Max range:** *7315km (4550 miles)* **Wing span:** *38.00m (125ft)* **Length:** *47.50m (155ft 6in)* **Height:** *13.60m (44ft 6in)* **Weight:** *100,000kg (220,000lb)* **Payload:** *201 passengers*

Towards the end of the 1970s, Boeing was faced with a problem: how to keep its highly successful Model 727 at the top of airliner sales. Subsequent improvement studies on the design of the basic airframe resulted in an aircraft which had little in common with its predecessor, but which kept the Boeing sales challenge alive. Designated the Model 757, the new aircraft eventually began to take its place in ever-growing numbers in the ranks of the world's major airlines, despite

RIGHT: *The 757-300 is the longest single-aisle twinjet ever produced.*

Boeing 757 (continued)

the fact that initial sales were disappointing. No new customers appeared until, in April 1980, three aircraft were ordered by Transbrasil and three by Aloha. After that, sales rocketed; the US giant Northwest purchased a total of 73 Model 757s to begin the replacement of its domestic 727 fleet alongside its European rival, the Airbus A320. The other launch customer for the 757 was Eastern Airlines.

ABOVE: *The 757 is the backbone of many airline fleets, particularly in the USA.*

> **MAJOR VARIANTS**
> **Boeing 757-100:** initial design with 150-seat capacity (not built)
> **Boeing 757-200:** definitive version forming the majority of the 757 series
> **757-200F:** freighter
> **757-200M:** passenger/freight combi version
> **757-300:** stretched version, trading range for passenger capacity; 252 passengers

> **RECOGNITION FEATURES**
> Low-mounted swept wing; twin podded underwing turbofans; long, narrow fuselage

Boeing 767

ABOVE: *A Boeing 767 in the colours of American Airlines.*

Specification (767-300ER)

Crew: *2/3* **Powerplant:** *two 21,800kg (47,950lb) thrust General Electric CF6-80C2B turbofans* **Max speed:** *965km/h (595mph)* **Service ceiling:** *10,725m (35,200ft)* **Max range:** *11,390km (7080 miles)* **Wing span:** *47.60m (156ft)* **Length:** *54.90m (180ft 3in)* **Height:** *15.80m (52ft)* **Weight:** *172,365kg (380,000lb) loaded* **Payload:** *242 passengers*

The Boeing 767 family of aircraft is intended to bridge the gap between the single-aisle Boeing 757 and the larger, twin-aisle 777. The family comprises three passenger models – the 767-200ER, 767-300ER and 767-400ER – and a freighter, which is based on the 767-300ER fuselage. The 767 Freighter is a derivative of the popular 767-300ER (extended range) passenger twinjet. All the advancements in avionics, aerodynamics, materials and propulsion that were developed for passenger versions of the 767 are incorporated in the freighter. Its design provides excellent operating characteristics.

MAJOR VARIANTS
767-200: first production version
767-200ER: extended range variant
767-300: stretched model
767-300F: freighter model
767-400: improved version; advanced avionics

RECOGNITION FEATURES
Low-mounted swept wing, broad in section between engines and wing root; twin podded underwing turbofans; wide body

Boeing 777

The Boeing 777, the largest twin-jet airliner in the world, was rolled out on 9 April 1994, and the aircraft made its maiden flight on 12 June that year. The 777 is the first Boeing airliner to feature a 'fly-by-wire' system, and was conceived in response to the inroads being made by the European Airbus into Boeing's traditional market. The 777 comes with a choice of turbofan engines (General Electric, Pratt & Whitney or Rolls-Royce) and is produced in several versions: the 777-200, the 777-200ER (Extended Range), and the 777-300. The latter was originally known as the 777 Stretch.

ABOVE: *The 777 was the first Boeing 'fly-by-wire' airliner.*

Specification (Model 777-300)

Crew: *3* **Powerplant:** *two 34,655kg (76,400lb) General Electric GE.90-75B turbofans* **Max speed:** *900km/h (560mph)* **Service ceiling:** *13,135m (43,100ft)* **Max range:** *10,800km (6720 miles)* **Wing span:** *60.90m (200ft)* **Length:** *63.75m (209ft)* **Height:** *18.50m (60ft 9in)* **Weight:** *299,375kg (660,000lb) loaded* **Payload:** *386 passengers*

MAJOR VARIANTS
777-200: first production model
777-200ER: extended-range variant
777-200LR: long-range version; more powerful engines
777-300: stretched variant; uprated engines
777-300ER: extended-range variant

RECOGNITION FEATURES
Low-mounted swept wing, tapering sharply towards the tip; twin podded underwing turbofans; swept tail surfaces; wide body

Boeing (McDonnell Douglas) DC-8

ABOVE: *A DC-8 of Capitol Airlines.*

Specification (Super 63)

Crew: *4* **Powerplant:** *four 8172kg (18,000lb) thrust Pratt & Whitney JT3D-3B turbofans* **Max speed:** *965km/h (600mph)* **Service ceiling:** *13,800m (42,000ft)* **Max range:** *9640km (6000 miles)* **Wing span:** *45.23m (148ft 5in)* **Length:** *47.98m (157ft 5in)* **Height:** *13.11m (43ft)* **Weight:** *151,950kg (335,000lb) loaded* **Payload:** *179 passengers*

MAJOR VARIANTS
DC-8 Series 10: initial production version
DC-8 Series 30: intercontinental model
DC-8 Super 61: enlarged model; 259 passengers
DC-8 Super 71: Super 61 airframes with improved engines/performance

RECOGNITION FEATURES
Low-mounted swept wing; four podded underwing turbojets; swept tail surfaces

The Douglas DC-8 made its first flight on 30 May 1958 and entered airline service about a year after the Boeing 707. The Series 30, 40 and 50 were the intercontinental versions, while the domestic models were the Series 10 and Series 20. In April 1965 Douglas announced three new variants of the DC-8. The first was the DC-8 Super 61, a high-capacity transcontinental aircraft with the same wing and engines as the DC-8-50; the second was the Super 62, which was only slightly longer than the standard aircraft but stretched just enough to match the seating capacity of the Boeing 707-320 and which had a completely redesigned engine installation; and the third was the Super 63, which combined the DC-8-61 fuselage with the Super 62 wing and uprated engines.

Boeing (McDonnell Douglas) DC-9

If the capacity for development is the hallmark of a great design, the DC-9/MD-80 family deserves a place in that category. The latest model carries very nearly twice as many passengers as the first, and weighs nearly twice as much. For many years the DC-9 provided the backbone of several European airlines' short-

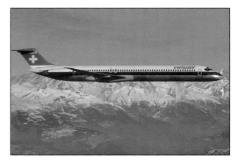

/medium-haul routes. Paradoxically, the very success of the DC-9 nearly brought disaster. The company was still spending money on DC-9 development; at the same time it had sold aircraft at low introductory prices, and the airliner was proving more expensive to build than anticipated. Eventually, the point was reached where Douglas was losing money on every DC-9 it delivered. Deliveries began to slip behind schedule, and some airline customers launched massive lawsuits to cover their estimated losses. Facing bankruptcy, Douglas was taken over by the McDonnell company of St Louis, Missouri, in April 1967, and the DC-9 became the MD-80.

ABOVE: *A DC-9 in the colours of the Swiss national carrier.*

Specification (DC-9 Series 50)

Crew: 2 **Powerplant:** *two 6575kg (14,500lb) thrust Pratt & Whitney JT8D-9 turbofans* **Wing span:** *28.47m (93ft 5in)* **Length:** *36.40m (119ft 3in)* **Height:** *8.38m (27ft 6in)* **Max speed:** *903km/h (561mph)* **Service ceiling:** *10,675m (35,000ft)* **Max range:** *2970km (1843 miles)* **Weight:** *44,450kg (98,000lb)* **Payload:** *115 passengers*

MAJOR VARIANTS
Series 10: initial production versions
Series 20: larger; improved engines
Series 30: lengthened fuselage
Series 50: lengthened fuselage
MD-80: lengthened; fuel-efficient engines

RECOGNITION FEATURES
DC-9 Series 50: relatively short, tapered, swept wing; twin turbojets mounted on rear fuselage; T-type tail

Boeing (McDonnell Douglas) MD-11

ABOVE: An MD-11 of LTU, a German holiday airline.

Specification

Crew: *2* **Powerplant:** *three 27,360kg (60,000lb) thrust Pratt & Whitney PW4460 turbofans* **Max speed:** *932km/h (579mph)* **Service ceiling:** *9935m (32,600ft)* **Max range:** *9270km (5760 miles)* **Wing span:** *51.66m (169ft 6in)* **Length:** *61.21m (200ft 10in)* **Height:** *17.60m (57ft 9in)* **Weight:** *273,300kg (602,500lb) loaded* **Payload:** *410 passengers*

Although the MD-11 obviously owes a great deal in design to the DC-10, there are sufficient changes to warrant its classification as a totally new aircraft. The fuselage is stretched to provide greater accommodation for both passengers and baggage, while the wings are lengthened and feature winglets. The aerodynamic design is more advanced than the DC-10's, resulting in greater efficiency, and the tailplane holds a fuel 'trim tank'. For the aircrew, the most obvious difference is the cockpit, where the three-man analogue display has been replaced by multi-function CRT displays.

MAJOR VARIANTS
MD-11P: first production model
MD-11 Combi: combined cargo/passenger variant
MD-11CF: convertible cargo/passenger model

RECOGNITION FEATURES
Low-mounted, sharply swept wing; two podded underwing turbofans and one mounted at base of tailfin; distinguished from DC-10 by winglets

Convair 440

One of the oldest airliners still in service today, the Convair 440 Metropolitan first flew in October 1955. It was developed from the earlier Model 340, featuring better soundproofing and uprated engines. Several further versions were produced, including the 540/580/600/640 series with two Rolls-Royce Dart turboprops. Conversions of the Convair airliners to turbine power began experimentally in the early 1950s, although it was only in the early and middle 1960s that the programme gained impetus. As well as aircraft converted from the Model 340, 186 Convair 440s were built, and some are still in service with their original customers, mostly in Latin America. A few serve as military transports.

ABOVE: *Convair 440s were used by American Airlines in the Philippines.*

Specification (Convair 440 Metropolitan)

Crew: *3* **Powerplant:** *two 1865kW (2500hp) Pratt & Whitney R-2800-CB17 radial engines* **Max speed:** *465km/h (289mph)* **Service ceiling:** *7590m (24,900ft)* **Max range:** *756km (470 miles)* **Wing span:** *32.10m (105ft 4in)* **Length:** *24.84m (81ft 6in)* **Height:** *8.60m (28ft 2in)* **Weight:** *22,270kg (49,100lb)* **Payload:** *52 passengers or 7000kg (16,000lb) of cargo*

MAJOR VARIANTS
440: initial production version
540/580/600/640: turboprop variants

RECOGNITION FEATURES
Low-mounted straight wing; twin radial engines or turboprops; tapered leading edge; tall fin with large fairing sweeping down to upper fuselage

Fokker F.27 Friendship

ABOVE: *A Fokker F.27 Friendship of British Midland Airways.*

Specification

Crew: *2/3* **Powerplant:** *two 1246kW (1670ehp) Rolls-Royce Dart 511 turboprops* **Max speed:** *428km/h (266mph)* **Service ceiling:** *8840m (29,000ft)* **Max range:** *1250km (775 miles)* **Wing span:** *29.00m (95ft 2in)* **Length:** *23.50m (77ft)* **Height:** *8.40m (27ft 6in)* **Weight:** *18,370kg (40,500lb) loaded* **Payload:** *40–52 passengers*

The first prototype of the Friendship flew on 24 November 1955, by which time the aircraft's commercial success was assured, 30 F.27s being on the company's order books by the spring of 1956. In April of that year Fokker entered into a licence agreement with Fairchild in the USA, and series production was begun almost simultaneously in both countries. The most important later series F.27 models were the F.27-200 (known as the F.27A in the USA), which had uprated engines, the F.27-300 and F-27-400 (designated F.27B and F.27C respectively in the United States). These models were more versatile, having a large freight loading door in the forward fuselage to permit mixed passenger and freight operations. The next version was the F.27-500, which appeared in November 1967 and resembled the F.27-200, except that it had a stretched fuselage.

MAJOR VARIANTS
F.27-200: uprated engines
F-27-300/400: mixed passenger/freight operations
F-27-500: stretched fuselage; passenger or freight configurations

---

RECOGNITION FEATURES
Long, slender, shoulder-mounted wing; twin turboprops; long fairing from tailfin to upper fuselage

Fokker F.28 Fellowship

Having achieved consider-able success with the turboprop-powered F.27, it was logical for Fokker to move into the jet market. Here the F.28 proved another winner for the Dutch company, offering low-cost, short-range transport from short runways, an aspect

that has made it particularly attractive to third world customers. Sales of the Fokker F.28, the prototype of which flew for the first time on 9 May 1967, have mostly been to European, Asian, African and South American operators, although several US operators adopted the type. The F.28-1000 was the original version, sized for up to 65 passengers. In 1970 Fokker introduced the Mk 2000. The next versions were the Mks 5000 and 6000, which flew in 1973 and which were, respectively, short- and long-fuselage versions of a more advanced aircraft with slatted wings, among other refinements. However, Fokker decided that few customers wanted the slatted wing and so two final versions, the Mks 3000 and 4000, were produced without slats but with all the other improvements.

ABOVE: *The F.28 was Fokker's first venture into the jet airliner market, and proved an outstanding success.*

Specification

Crew: *2/3* **Powerplant:** *two 4468kg (9850lb) thrust Rolls-Royce Spey Mk 555-15 turbofans* **Max speed:** *843km/h (523mph)* **Service ceiling:** *10,670m (35,000ft)* **Max range:** *2100km (1300 miles)* **Wing span:** *23.58m (77ft 4in)* **Length:** *27.40m (89ft 11in)* **Height:** *8.50m (27ft 10in)* **Weight:** *29,485kg (65,000lb)* **Payload:** *85 passengers*

MAJOR VARIANTS
F.28-1000: initial production version
F.28-2000: stretched fuselage; 79 passengers
F.28-3000 and 4000: improved versions of F.28-1000 and F.28-2000
F.28-5000 and 6000: short and long fuselage advanced aircraft

---

RECOGNITION FEATURES
Low-mounted, slightly swept wing; twin turbofans mounted on rear fuselage; T-type tail; sharply tapered rear fuselage

Fokker 100

![Fokker 100 aircraft]

ABOVE: *The Fokker 100 is a stretched version of the F.28 Fellowship. American Airlines was a principal customer.*

Specification (Fokker 100)

Crew: *2* **Powerplant:** *two 6160kg (13,600lb) thrust Rolls-Royce Tay 620-15 turbofans* **Max speed:** *845km/h (524mph)* **Service ceiling:** *11,278m (37,000ft)* **Max range:** *2505km (1555 miles)* **Wing span:** *28.10m (92ft 1in)* **Length:** *35.50m (116ft 6in)* **Height:** *8.50m (27ft 10in)* **Weight:** *43,090kg (95,000lb) loaded* **Payload:** *122 passengers*

The Fokker 100 is an enlarged and modernized version of the F.28 Fellowship. The type first flew on 30 November 1986, and customer deliveries began in February 1988. Production ended in early 1997, after 283 had been built. The launch customer was Swissair, which ordered eight aircraft to replace its early model DC-9s in July 1984, but Fokker had to wait for a year before another airline placed an order. KLM ordered 10 in May 1985; a further 75 were eventually ordered by American Airlines. The Fokker 100 was offered in a number of versions, including a freighter and a VIP transport. Many orders were cancelled after Fokker went into liquidation in 1996.

MAJOR VARIANTS
Fokker 100/70: 80-seat version powered by Rolls-Royce Tay engines; 45 built

---

RECOGNITION FEATURES
Low-mounted swept wing; twin turbofans mounted on rear fuselage; T-type tail

Ilyushin Il-18

ABOVE: *An Ilyushin Il-18 of Malev, the Hungarian airline.*

Unsophisticated and crude by western standards, the Ilyushin Il-18 (NATO reporting name 'Coot') became a mainstay of the Soviet civil aviation scene, and did much to expand the services of Aeroflot, the former Soviet Union's state-run airline. Still in limited service today, the Il-18 also provided an excellent platform for special mission variants with both civil and military applications, including electronic intelligence gathering and anti-submarine warfare.

Specification (Il-18)

Crew: *5* **Powerplant:** *four 2984kW (4000ehp) Ivchenko A1-20K turbo-props* **Max speed:** *650km/h (404mph)* **Service ceiling:** *10,750m (35,268ft)* **Max range:** *4800km (2980 miles)* **Wingspan:** *37.4m (122ft 8in)* **Length:** *35.9m (117ft 9in)* **Height:** *10.16m (33ft 4in)* **Weight:** *61,200kg (134,922lb) loaded* **Payload:** *84–110 passengers*

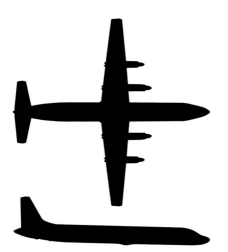

MAJOR VARIANTS
Il-20: electronic intelligence aircraft; carries a ventral canoe housing side-ways-looking radar, and signals intelligence sensors and optics in fairings on the sides of the forward fuselage
Il-38: anti-submarine warfare variant. NATO reporting name 'May'
Il-18D: atmospheric research aircraft

RECOGNITION FEATURES
Low-mounted straight wing; four turbofan engines; low-mounted tailplane set to rear of fin

Ilyushin Il-62

ABOVE: *An attractive but noisy airliner, the Il-62 was the first long-range, four-jet airliner produced in the Soviet Union.*

Specification (Il-62M)

Crew: 5 **Powerplant:** *four 10,985kg (24,200lb) thrust Soloviev D-30KU turbofans* **Max speed:** *900km/h (560mph)* **Service ceiling:** *12,800m (42,000ft)* **Max range:** *7800km (4850 miles)* **Wing span:** *43.20m (141ft 9in)* **Length:** *53.12m (174ft 3in)* **Height:** *12.35m (40ft 6in)* **Weight:** *165,000kg (363,762lb) loaded* **Payload:** *174 passengers*

The Ilyushin Il-62 (NATO reporting name 'Classic'), which flew for the first time in January 1963, was the first commercial, long-range, four-jet aircraft produced in the Soviet Union. After proving flights by three pre-production aircraft and a second prototype, an Il-62 service with Aeroflot was inaugurated on the Moscow–Khabarovsk and Moscow–Novosibirsk routes. On 15 September 1967, the type began to replace the Tu-114 on the Moscow–Montreal route, this service continuing on to New York from 15 July 1968. The Il-62M had more powerful engines and extended range, and made its appearance in 1971. The Il-62M continued in production until 1990 and the type remains operational in various parts of the world.

MAJOR VARIANTS
Il-62: initial production version
Il-62M: new engines; increased fuel capacity
Il-62MK: increased max take-off weight; 195 passengers

RECOGNITION FEATURES
Low-mounted swept wing; four turbofans mounted in pairs on rear fuselage; swept tail surfaces; T-type tail

Ilyushin Il-86

The Ilyushin Il-86 (NATO reporting name 'Camber') was Russia's first attempt at building a modern wide-bodied jet airliner, but it was not a success. The first production aircraft flew on 24 October 1977. By this time, the Il-86 was running well behind schedule and it was clear that it would not be in quantity service by its target date of 1980. It was also failing to meet its expected performance requirements. The Il-86 was intended to handle Aeroflot's high-density tourist routes, such as Moscow–Leningrad or Moscow–Kiev. It was also intended to replace the Il-62M on prestige international routes, which it failed to do. In the end, production of the Il-86 ended in 1994, with 104 built.

ABOVE: *Although its concept was valid, the Ilyushin Il-86 has not been a success, Russian airlines preferring to buy western types.*

Specification

Crew: *3* **Powerplant:** *four 12,983kg (28,660lb) thrust Kuznetsov NK-86 turbofans* **Max speed:** *900km/h (558mph)* **Service ceiling:** *11,000m (36,080ft)* **Max range:** *4600km (2857 miles)* **Wing span:** *48.10m (157ft 8in)* **Length:** *59.40m (195ft 8in)* **Height:** *15.80m (51ft 8in)* **Weight:** *206,000kg (454,024lb)* **Payload:** *350 passengers; 42,000kg (92,600lb) of cargo*

> MAJOR VARIANTS
> Il-87: airborne command post; has large dorsal canoe fairing

> RECOGNITION FEATURES
> Low-mounted swept wing; four podded underwing turbofans; widebody; swept tail surfaces

Ilyushin Il-96

ABOVE: *The Ilyushin Il-96 was an attempt to remedy the shortcomings of the earlier Il-86 design.*

Specification (Il-96)

Crew: *3/5* **Powerplant:** *four 14,717kg (32,275lb) thrust Soloviev PS-90A turbofans* **Max speed:** *900km/h (559mph)* **Service ceiling:** *14,600m (47,900ft)* **Max range:** *7500km (4660 miles)* **Wing span:** *57.66m (189ft 2in)* **Length:** *55.35m (181ft 7in)* **Height:** *17.57m (57ft 8in)* **Weight:** *216,000kg (476,200lb) loaded* **Payload:** *300 passengers*

Developed from the earlier Il-86, which suffered from a poor range, the Il-96 turned out to be virtually a new design. Almost the only components left unaltered, or only slightly modified, were major sections of the fuselage (though this was made much shorter) and the four units of the landing gear. The first prototype of the Il-96, SSSR-96000, flew from Khodinka on 28 September 1988, and the type made its international debut at the Paris Air Show in the following June. Aeroflot placed orders for about 100 aircraft for service on its long-range, high-density routes both at home and overseas.

MAJOR VARIANTS

Il-96: initial production version
Il-96M: medium-range variant; 350 seats
Il-90: twin-engine version

RECOGNITION FEATURES

Low-mounted swept wings with winglets; four podded underwing turbofans; swept tail surfaces with low-mounted tailplane

Lockheed L-188A Electra

First flown on 6 December 1957, the Lockheed Electra short-/medium-range airliner was an immediate success, the company having 144 orders on its books by the time the prototype made its maiden flight. Brazilian airline VARIG was perhaps the most faithful Electra operator ever. Fifteen aircraft were delivered, beginning in the early 1960s, and only one was lost between then and 1991, when they were retired. VARIG's Electras operated the daily air-bridge shuttle service between Rio de Janeiro and Sao Paulo. One of the reasons why they continued for so long is that the airport they used in Rio, Santos Dumont, was close to the city centre and was closed to jet traffic. Principal factors, however, were the reliability of the Allison engines and passenger loyalty. The Electra was the first turboprop airliner designed and built in the United States, and is still in limited passenger service around the world.

ABOVE: *American Airlines was a launch customer of the Electra.*

Specification

Crew: *3* **Powerplant:** *four 2798kW (3750ehp) Allison 501-D13A turboprops* **Max speed:** *600km/h (373mph)* **Service ceiling:** *8656m (28,400ft)* **Max range:** *4458km (2770 miles)* **Wing span:** *30.00m (99ft)* **Length:** *32.14m (104ft 5in)* **Height:** *10.25m (32ft 9in)* **Weight:** *51,257kg (113,000lb) loaded* **Payload:** *66–98 passengers*

MAJOR VARIANTS
L-188A: initial production version
L-188C: increased fuel capacity

RECOGNITION FEATURES
Long fuselage; relatively short wing with four turboprops and square-cut wingtips; rounded tailfin

Lockheed Martin L-1011 TriStar

ABOVE: *This Tristar was the personal transport of the late King Hussein of Jordan.*

Specification (TriStar L-1011-200)

Crew: *2/4* **Powerplant:** *three 22,680kg (50,000lb) thrust Rolls-Royce RB211-524B turbofans* **Max speed:** *975km/h (605mph)* **Service ceiling:** *12,800m (42,000ft)* **Max range:** *6335km (3980 miles)* **Wing span:** *47.35m (155ft 3in)* **Length:** *54.35m (178ft 8in)* **Height:** *16.90m (55ft 3in)* **Weight:** *225,000kg (496,000lb) loaded* **Payload:** *400 passengers*

The market requirements that had led to the development of the McDonnell Douglas DC-10 in 1966 also resulted in the Lockheed TriStar high-density jet airliner programme. The project, designated L-1011, was launched in March 1968, by which time 144 orders and options were in place, and the first aircraft flew on 16 November 1970. The initial version was the Lockheed L-1011-1, which entered regular airline service with Eastern Air Lines on 26 April 1972. The Series 100 TriStars followed, with increased range and power, and several further developments took place in subsequent years.

External, it is impossible to differentiate between the L-1011-1, -50, -100 and -200 models of the TriStar; the primary modifications include type of engine, tyre, wheel-rim and oleo strength, and internal fuel tankage. In an attempt to bring about a radical improvement of the TriStar's range capability, Lockheed introduced the L-1011-500, this aircraft receiving FAA certification in December 1979. Powered by RB-211-524Bs or B4s, the -500 had a shorter fuselage, six Class A doors, an engine No 2 fairing, and no tail skid. The wingtips were lengthened by 1.37m (4ft 6in), with load relief against

Lockheed Martin L-1011 TriStar (continued)

gusts and turbulence catered for by the ACS (Active Control System). To guard against excessive accelerations at high Mach numbers, an RSB (Recovery Speed Brake) was fitted, which automatically deployed the speed brakes at Mach 0.85. The TriStar K.Mk 1/C. Mk 2 is a tanker/passenger conversion operated by the Royal Air Force.

ABOVE: *A Tristar of Delta Airlines. The Tristar can be differentiated from the DC-10/ MD-11 by its third engine, which is set much lower on the tail.*

MAJOR VARIANTS
L1011: initial production version
L-1011-100 Series: extended range variant
L-1011-200 Series: increased range
L-1011-500: fuselage/wing modifications

RECOGNITION FEATURES
Low-mounted, sharply swept wing; wide body; two podded turbofans mounted under wings, one in tail unit; all variants externally similar except **Model 500**

Tupolev Tu-134

ABOVE: *A Tupolev Tu-134 in the livery of Air Kazakhstan.*

Specification (Tu-134A)

Crew: *3* **Powerplant:** *two 6790kg (14,990lb) thrust Soloviev D-30 turbofans* **Max speed:** *885km/h (550mph)* **Service ceiling:** *11,900m (39,000ft)* **Max range:** *3020km (1876 miles)* **Wing span:** *29.00m (95ft 2in)* **Length:** *37.05m (121ft 6in)* **Height:** *9.14m (30ft)* **Weight:** *47,000kg (103,600lb) loaded* **Payload:** *80 passengers*

Although the Tu-134's design was based on that of the earlier Tu-104 and Tu-124, it incorporated so many changes that an entirely new bureau number was allocated. Work on the Tu-134 (NATO reporting name 'Crusty') project began in June 1962, and the prototype flew in December 1963, being followed by five pre-production aircraft. The type entered service with Aeroflot on domestic routes in 1966. The original 64-seat Tu-134 was followed in 1968 by a stretched version, the 80-seat Tu-134A. The Tu-134A continues to serve as a military transport in Russia and several other countries.

> **MAJOR VARIANTS**
> **Tu-134:** initial production version
> **Tu-134A:** stretched variant

> **RECOGNITION FEATURES**
> Low-mounted swept wing with undercarriage nacelles protruding past trailing edge; twin turbofans mounted on rear fuselage; T-type tail

Tupolev Tu-154

Although it is gradually being replaced, the Tu-154 (NATO reporting name 'Careless') remains a major airline type. In widespread service with Russian domestic airlines, it also equips the civil airlines of nations that were allied to the former Soviet Union. Although it does not compare with western types in terms of sophistication, the Tu-154 exhibits typical Russian design characteristics in that it is very strong and is able to operate from semi-prepared airstrips. A notable feature are the undercarriage nacelles, which project beyond the wing trailing edge. The sturdy main units retract backwards into the nacelles, the bogies somersaulting to lie flat within the fairings.

ABOVE: *An Aeroflot Tu-154 pictured in Soviet times.*

Specification (Tu-154M)

Crew: *3* **Powerplant:** *three 10,591kg (23,380lb) thrust Soloviev D-30-KU turbofans* **Max speed:** *950km/h (590mph)* **Service ceiling:** *11,900m (39,000ft)* **Max range:** *2750km (1700 miles)* **Wing span:** *37.55m (123ft 2in)* **Length:** *47.90m (157ft 1in)* **Height:** *11.40m (37ft 5in)* **Weight:** *100,000kg (220,460lb)* **Payload:** *151 passengers*

MAJOR VARIANTS
Tu-154B: version with increased all-up weight
Tu-154C: freighter version
Tu-154M: variant with uprated turbofans

RECOGNITION FEATURES
Low-mounted swept wing with protruding undercarriage nacelles; three turbojets mounted on rear fuselage; T-type tail

Tupolev Tu-204/214

ABOVE: *The Tu-204 suffered from the collapse of the Soviet Union, which resulted in anticipated Aeroflot orders being slashed.*

Specification (Tu-204)

Crew: *3* **Powerplant:** *two Perm PSA-90 or Rolls-Royce RB-211 turbofans* **Max speed:** *825km/h (512mph)* **Service ceiling:** *11,000m (36,080ft)* **Max range:** *6330km (3931 miles)* **Wing span:** *42.00m (137ft 9in)* **Length:** *46.00m (150ft 11in)* **Height:** *13.90m (45ft 7in)* **Weight:** *107,900kg (237,812lb) loaded* **Payload:** *214 passengers; 21,000kg (46,269lb) of cargo*

MAJOR VARIANTS
Tu-204: for medium haul routes
Tu-214: combination passenger/cargo
Tu-224: shortened version for commuter services

RECOGNITION FEATURES
Low-mounted swept wing; twin podded underwing turbofans; winglets; swept tail surfaces; resembles a Boeing 757

Designed to replace the Tu-154 in Aeroflot service, Tupolev's Tu-204 was designed to match the latest western airliners, while still meeting Soviet requirements. By the time the prototype made its first flight on 2 January 1989, Tupolev had received firm orders for 80 and provisional orders for 350 aircraft from Aeroflot, but these later lapsed when the Soviet Union disintegrated and Aeroflot became fragmented. Some of the fragments of the old Aeroflot within Russia itself placed new orders for small numbers of Tu-204s, but in general the new Russian and former Soviet civil operators looked to the West for their equipment.

Tupolev Tu-330

The Tupolev Tu-330 is a next-generation widebody cargo transport based on the successful Tu-214, using much of the technology applied to the latter aircraft, including about 75 per cent of its components. The aircraft is designed to replace the An-12 completely and the Il-76 partially on the majority of Russian cargo routes. The Tu-330 is a high-wing design with short take-off and landing capability. The type was a contender for a Russian Air Force STOL transport contract, but this was awarded to the Antonov An-70.

ABOVE: *A model of the proposed Tupolev Tu-330.*

Specification

Crew: *3* **Powerplant:** *two 16,140kg (35,573lb) thrust Aviadvigatel PS-90A turbofans* **Max speed:** *850km/h (528mph)* **Service ceiling:** *12,000m (39,360ft)* **Max range:** *5600km (3477 miles)* **Wing span:** *43.50m (142ft 8in)* **Length:** *42.00m (137ft 9in)* **Height:** *14.00m (46ft)* **Weight:** *103,000kg (227,000lb)* **Payload:** *30 tonnes (27 tons)*

MAJOR VARIANTS
Tu-330: initial production version
Tu-330TG: tanker variant

RECOGNITION FEATURES
High-mounted, swept wing with anhedral and prominent winglets; twin podded turbofans under inboard wing sections; swept tail surfaces; upswept rear fuselage to accommodate cargo ramp

Avro Lancaster

ABOVE: *The Battle of Britain Memorial Flight's Lancaster bearing the 'KM' code of No 44 (Rhodesia) Squadron.*

Specification (Lancaster Mk III)

Crew: *7* **Powerplant:** *four 1233kW (1640hp) Rolls-Royce Merlin 28 or 38 12-cylinder V-type engines* **Max speed:** *462km/h (287mph)* **Service ceiling:** *5790m (19,000ft)* **Max range:** *2784km (1730 miles) with a 5443kg (12,000lb) bomb load* **Wing span:** *31.09m (102ft)* **Length:** *21.18m (69ft 6in)* **Height:** *6.25m (20ft 6in)* **Weight:** *29,484kg (65,000lb) loaded* **Armament:** *two 7.7mm (0.303in) machine guns in nose turret, two 7.7mm (0.303in) machine guns in dorsal turret and four 7.7mm (0.303in) machine guns in tail turret; maximum internal bomb load 8165kg (18,000lb)*

One of the most famous bomber aircraft of all time, the Avro Lancaster was developed from the Avro Manchester, a design that suffered from the unreliability of its two Rolls-Royce Vulture engines. While production of the Manchester was in progress one airframe, BT308, was designated a 'four-engined Manchester' and fitted with four Rolls-Royce Merlin XX engines. This was the first prototype Lancaster, which first flew on 9 January 1941. The first operational sortie with Lancasters was on 3 March 1942, when four aircraft of No 44 Squadron laid mines in the Heligoland Bight. Deployment of the Lancaster III, with Packard-built Merlin engines, enabled Bomber Command to use first the 3624kg (8000lb) bomb, then the 5436kg (12,000lb) Tallboy, and finally the 9966kg (22,000lb) Grand Slam, recessed in the doorless bomb bay. Specially modified Lancasters of No 617 Squadron RAF also carried out the famous attack on the Mohne, Eder and Sorpe dams in May 1943.

The last Lancaster raid of the war was made against an SS barracks at Berchtesgaden on 25

Avro Lancaster (continued)

April 1945. During the war Lancasters flew 156,192 sorties, dropping 608,612 tons of bombs. Losses in action were 3431 aircraft, a further 246 being destroyed in operational accidents. At its peak strength in August 1944 no fewer than 42 Bomber Command squadrons were armed with Lancasters.

Total Lancaster production, all variants, was 7374 aircraft. Two Lancasters are still flying, one with the Battle of Britain Memorial Flight and the other with the Canadian Warplane Heritage Museum.

ABOVE: *The Battle of Britain memorial flight Lancaster in the markings of No 9 Squadron.*

MAJOR VARIANTS
Lancaster Mk I: basic bomber version
Lancaster Mk I (Special): Mk I modified to carry Tallboy and Grand Slam bombs
Lancaster Mk II: variant fitted with Bristol Hercules radial engines
Lancaster Mk III: bomber variant
Lancaster Mks IV and V: redesignated Lincoln Mks I and II
Lancaster Mk VI: variant equipped for electronic countermeasures
Lancaster Mk VII: bomber variant built by Austin Motors
Lancaster Mk X: bomber variant built in Canada
Lancaster GR.3: maritime patrol variant
Lancaster PR 1: photographic reconnaissance modification of Mk I

RECOGNITION FEATURES
Four piston engines; twin tailfins; nose, mid-upper and rear gun turrets

Boeing B-17 Flying Fortress

ABOVE: *A Boeing B-17G pictured at March Field in 1981.*

Specification (B-17G)

Crew: *10* **Powerplant:** *four 895kW (1200 hp) Wright Cyclone R-1820-97 radial engines* **Max speed:** *462km/h (287mph)* **Service ceiling:** *10,850m (35,000ft)* **Max range:** *3220km (2000 miles)* **Wing span:** *31.62m (103ft 9in)* **Length:** *22.78m (74ft 9in)* **Height :** *5.82m (19ft 1in)* **Weight:** *32,660kg (72,000lb) loaded* **Armament:** *twin 12.7mm (0.5in) machine guns under nose, aft of cockpit, under centre fuselage and in tail, and single-gun mountings in sides of nose, in radio operator's hatch and waist positions; maximum bomb load 7983kg (17,600lb)*

The B-17 Flying Fortress was designed in response to a United States Army Air Corps requirement, issued in 1934, for a long-range, high-altitude daylight bomber. The prototype, bearing the company designation Boeing Model 299, flew for the first time on 28 July 1935. Although the prototype was later destroyed in an accident, the cause was attributed to human error and the project went ahead. Thirteen Y1B-17s and one Y1B-17A were ordered for evaluation, and after the trials period these were designated B-17 and B-17A respectively. The first production batch of 39 B-17Bs were all delivered by the end of March 1940; meanwhile a further order had been placed for 38 B-17Cs, which were powered by four Wright 895kW (1200hp) Cyclone engines and featured some minor changes. The B-17D was generally similar to the C model, and the Cs in service were subsequently modified to D standard.

A new tail design, the main recognition feature of all subsequent Fortresses, was introduced with the B-17E, together with improved armament which for the first time included a tail gun position. The B-17E was the first version of the Flying Fortress to see combat in the European Theatre of Operations. The RAF received 42 B-17Es in 1942 under the designation Fortress IIA.

Boeing B-17 Flying Fortress (continued)

A total of 512 B-17Es were produced, this variant being followed into service by the further refined B-17F, which entered production in April 1942. Total production of the B-17F was 3400, including 61 examples which were converted to the long-range reconnaissance role as the F-9. Another 19 were delivered to RAF Coastal Command as the Fortress II. The major production model was the B-17G, which featured a chin gun turret. Ten B-17Gs were converted for reconnaissance as the F-9C, while the US Navy and Coast Guard used 24 PB-1Ws and 16 PB-1Gs for maritime surveillance and aerial survey. About 130 were modified for air-sea rescue duties as the B-17H or TB-17H, with a lifeboat carried under the fuselage and other rescue equipment.

ABOVE: *A wartime colour image of a Boeing B-17E Flying Fortress. Note the early-type insignia, used by the Army Air Corps.*

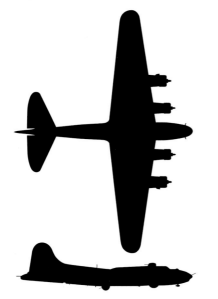

MAJOR VARIANTS
B-17B: initial production version
B-17C: reengined variant
B-17D: modified B-17C; extra pair of MGs
B-17E: modified tail; tail gun defensive position
B-17F: new engines; strengthened structural features
B-17G: heavier firepower; chin turret

RECOGNITION FEATURES
Low-mounted, straight wing with four radial engines; long cockpit fairing with dorsal gun turret; broad tailfin with large fairing extending to fuselage; tail and chin turrets

de Havilland DH.82A Tiger Moth

ABOVE: *This DH.82 Tiger Moth was originally an RAF trainer.*

Specification

Crew: *2* **Powerplant:** *one 97kW (130hp) de Havilland Gipsy Major 4-cylinder in-line engine* **Max speed:** *161km/h (100mph)* **Service ceiling:** *4270m (14,000ft)* **Max range:** *483km (300 miles)* **Wing span:** *8.94m (29ft 4in)* **Length:** *7.29m (23ft 11in)* **Height:** *2.67m (8ft 9in)* **Weight:** *828kg (1825lb) loaded*

The line of training and sports biplanes that resulted in the Tiger Moth began with the DH.60 of 1925, named Moth in recognition of Geoffrey de Havilland's renown as a lepidopterist. By the end of 1925 20 Cirrus-engined Moths had been completed, of which 16 had been delivered to six government-sponsored flying clubs and two to private owners. Another 35 were built in 1926, of which 14 were exported, and by the end of 1928 the production total had reached 403, with more being turned out at the rate of 16 per week. The light aeroplane that made the greatest impact on sporting aviation throughout the world in the 1920s was the DH.60G Gipsy Moth, which was flown in almost every country that supported flying facilities. The Gipsy Moth continued in production until 1943, by which time a total of 595 had been produced in England, in addition to 40 built by Morane-Saulnier in France,

de Havilland DH.82A Tiger Moth (continued)

18 by the Moth Aircraft Corporation of Massachusetts, USA, and 32 by the Larkin Aircraft Supply Co Ltd of Melbourne, Australia.

Probably the most famous (and certainly the most attractive) basic training aircraft of all time, the DH.82A Tiger Moth first flew on 26 October 1931 and large-scale production began almost immediately, mostly for the Royal Air Force. This classic little aircraft was also licence built in Canada, New Zealand, Australia, Portugal, Norway and Sweden. No fewer than 8700 Tiger Moths were produced. After World War II Tiger Moths flooded into the civil market, while others continued to serve in the RAF for a number of years until replaced by the Percival Prentice and de Havilland Chipmunk. Among the famous exponents of Tiger Moth flying was the Tiger Club, whose aircraft (The Bishop, The Archbishop, The Deacon and The Canon single-seat conversions) became well known for their aerobatic displays. Tiger Moths are far from rare, many remaining in the hands of private owners.

MAJOR VARIANTS
DH.82: initial version
DH.82A: Gypsy Major engine; structural improvements
DH.82C: winterised version made in Canada

RECOGNITION FEATURES
Biplane with staggered, slightly swept wings; tandem cockpits; fixed undercarriage; distinctive 'de Havilland' tail unit

de Havilland Mosquito

ABOVE: *De Havilland Mosquito B.IVs of No 105 Squadron RAF.*

Specification (FB.Mk VI)

Crew: 2 **Powerplant:** *two 1104kW (1480hp) Rolls-Royce Merlin 21 or 23 engines* **Max speed:** *595km/h (370mph)* **Service ceiling:** *10,515m (34,500ft)* **Max range:** *2744km (1705 miles)* **Wing span:** *16.51m (54ft 2in)* **Length:** *13.08m (42ft 11in)* **Height:** *5.31m (17ft 5in)* **Weight:** *9072kg (20,000lb) loaded* **Armament:** *four 20mm (0.79in) cannon and four 7.7mm (0.303in) fixed machine guns, plus ordnance up to 907kg (2000lb)*

> MAJOR VARIANTS
> Numerous, but all externally similar except for some radar-equipped versions, which had a redesigned nose

> RECOGNITION FEATURES
> Wing with straight leading edge and tapered trailing edge; twin engines, propellers in line with nose of aircraft; low-mounted tailplane, extending aft of tailplane

Known as the 'wooden wonder' because of its all-wood construction, the de Havilland DH.98 Mosquito was, without doubt, one of the most versatile and successful aircraft of World War II. It saw service throughout the world as a day and night fighter, fighter-bomber, high-altitude bomber, pathfinder, anti-shipping strike aircraft, reconnaissance aircraft and trainer. The prototype flew for the first time on 25 November 1940. The major production version was the FB.Mk VI fighter-bomber, of which 2718 were built during and after the war. Squadrons equipped with it carried out some daring low-level precision attacks during the last year of the war, including the raid on Amiens prison in February 1944 and attacks on Gestapo head-quarters buildings in Norway and the Low Countries.

de Havilland (Canada) Chipmunk

Originally designed by de Havilland (Canada), the Chipmunk T.10 was developed by the parent company to meet RAF basic training requirements, which it fulfilled until replaced by the Scottish Aviation Bulldog in the 1970s. Canadian production came to 218 examples, and a further 1014 were built in the UK, the latter comprising military T.10s and civilian Mk 21s. Sixty were built under licence in Portugal and large numbers of ex-RAF machines were subsequently civilianized as Mks 22 or 22A. Canadian-built Chipmunks carried the designation T.30.

ABOVE: *A Chipmunk T.10 of the RAF Flying Training Command.*

Specification

Crew: 2 **Powerplant:** *one de Havilland Gipsy Major 8 4-cylinder in-line engine* **Max speed:** *222km/h (138mph)* **Service ceiling:** *4880m (16,000ft)* **Max range:** *480km (300 miles)* **Wing span:** *10.46m (34ft 4in)* **Length:** *7.82m (25ft 8in)* **Height:** *2.16m (7.1ft)* **Weight:** *907kg (2000lb) loaded*

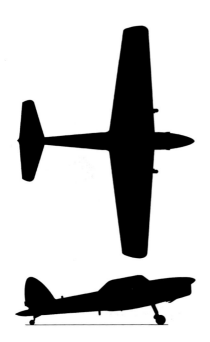

MAJOR VARIANTS
DHC-1: initial production version
T.10: RAF trainer variant
Mk 22/22A: civilianized versions

RECOGNITION FEATURES
Single-engine, low-wing monoplane; fixed undercarriage; 'de Havilland' tail, with fin set slightly forward of tailplane

de Havilland (Hawker Siddeley) DH.110 Sea Vixen

ABOVE: *Pictured at Duxford, this Sea Vixen FAW.2 carries the winged fist insignia of No 899 Naval Air Squadron.*

Specification (FAW.2)

Crew: *2* **Powerplant:** *two 5094kg (11,230lb) thrust Rolls-Royce Avon 208 turbojets* **Max speed:** *1110kh/h (690mph)* **Service ceiling:** *14,640m (48,000ft)* **Max range:** *965km (600 miles)* **Wing span:** *15.54m (51ft)* **Length:** *17.02m (55ft 7in)* **Height:** *3.28m (10ft 9in)* **Weight:** *18,858kg (41,575lb) loaded* **Armament:** *four Firestreak or Red Top AAMs; Bullpup ASMs on underwing pylons*

The de Havilland Sea Vixen originated in the DH.110, which had been in competition with the Gloster Javelin for an RAF all-weather fighter requirement, but which had suffered a catastrophic breakup at the 1952 Farnborough air display. In 1956, the surviving DH.110 prototype underwent carrier trials, and the first fully navalized machine, with folding wings, flew on 20 March 1957. Known initially by the designation FAW.20, the aircraft was later named Sea Vixen and re-designated FAW.1. In 1961, two FAW.1s received extra fuel tanks in forward extensions of the tail booms, and these served as the prototype FAW.2, which was issued to squadrons in 1965.

> **MAJOR VARIANTS**
> **Mk 1:** initial production version
> **Mk 2:** structural modifications to Mk 1; enlarged tail booms

> **RECOGNITION FEATURES**
> Swept wings; central fuselage nacelle with cockpit and engines; twin tail booms with broad tailplane and twin fins

Douglas DC-3

Whereas the Douglas DC-2 was designed to a TransWorld Airlines (TWA) specification, its successor, the DC-3, began life as the DST (Douglas Sleeper Transport) and was designed for a new carrier, American Airlines. When the type entered service in 1936, no one could foresee that, within three years, the DC-3 would account for 90 per cent of the world's airline trade. American Airlines eventually operated the largest prewar DC-3 fleet, taking delivery of 66 aircraft. Licence manufacture of the airliner was undertaken by Nakajima in Japan from 1938, and Soviet licence production as the PS-84 (later Lisunov Li-2) began in 1940. Huge numbers were ordered from September 1940 for the US Army Air Corps as the C-47 and C-53, and US Navy as the R4D-1, and many civilian DC-3s were impressed for military service. The type saw widespread service with the RAF, who named it the Dakota, and with other Allied air forces. About 18,000 DC-3s and their military variants were built, and an estimated

ABOVE: *In the years after World War II the DC-3 helped to get many small airlines such as Air Oasis off the ground.*

Specification

Crew: *2* **Powerplant:** *two 746kW (1000hp) Wright Cyclone SGR-1820 radials* **Max speed:** *298km/h (185mph)* **Service ceiling:** *7070m (23,200ft)* **Max range:** *2414km (1500 miles)* **Wing span:** *28.96m (95ft)* **Length:** *19.65m (64ft 5in)* **Height:** *4.97m (16ft 3in)* **Weight:** *10,886kg (24,000lb) loaded* **Payload:** *21 passengers*

2000 were still in commercial use around the world in the early 21st century. One frequently seen Dakota is the example preserved in flying condition by the RAF's Battle of Britain Memorial Flight (BBMF). Douglas C47 (DC3) Dakota ZA947 was manufactured in March 1942 and initially issued to the United States Army Air Force. In September that year the aircraft was transferred to the Royal Canadian Air Force (RCAF) and served mainly in Canada, but was later used in Europe until declared surplus to requirements in 1971. The aircraft was adopted by Strike Command and issued to the BBMF in March 1993 after Air Atlantique at Coventry had completed necessary engineering and structural work. The Dakota is a year-round workhorse for the BBMF, being used in a variety of roles.

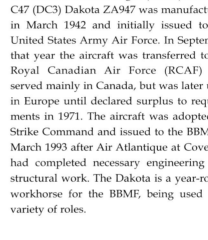

MAJOR VARIANTS
Numerous variants and roles, although all aircraft externally similar

DC-3: main original production version
C-47 and C-53: US Army Air Corps version
R4D-1: US Navy version
Dakota: RAF version
AC-47D: gunship
Lisunov Li-2: Russian licence-built version

RECOGNITION FEATURES
Low-mounted wing with distinctive sweepback on leading edge and straight trailing edge; twin piston engines; semi-retractable landing gear; low-mounted tailplane

Hawker Hunter

In a career spanning a quarter of a century the Hunter equipped 30 RAF fighter squadrons, in addition to numerous units of foreign air forces. The aircraft was licence built in Holland and Belgium; principal customers for British-built aircraft were India, Switzerland and Sweden. Indian Hunters saw considerable action in the 1965 and 1971 conflicts with Pakistan, 10 Hunters being lost in the three-week air war of 1965 and 22 in the 1971 battle, some of these being destroyed on the ground. The grand total of Hunter production, including two-seat trainers, was 1972 aircraft, and over 500 were subsequently rebuilt for sale overseas.

The Hunter F.Mk 1, which entered service early in 1954, suffered from engine surge problems during high-altitude gun-firing trials, resulting in some modifications to its Rolls-Royce Avon turbojet, and this – together with increased fuel capacity and provision for underwing tanks – led to the Hunter F.4. The Hunter Mks 2 and 5 were variants powered by the Armstrong Siddeley Sapphire

ABOVE: The two-seat Hawker Hunter T.7, seen here, gave many military pilots their first taste of fast jet flying.

MAJOR VARIANTS
F.1: initial production version
F.4: Avon 115 engine; increased fuel capacity
F.5: Sapphire 101 engine
F.6: Avon 203 engine; increased fuel capacity
FR.10: reconnaissance version
T.8: two-seat Navy version

ABOVE: *Hawker Hunter T.67s of the Royal Kuwaiti Air Force.*

Specification (Hunter F.6)

Crew: *1* **Powerplant:** *one 3628kg (8000lb) thrust Rolls-Royce Avon 122 turbojet* **Max speed:** *1117km/h (694mph)* **Service ceiling:** *14,325m (47,000ft)* **Max range:** *689km (429 miles)* **Wing span:** *10.26m (33ft 8in)* **Length:** *13.98m (45ft 10in)* **Height:** *4.02m (13ft 2in)* **Weight:** *7802kg (17,200lb) loaded* **Armament:** *four 30mm (1.18in) Aden cannon; underwing pylons with provision for two 453kg (1000lb) bombs and 24 76cm (3in) rockets*

engine. The Hunter F6, with a more powerful Avon engine, subsequently equipped 15 squadrons of RAF Fighter Command. The Hunter FGA.9 was a development of the F.6 optimized for ground attack, as its designation implies. The Hunter Mks 7, 8, 12, T52, T62, T66, T67 and T69 were all two-seat trainer variants, while the FR.10 was a fighter-reconnaissance version, converted from the F.6. The GA.11 was an operational trainer for the Royal Navy.

RECOGNITION FEATURES
Streamlined, swept-wing jet fighter; wing root air intakes; single engine; bulges for collecting ammunition cases under lower front fuselage (most variants)

Hawker Hurricane

The Hawker Hurricane prototype (K5083) flew on 6. November 1935. The fighter subsequently played a vital part in the Battle of Britain, and served as an effective fighter-bomber in the Middle East and Burma. Large numbers were exported to the Soviet Union.

In 1941 the Hurricane was adopted by the Royal Navy for fleet protection duties, the first Sea Hurricane Mk 1As being deployed on escort carriers in 1941. As Hurricanes were progressively withdrawn from first-line RAF squadrons they were converted for naval use as Sea Hurricanes Mks IB, IIC and XIIA. Overall Hurricane production in the UK was 13,080 by Hawker, Gloster and Austin Motors; another 1451 Mks X, XI, XII and XIIA, fitted with Packard-built Rolls-Royce Merlins, were produced by the Canadian Car and Foundry Co.

ABOVE: *Flaps and wheels down, the Battle of Britain Memorial Flight's Hawker Hurricane cruises in to land.*

Specification (Hurricane Mk 2c)

Crew: 1 **Powerplant:** *one 1089kW (1460hp) Rolls-Royce Merlin XX 12-cylinder V-type* **Max speed:** *518km/h (322mph)* **Service ceiling:** *9785m (32,100ft)* **Max range:** *1448km (900 miles)* **Wing span:** *12.19m (40ft)* **Length:** *9.81m (32ft 2in)* **Height:** *3.98m (13ft 1in)* **Weight:** *3674kg (8100lb) loaded* **Armament:** *two 20mm (0.79in) cannon in each wing*

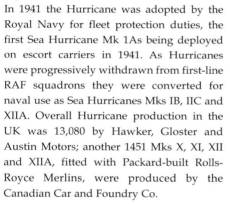

MAJOR VARIANTS
Mk I: initial production version
Mk IIA: Merlin XX engine
Mk IIB: 12 machine guns
Mk IIC: four 20mm (0.79in) cannon
Mk IV: ground-attack version
Mk V: Merlin 32 engine
Sea Hurricane: navalized version

RECOGNITION FEATURES
Low-wing monoplane; single engine; broad, rounded tailfin; 'hump-backed' appearance

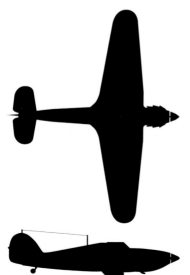

MiG-MAPO (Mikoyan) MiG-15/MiG-17

ABOVE: *A defecting Angolan MiG-17, right, escorted by a South African Mirage F.1Z.*

Specification (MiG-15B)

Crew: *1* **Powerplant:** *one 2700kg (5952lb) thrust Klimov VK-1 turbojet* **Max speed:** *1100km/h (684mph) at 7625m (25,000ft)* **Service ceiling:** *15,545m (51,000ft)* **Max range:** *1424km (885 miles) with slipper tanks* **Wing span:** *10.08m (33ft)* **Length:** *11.05m (36ft 3in)* **Height:** *3.40m (11ft 1in)* **Weight:** *5700kg (12,566lb) loaded* **Armament:** *one 37mm (1.5in) N-37 and two 23mm (0.9in) NS-23 cannon; up to 500kg (1102lb) of underwing stores*

One of the most famous jet fighters of all time, and certainly one of the most outstanding combat aircraft of the postwar years, the MiG-15 (NATO reporting name 'Fagot') was designed by a Russo-German team headed by Artem I. Mikoyan and Mikhail I. Guryevich. The type flew for the first time on 30 December 1947 and entered series production in the following year. The first MiG-15s were powered by a Rolls-Royce Nene copy, designated RD-45. An uprated variant was designated MiG-15B, and was serving in large numbers with the Soviet Air Force by the end of 1950. Production of the MiG-15 eventually reached some 18,000 aircraft, this figure including a tandem two-seat trainer version, the MiG-15UTI. The MiG-15 was built under licence in the People's Republic of China as the Shenyang F-2, in Poland as the LIM-1 and in Czechoslovakia as the S-102. The MiG-15 saw a great deal of action in its heyday, starting with the Korean War, where it fought the North American F-86 Sabre in history's first jet-versus-jet air battles.

When the MiG-17 (NATO reporting name 'Fresco') first appeared in the early 1950s, western observers at first believed that it was

MiG-MAPO (Mikoyan) MiG-15/MiG-17 (continued)

an improved MiG-15, with new features that reflected the technical lessons learned during the Korean War. In fact, design of the MiG-17 had begun in 1949, the new type incorporating a number of aerodynamic refinements that included a new tail on a longer fuselage and a thinner wing with different section and planform and with three boundary layer fences to improve handling at high speed. The basic version, known to NATO as Fresco-A, entered service in 1952.

ABOVE: *A MiG-15UTI trainer supplied in 1962 to the Finnish Air Force to prepare for the arrival of MiG-21F-13 fighters the following year.*

MAJOR VARIANTS
MiG-15: initial production version
MiG-15B: uprated engine
MiG-15UTI: two-seat trainer
Shenyang F-2: licence-built Chinese variant
MiG-17: initial production version
MiG-17F: uprated engine with afterburner
MiG-17P: all-weather interceptor
MiG-17PFU: SAM armed interceptor (no cannon)

RECOGNITION FEATURES
Both **MiG-15** and **MiG-17** have mid-mounted swept wings with boundary layer fences on upper surface, but **MiG-17** has more pronounced sweepback, more rounded wingtips and trailing edge wing root extensions; both types have a high, broad tailfin with high-mounted tailplane, and nose intakes

North American B-25 Mitchell

ABOVE: *The B-25 Mitchell was one of the most effective medium bombers of World War II.*

Specification (B-25D)

Crew: *5* **Powerplant:** *two 1268kW (1700hp) Wright R-2600-13 18-cylinder two-row radials* **Max speed:** *457km/h (284mph)* **Service ceiling:** *6460m (21,200ft)* **Max range:** *2454km (1525 miles)* **Wing span:** *20.60m (67ft 7in)* **Length:** *16.12m (52ft 10in)* **Height:** *4.82m (15ft 10in)* **Weight:** *18,960kg (41,800lb) loaded* **Armament:** *six 12.7mm (0.5in) machine guns; ordnance load of 1361kg (3000lb)*

The North American B-25 was designed as a tactical bomber, but found a valuable second role as a potent anti-shipping aircraft in the Pacific Theatre. The prototype, bearing the company designation NA-40, flew for the first time in January 1939, and the first batch of production B-25s was delivered from February 1941, further deliveries comprising 40 B-25As and 120 B-25Bs, the former with self-sealing tanks and the latter with dorsal and ventral turrets but no tail gun position. On 16 April 1942, the Mitchell leapt into the headlines when the aircraft carrier USS *Hornet*, from a position at sea 1075km (668 miles) from Tokyo, launched 16 B-25Bs of the 17th AAF Air Group, led by Lt Col. J.H. Doolittle, for the first attack on the Japanese homeland. Total production of all Mitchell variants was 9816 aircraft.

MAJOR VARIANTS
B-25A: initial production version
B-25B: no tail gun position
B-25C: autopilot equipped
B-25G: anti-shipping variant

RECOGNITION FEATURES
Glazed nose; tail gun position; twin tailfins; twin engines; slight anhedral on outer wing panels

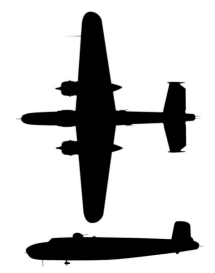

North American P-51 Mustang

The North American P-51 Mustang was initially produced in response to a 1940 RAF requirement for a fast, heavily armed fighter able to operate effectively at altitudes in excess of 6100m (20,000ft). North American built the prototype in 117 days, and the aircraft, designated NA-73X, flew on 26 October 1940. The first of 320 production Mustang Is for the RAF flew on 1 May 1941, powered by a 820kW (1100hp) Allison V-1710-39 engine. The USAAF, somewhat belatedly, realized the fighter's potential and evaluated two early production Mustang Is under the designation P-51. The first two USAAF Mustang variants, both optimized for ground attack and designated A-36A and P-51A, were fitted with Allison engines. Trials with Mustangs fitted with Packard-built Rolls-Royce Merlin 61 engines showed a dramatic improvement in performance, and production of the Merlin-powered P-51B got under way in the autumn of 1942. Complaints about the poor visibility from the Mustang's cockpit led North American to test two P-51Bs with a one-piece sliding canopy

ABOVE: *This P-51D Mustang bears the code letters of the 363rd Fighter Squadron, 357th Fighter Group, based in the UK during World War II.*

MAJOR VARIANTS
Mustang IA: initial production version for RAF
P-51A: initial production variant for USAAF
P-51B: Packard-built Merlin engine
P-51D: one-piece sliding canopy; cut-down rear fuselage
P-51H: lightened version; increased top speed

Specification (P-51D)

Crew: *1* **Powerplant:** *one 1112kW (1490hp) Packard Rolls-Royce Merlin V-1650-7 engine* **Max speed:** *704km/h (437mph) at 7620m (25,000ft)* **Service ceiling:** *12,770m (41,900ft)* **Max range:** *3347km (2080 miles)* **Wing span:** *11.28m (37ft)* **Length:** *9.85m (32ft 3in)* **Height:** *3.71m (12ft 2in)* **Weight:** *5493kg (12,100lb) loaded* **Armament:** *six 12.7mm (0.5in) machine guns in the wings, plus provision for up to two 454kg (1000lb) bombs or six 12.7cm (5in) rockets*

and cut-down rear fuselage, in which guise it became the P-51D. The first production P-51Ds began to arrive in England in the late spring of 1944 and quickly became the standard equipment of the USAAF Eighth Fighter Command.

In the Pacific, Mustangs were operating from the captured Japanese islands of Iwo Jima and Okinawa from April 1945, escorting B-29s to their targets and neutralizing the Japanese Air Force on the ground. The fastest Mustang version, which saw service in the Pacific towards the end of the war, was the P-51H, with a top speed of 784km/h (487mph). The Mustang continued to serve with some 20 air forces around the world for years after the end of WWII, and gave valiant service during the early months of the Korean War with US, Australian, South African and South Korean air units.

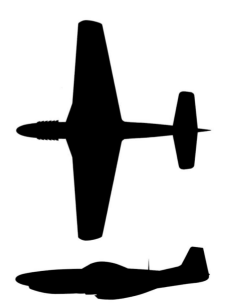

RECOGNITION FEATURES
Square-cut wing; long radiator under mid-fuselage; angular tailfin with fairing; raised cockpit canopy; single engine

North American F-86 Sabre

The F-86 Sabre originated as a swept-wing version of an earlier design, the NA-134, the first of two XP-86 flying prototypes making its first flight on 8 August 1947 under the power of a General Electric J35 turbojet. The first operational F-86As were delivered to the 1st Fighter Group early in 1949. Production of the F-86A ended with the 554th aircraft in December 1950, a date that coincided with the arrival of the first F-86As in Korea with the 4th Fighter Wing. During the next two and a half years, Sabres were to claim the destruction of 810 enemy aircraft, 792 of them MiG-15s. The next Sabre variants were the F-86C penetration fighter (which was redesignated YF-93A and which flew only as a prototype) and the F-86D all-weather fighter, which had a complex fire-control system and a ventral rocket pack; 2201 were built, the F-86L being an updated version. The F-86E was basically an F-86A with power-operated controls and an all-flying tail; 396 were built before the variant was replaced by

ABOVE: *An F-86F Sabre of the Japanese Air Self-Defense Force, one of the largest overseas customers for the type.*

MAJOR VARIANTS

F-86A: initial production version
F-86D: all-weather fighter; fire-control system; ventral rocket pack
F-86E: power-operated controls; all-flying tail
F-86F: major production version
F-86H: fighter-bomber version; four 20mm (0.79in) cannon
Sabre Mk 4: RAF versions

ABOVE: *The Sabre was a graceful aircraft and a delight to fly.*

Specification (F-86E)

Crew: *1* **Powerplant:** *one 2358kg (5200lb) thrust General Electric J47-GE-13 turbojet* **Max speed:** *1086km/h (675mph)* **Service ceiling:** *14,720m (48,300ft)* **Max range:** *1260km (765 miles)* **Wing span:** *11.30m (37ft 1in)* **Length:** *11.43m (37ft 6in)* **Height:** *4.47m (14ft 8in)* **Weight:** *7419kg (14,720lb) loaded* **Armament:** *six 12.7mm (0.5in) Colt-Browning MG; up to 907kg (2000lb) of underwing stores*

the F-86F, the major production version with 2247 examples being delivered. The F-86H was a specialized fighter-bomber armed with four 20mm (0.79in) cannon and capable of carrying a tactical nuclear weapon. The F-86K was essentially a simplified F-86D; and the designation F-86J was applied to the Canadair-built Sabre Mk 3. Most of the Sabres built by Canadair were destined for NATO air forces; the RAF, for example, received 427 Sabre Mk 4s. The Sabre Mk 6 was the last variant built by Canadair. The Sabre was also built under licence in Australia as the Sabre Mk 30/32, powered by a Rolls-Royce Avon turbojet. The total number of Sabres built by North American, Fiat and Mitsubishi was 6208, with a further 1815 produced by Canadair.

RECOGNITION FEATURES
Swept flying surfaces; nose intake with pronounced 'lip'; single-seat cockpit

Supermarine Spitfire

A contract for the production of 310 Spitfires was issued by the Air Ministry in June 1936, and the first examples were delivered to No 19 Squadron at Duxford in August 1938. Eight other squadrons had equipped with Spitfires by September 1939, and two Auxiliary Air Force units, Nos 603 and 609, were undergoing operational training. Production of the Spitfire Mk I, which was powered by a 768kW (1030hp) Merlin II or III engine, eventually reached 1566 aircraft. It was this variant that saw the most combat in the Battle of Britain, the Mk II with the 877kW (1175hp) Merlin XII engine being issued to the squadrons of Fighter Command in September 1940. The major Spitfire production version was the Mk V, with 6479 examples completed. The Spitfire V, however, failed to provide the overall superiority Fighter Command needed so badly, and so a Mk V airframe was married with a Merlin 61 engine. The resulting combi-

ABOVE: *A Spitfire VB with the code letters of No 310 Squadron, the first Czech squadron to form within the RAF during World War II.*

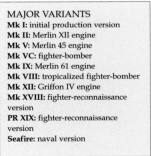

MAJOR VARIANTS
Mk I: initial production version
Mk II: Merlin XII engine
Mk V: Merlin 45 engine
Mk VC: fighter-bomber
Mk IX: Merlin 61 engine
Mk VIII: tropicalized fighter-bomber
Mk XII: Griffon IV engine
Mk XVIII: fighter-reconnaissance version
PR XIX: fighter-reconnaissance version
Seafire: naval version

ABOVE: *A Spitfire Mk IX in the markings of No 222 Squadron, which operated Spitfires from March 1940 to December 1944.*

Specification (Spitfire Mk VB)

Crew: *1* **Powerplant:** *one 1074kW (1440hp) Rolls-Royce Merlin 45/46/50 V-12 engine* **Max speed:** *602km/h (374mph)* **Service ceiling:** *11,280m (37,000ft)* **Max range:** *756km (470 miles)* **Wing span:** *11.23m (36ft 10in)* **Length:** *9.11m (29ft 11in)* **Height:** *3.48m (11ft 5in)* **Weight:** *3078kg (6785lb) loaded* **Armament:** *two 20mm (0.79in) cannon and four 7.7mm (0.303in) machine guns*

nation was the Spitfire Mk IX, which for a stop-gap aircraft turned out to be a resounding success. Deliveries to the RAF began in June 1942 and 5665 were built, more than any other mark except the Mk V.

The Spitfire Mk X and XII were unarmed PR variants, while the Mk XII was the first Griffon-powered version, being followed by the Mk XIV. The Spitfire XVI, which entered service in 1944, was a ground-attack version similar to the Mk IX, but with a Packard-built Merlin 266 engine. The Spitfire XVIII was a fighter-reconnaissance variant, just beginning to enter service at the end of WWII, as was the PR Mk XIX. The last variants of the Spitfire, produced until 1947, were the Mks 21, 22 and 24. They bore very little resemblance to the prototype Mk I of a decade earlier. Total production of the Spitfire was 20,351 plus 2334 examples of the naval version, the Seafire. Many Spitfires still fly on the airshow circuit.

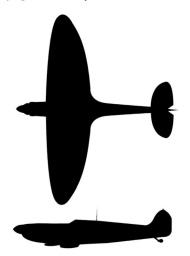

RECOGNITION FEATURES
Low-wing single-engined mono-plane; early marks have distinctive elliptical wing; later marks have square-cut wingtips

COMMUTER & EXECUTIVE AIRCRAFT

Aero Commander

The prototype Aero Commander 520 was first flown in 1948, production beginning in 1951. Since its introduction, the Aero Commander has been continuously improved, including stretched versions and variants fitted with more powerful piston and turboprop engines.

ABOVE: *An Aero Commander 500S (Rockwell Shrike Commander).*

The first version was the Commander 520, with a 179kW (240hp) Lycoming GO-435-C2 piston engine; the 560 had a 201kW (270hp) Lycoming GO-480-B. The 500, a four-seat version, was renamed the Shrike Commander in 1967, while the Grand Commander (later renamed Courser Commander) of 1961 was a 5/9-seat variant. The Turbo Commander, first flown in 1964, was powered by 428kW (575hp) Garrett TPE 331 turboprops. US military designations for the Aero Commander were L-26, U-4 and U-9.

Specification (560E)

Crew: 2 **Powerplant:** *two 201kW (270hp) Lycoming GO-480-B piston engines* **Max speed:** *357km/h (222mph)* **Service ceiling:** *6862m (22,500ft)* **Max range:** *2615km (1625 miles)* **Wing span:** *15.09m (49ft 6in)* **Length:** *10.70m (35ft 1in)* **Height:** *4.49m (14ft 6in)* **Weight:** *2944kg (6500lb)* **Payload:** *5 passengers*

MAJOR VARIANTS
520: initial production version
570: upgraded engine
500/Shrike Commander: four-seat version
Grand Commander/Courser Commander: 5/9-seat variant
Turbo Commander: upgraded engine

RECOGNITION FEATURES
560E: high-mounted wing; twin piston engines; tricycle undercarriage; upswept rear fuselage; dihedral tailplane

Aerospatiale SN601 Corvette

ABOVE: *An Aerospatiale Corvette in the colours of the Danish commuter airline Sterling.*

Specification

Crew: *2* **Powerplant:** *two 1134kg (2500lb) thrust Pratt & Whitney (Canada) JT15D-4 turbofans* **Max speed:** *760km/h (472mph)* **Service ceiling:** *12,500m (41,000ft)* **Max range:** *1555km (967 miles)* **Wing span:** *12.70m (42ft 2.5in)* **Length:** *13.83m (45ft 4.5in)* **Height:** *4.23m (13ft 10in)* **Weight:** *6600kg (14,550lb) loaded* **Payload:** *6–14 passengers*

MAJOR VARIANTS
SN601: major production version

RECOGNITION FEATURES
Low-mounted, swept wing, mostly fitted with tip tanks; twin turbofans mounted on rear fuselage; swept tail surfaces

The first prototype Corvette, designated SN600, flew in July 1960 and crashed eight months later, but the information gleaned while testing it enabled Aerospatiale to develop a production version, the SN601, which flew in 1972. The aircraft received its certification in September 1974 and deliveries started immediately afterwards, the 40th and last aircraft being produced in 1978. As well as its executive transport role the Corvette was designed to act as an air ambulance, light transport, trainer and radar calibration aircraft.

Beriev Be-103

The Be-103 light multi-purpose amphibious aircraft is a monoplane with low-set water-displacement wing with a root strake, all-moving horizontal tail located in the propeller blow zone, and tricycle landing gear. A unique feature of the amphibious aircraft includes implementation of a water-displacement wing concept, which improves seaworthiness and stability when moving on water. The low-set wing (in relation to hull) provides for wing-in-ground effect during take-off and landing. Thanks to this feature the aircraft does not need flaps and can skim on the wing trailing edges. This also makes aircraft construction simpler.

ABOVE: *The Beriev Be-103 Amphibian is manufactured in the United States.*

Specification

Crew: *1* **Powerplant:** *two 157kW (210hp) Teledyne Continental IO-360-ES4 piston engines* **Max speed:** *240km/h (150mph)* **Service ceiling:** *5020m (16,465ft)* **Max range:** *1070km (664 miles)* **Wing span:** *12.72m (41ft 9in)* **Length:** *10.65m (34ft 11in)* **Height:** *3.75m (12ft 4in)* **Weight:** *2270kg (5003lb)* **Payload:** *6 passengers*

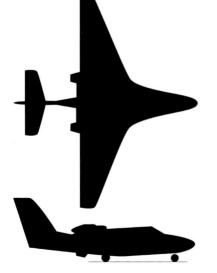

MAJOR VARIANTS
Roles envisaged for the Be-103 include casevac patrol, cargo/passenger transportation, fire protection monitoring, ecology monitoring of water areas, and tourism

RECOGNITION FEATURES
Single-step hull; mid-mounted wing; twin piston engines mounted on pylons on rear fuselage

Bombardier BD-100 Challenger 300

ABOVE: *A relative newcomer to the business jet market, the Bombardier Challenger has trans-continental range.*

Specification

Crew: *2* **Powerplant:** *two 3647kg (8050lb) thrust Honeywell AS907 turbofans* **Max speed:** *870km/h (540mph)* **Service ceiling:** *13,716m (45,000ft)* **Max range:** *5741km (3565 miles)* **Wing span:** *19.46m (63ft 10in)* **Length:** *20.93m (68ft 11in)* **Height:** *6.17m (20ft 3in)* **Weight:** *17,010kg (37,490lb)* **Payload:** *8–16 passengers*

The Challenger 300, originally known as the Continental Business Jet BD-100, is a medium-sized transcontinental business jet developed by Bombardier Aerospace of Canada. The aircraft was renamed in September 2002. The aircraft carries up to eight passengers in a cabin with stand-up headroom over a non-stop range of 5744km (3569 miles), i.e. coast-to-coast range across America, using a take-off airfield length of less than 1525m (5000ft). The Challenger was launched in 1999 and a flight test programme involving five aircraft is under way. The prototype flew for the first time in August 2001.

MAJOR VARIANTS
BD-100: initial production version

RECOGNITION FEATURES
Low-mounted swept wing with winglets; two turbofans mounted on rear fuselage; T-type tail

Bombardier BD-700 Global Express

Having acquired the established and successful business jet manufacturers Canadair and Learjet, Bombardier announced in 1991 that it intended to produce a new aircraft – the Global Express – to compete with Gulfstream at the top end of the business jet market. The result was the elegant BD-700, which first flew in 1996 and was intended to capture the lion's share of an anticipated 500–800 orders for long-range business jets over the following 15 years.

ABOVE: *The Bombardier Global Express is possibly the most elegant business jet in service today.*

Specification

Crew: *2* **Powerplant:** *two BMW/Rolls-Royce BR712A2-2 turbofans* **Max speed:** *850km/h (527mph)* **Service ceiling:** *15,555m (51,000ft)* **Max range:** *10,158km (6308 miles)* **Wing span:** *28.60m (94ft)* **Length:** *30.30m (99ft 5in)* **Height:** *7.60m (24ft 10in)* **Weight:** *41,280kg (90,981lb) loaded* **Payload:** *19 passengers*

MAJOR VARIANTS
BD-700 Special Missions: a developed version by Raytheon E-systems to meet the UK's Airborne Stand-Off Radar (Astor) requirement.

RECOGNITION FEATURES
Low-mounted swept wing tapering sharply towards the tips; winglets; twin turbofans mounted on rear fuselage; swept tail surfaces; T-type tail

Britten-Norman BN-2 Islander/ BN-2A Trislander

ABOVE: *This Trislander is operated by Aurigny, the principal commuter airliner serving the Channel Islands.*

Specification (BN-2 Islander)

Crew: *2* **Powerplant:** *two 194kW (260hp) Lycoming O-540-E4C5 piston engines* **Max speed:** *257km/h (160mph)* **Service ceiling:** *6000m (19,700ft)* **Max range:** *670km (425 miles)* **Wing span:** *14.94m (49ft)* **Length:** *10.87m (35ft 8in)* **Height:** *4.16m (13ft 8in)* **Weight:** *2857kg (6300lb) loaded* **Payload:** *9 passengers*

One of Britain's greatest civil aviation success stories of the postwar years did not originate with a main manufacturer, but with a small company established at Bembridge Aerodrome on the Isle of Wight by two aeronautical engineers, John Britten and Desmond Norman. Their BN-2 Islander design and its many developments have sold widely around the world, its toughness and dependability having proved ideal for many small operators, both civil and military. Design work on the BN-2 began in 1963, and the prototype flew on 13 June 1965. British launch customers in 1967 were Glos-Air and Loganair. The Islander is superbly suited to conditions in difficult terrain. Variants include the BN-2 Defender, with two wing hardpoints, and the BN-2T, with Allison turboprops.

A simple way of extending the Islander design to carry far greater loads was to stretch the fuselage and install a third engine halfway up the tailfin. The result was the Trislander, offering 17 seats in maximum density as opposed to nine in the Islander. The first Trislander was G-ATWU, the converted production prototype of the Islander, which flew on 11 September 1970. The name Trislander was adopted in January 1971, UK

Britten-Norman BN-2 Islander/BN-2A Trislander (continued)

certification was granted in May, and the first customer delivery to Aurigny Airlines in the Channel Islands followed on 29 June, only 292 days after the aircraft's maiden flight. Further developments of the Trislander included the BN-2A Mk III-2 with an extended nose, the BN-2A Mk III-3 with an automatic propeller feathering system, and the BN-2A Mk III-4, which had a standby tail cone rocket system to provide extra thrust in the event of an engine failure on take-off.

ABOVE: *A turboprop-powered BN-2T Islander registered G-BLNK, which started life as a piston-engined BN-2B.*

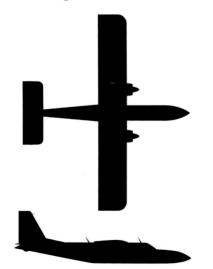

MAJOR VARIANTS
BN-2: initial production version
BN-2A: increased max take-off weight; structural additions
BN-2A-3: uprated engine; extended wingtips
BN-2B: improved variant
BN-2 Defender: wing hardpoints
BN-2A Mk III-2: extended nose
BN-2A Mk III-3: auto propeller feathering system
BN-2A Mk III-4: standby tail rocket system

RECOGNITION FEATURES
Islander: high-mounted straight wing; twin piston engines; fixed landing gear with mainwheel struts attached to engine nacelles
Trislander: high-mounted straight wing with dihedral tips; two piston engines mounted on wing and one on tailfin; long, slim fuselage

Canadair (Bombardier) Regional Jet

ABOVE: *The CRJ is an economical and quiet choice for airlines.*

Specification (CRJ-200)

Crew: *2* **Powerplant:** *two 4176kg (9220lb) thrust General Electric CF34-3B1 turbofans* **Max speed:** *851km/h (528mph)* **Service ceiling:** *13,725m (45,000ft)* **Max range:** *3713km (2305 miles)* **Wing span:** *21.21m (69ft 7in)* **Length:** *26.77m (87ft 10in)* **Height:** *6.22m (20ft 5in)* **Weight:** *24,040kg (53,000lb) loaded* **Payload:** *50 passengers*

MAJOR VARIANTS
CRJ100: initial production version
CRJ200: version with improved CF3403B1 engines
CRJ700: 70-seat version of the CRJ200
CRJ900: 90-seat version of the CRJ700

RECOGNITION FEATURES
Low-mounted swept wing, tapering sharply; prominent winglets; twin turbofans mounted on rear fuselage; swept tail surfaces; T-type tail

The Canadair (Bombardier) Regional Jet (CRJ) is a ground-breaking aircraft. It was the first of a new breed of regional jets that swept the airline marketplace during the 1990s, a breed that is still the fastest-growing segment in the industry. Based on the proven Challenger business jet family, the CRJ has produced a whole new family of its own, with a range of variants both in production and under development. As well as commuter and regional airlines, the CRJ has been purchased by major corporations attracted by its economy and low noise signature.

Cessna Citation

Cessna began production of the Citation I medium-range executive jet in 1971, and this was followed by a stretched version, the Citation II. Introduced in 1979, and bearing little resemblance to its straight-winged predecessors, the Citation III was the first of the Cessna jets to provide a truly intercontinental range but, like its contemporary the Gates 55 Longhorn, sales did not match those of the previous generation. Both aircraft were powered by a pair of Garrett TFE731 engines and both represented a major new design departure by their parent companies; they were also, aesthetically, very attractive aircraft. In the case of the Citation III, however, a generally poor economic climate brought an end to Cessna's production run after only 189 had left the factory line. The majority of these went to existing Citation customers in the United States, who were trading-in their older models.

ABOVE: *The Citation III was not as successful as expected.*

Specification (Citation III)

Crew: *2* **Powerplant:** *two 1653kg (3650lb) thrust Garrett TFE731-3B-100S turbofans* **Max speed:** *541km/h (336mph)* **Service ceiling:** *15,544m (51,000ft)* **Max range:** *4352km (2704 miles)* **Wingspan:** *16.33m (53ft 6in)* **Length:** *16.93m (55ft 5in)* **Height:** *5.16m (16ft 9in)* **Weight:** *9979kg (22,000lb)* **Payload:** *10 passengers*

MAJOR VARIANTS
Citation II: stretched version
Citation III: extended range
Citation V: stretched version
Citation X: swept wing; more powerful engines

RECOGNITION FEATURES
Citation I and II: low-mounted straight wing; twin turbofans on rear fuselage; low-mounted tailplane
Citation III: low-mounted swept wing; twin turbofans mounted on rear fuselage; T-type tail

Cessna Model 401 Series

ABOVE: *The Cessna Model 401 Series continues to be popular.*

Specification (Model 421 Golden Eagle)

Crew: *1* **Powerplant:** *two 375hp Continental GTSIO-520D piston engines* **Max speed:** *418km/h (260mph)* **Service ceiling:** *8077m (26,500ft)* **Max range:** *1609km (1000 miles)* **Wing span:** *12.67m (41ft 10in)* **Length:** *11.00m (36ft 1in)* **Height:** *3.61m (11ft 10in)* **Weight:** *3289kg (7250lb) loaded* **Payload:** *6-8 passengers*

MAJOR VARIANTS
401: initial production version
402: convertible cabin
414: new pressurized version
421B Golden Eagle: lengthened; enlarged nose section; strengthened undercarriage

---

RECOGNITION FEATURES
Low-mounted straight wing; twin piston engines; low-set tailplane; raked tailfin; wingtip tanks. **Model 402** has square windows, other models have round windows.

The first version of this light executive transport, the Cessna 401, flew for the first time on 26 August 1965. The Model 402, with a similar airframe and powerplant but a convertible cabin, enabling it to be changed from a 10-seat commuter to a light cargo transport, was announced simultaneously. A new pressurized version, the Model 414, appeared in November 1968. Another version is the Model 421B Golden Eagle, which was developed from the earlier Model 421A. Principal changes comprise an increase of 0.71m (2ft 4in) in overall length as a result of enlarging the nose section of the fuselage to provide more baggage and avionics capacity, an extension of 0.61m (2ft) to maintain take-off and cruise performance without the need to increase engine power, and a strengthened undercarriage.

Dassault Falcon 50

The Falcon 50 was developed by Avions Marcel Dassault to meet a perceived demand for a business jet with non-stop trans-oceanic and transcontinental capability. Three prototypes were built, the first flying on 7 November 1976. On 31 March 1979, the Falcon 50 established a new world record for its category by flying non-stop from Bordeaux to Washington, a distance of 6099km (3787 miles). The latest version of the Falcon 50, and the only one now produced, is the Falcon 50EX, which has an updated avionics suite and Allied Signal TFE 731-40 turbofans. The EX flew for the first time on 10 April 1996. Four Falcon 50s are with French Naval Air Arm for maritime surveillance.

ABOVE: *Easily distinguishable from the other members of the Falcon family by its trio of engines, the Falcon 50 is notable for its long range.*

Specification (Falcon 50EX)

Crew: *2* **Powerplant:** *three Allied Signal TFE 731-40 turbofans* **Max speed:** *900km/h (560mph)* **Service ceiling:** *14,900m (48,878ft)* **Max range:** *6482km (4025 miles)* **Wing span:** *18.90m (61ft 10in)* **Length:** *18.50m (60ft 9in)* **Height:** *6.90m (22ft 10in)* **Weight:** *18,010kg (39,694lb)* **Payload:** *9 passengers*

MAJOR VARIANTS
Falcon 50: initial production version
Falcon 50EX: updated avionics; upgraded engine

RECOGNITION FEATURES
Low-mounted swept wing; three tail-mounted turbofans; mid-mounted tailplane

Dassault Falcon 100

ABOVE: *The Dassault Falcon 100 was developed to meet a demand for a short-range executive jet.*

Specification

Crew: *2* **Powerplant:** *two 1465kg (3230lb) thrust Garrett TFE731 turbofans* **Max speed:** *912km/h (566mph)* **Service ceiling:** *15,555m (51,000ft)* **Max range:** *2900km (1800 miles)* **Wing span:** *13.10m (42ft 11in)* **Length:** *13.80m (45ft 5in)* **Height:** *4.60m (15ft 1in)* **Weight:** *8500kg (18,740lb) loaded* **Payload:** *8 passengers*

Originally known as the Falcon 10, the prototype Falcon 100 flew for the first time on 1 December 1970. Production aircraft were assembled at Istres using airframe components supplied by Potez (fuselage), CASA of Spain (wings), IAM of Italy (nose assembly and tail unit) and Latecoere (doors, fin and other small components). Although most of the Falcon 100s built were sold to commercial customers, mainly in North America, six were delivered to the French Navy for use as instrument, navigation and radar trainers, for communications duties, calibration of shipboard radars and medevac missions.

MAJOR VARIANTS
Mystere-Falcon 10MER: version for the French Navy

RECOGNITION FEATURES
Low-mounted swept wing; twin turbofans mounted on rear fuselage; three round cabin windows on either side of fuselage

Dassault Falcon 200

The Falcon 200 was based on the Mystere 20, which first flew in 1963 and which was later renamed Falcon 20 (Fan Jet Falcon in the USA). The Falcon 20 proved adaptable to many roles beyond its primary task of transporting business customers, having been used for airline pilot training, airways and navaid calibration, high-altitude aerial photography and mapping, electronic countermeasures training, medevac, military transport and airborne sensing. The aircraft was marketed as the Falcon 200 from 1980.

ABOVE: *The Falcon 200 has been adapted to many tasks other than its main function as a business jet.*

Specification

Crew: *2* **Powerplant:** *two Garrett ATF3 turbofans* **Max speed:** *870km/h (540mph)* **Service ceiling:** *15,555m (51,000ft)* **Max range:** *4650km (2888 miles)* **Wing span:** *16.30m (53ft 6in)* **Length:** *17.20m (56ft 3in)* **Height:** *5.30m (17ft 5in)* **Weight:** *10,545kg (23,348lb)* **Payload:** *12 passengers*

> MAJOR VARIANTS
> **Falcon 20:** initial production version
> **Hu-25A Guardian:** search and rescue/offshore surveillance aircraft
> **Hu-25C:** anti-smuggling variant with APG-66 radar

> RECOGNITION FEATURES
> Low-mounted swept wing; twin turbofans mounted on rear fuselage; mid-mounted tailplane; five circular windows on each side of fuselage

Dassault Falcon 900

ABOVE: *The Falcon 900 shares its tri-jet configuration with the 50.*

Specification

Crew: *2* **Powerplant:** *three 2038kg (4500lb) thrust Garrett TFE731-5AR-1C turbofans* **Max speed:** *922km/h (572mph)* **Service ceiling:** *15,544m (51,000ft)* **Max range:** *7222km (4488 miles)* **Wing span:** *19.35m (63ft 5in)* **Length:** *20.20m (66ft 7in)* **Height:** *7.50m (24ft 9in)* **Weight:** *20,639kg (45,500lb)* **Payload:** *19 passengers*

MAJOR VARIANTS
900: initial production version
900B: upgraded engines; increased range
900EX: long-range version of 900B

RECOGNITION FEATURES
Low-mounted swept wing; three tail-mounted turbofan engines; mid-mounted tailplane with anhedral

In the hard-fought arena of executive jet sales, the Dassault Falcon series is unquestionably the best-selling family of business jets, with a pedigree that stretches back over several decades. The first of the line was the Mystere XX; this flew on 1 January 1965 and deliveries soon began to the type's American distributor, Pan American Business Jets Inc. It was initially marketed as the Fan Jet Falcon, before being renamed Falcon 20. Latest in the series is the Falcon 900, the first of which, named Spirit of Lafayette, flew on 21 September 1984. The second aircraft set a new distance record for its class when it flew non-stop from Paris to Dassault's US distribution centre at Little Rock, Arkansas, covering a distance of 7973km (4954 miles) at Mach 0.84.

de Havilland (Canada) Dash-7

Since the mid-1940s, when the DHC-2 Beaver was introduced, de Havilland Canada has maintained a reputation for building strong and reliable light utility transports. The Dash-7 has become one of the world's leading Short Take-Off and Landing (STOL) airlin-

ers. The first prototype flew on 27 March 1975. By the time the aircraft received full certification in Canada and the United States, Canadair had already rolled out the first production aircraft. Several of the commuter airlines who have bought the Dash-7 have made use of the 'Separate Access Landing System' concept which has been promoted by de Havilland. This involves the use of limited sections of runways or stub sections of runways which are available only because of the unique ability of the aircraft to manoeuvre onto such sections outside the general flow of the airport's traffic.

ABOVE: *One of the Dash-7's attractive features is that it can use limited sections of runways.*

Specification

Crew: *2* **Powerplant:** *four 835kW (1120shp) Pratt & Whitney PT6A-50 turboprops* **Max speed:** *426km/h (265mph)* **Service ceiling:** *7193m (23,600ft)* **Max range:** *1295km (805 miles)* **Wing span:** *28.35m (93ft)* **Length:** *24.58m (80ft 8in)* **Height:** *7.98m (26ft 2in)* **Weight loaded:** *19,958kg (44,000lb)* **Payload:** *50 passengers*

MAJOR VARIANTS
Several sub-series, but all externally similar

RECOGNITION FEATURES
High-mounted, straight wing; four turboprops; T-type tail

de Havilland Canada DHC-8 Dash-8

ABOVE: *The Dash-8 has sold well, although it is in direct competition with Europe's ATR-42/72 and regional jet commuters.*

Specification (DHC-8)

Crew: *2* **Powerplant:** *two 1492kW (2000shp) Pratt & Whitney Canada PW120A turboprops* **Max speed:** *500km/h (310mph)* **Service ceiling:** *7620m (15,000ft)* **Max range:** *2010km (1250 miles)* **Wing span:** *25.90m (85ft)* **Length:** *22.50m (73ft)* **Height:** *7.50m (24ft 6in)* **Weight:** *15,650kg (34,500lb) loaded* **Payload:** *36 passengers*

First flown in 1983, the de Havilland Canada DHC-8 'Dash-8' was designed to fill an identified gap between the 20-seat DHC-6 Twin Otter and the 50-seat Dash-7. The aircraft was intended from the outset to operate with minimum noise pollution, while retaining maximum efficiency. At the start of the Dash-8 development programme, a Canadian writer compared the aircraft with four major rivals, and concluded that the Toronto product would be 'the benchmark against which the others are measured'. Although the competition was perhaps tougher than DHC expected, some 567 Dash-8s had been sold by August 1998, and of these 494 had been delivered. The Franco-German ATR-42/72, the Canadian turbo-prop's main rival, was only slightly behind in the marketplace with 560 sold, although it started more than a year later. For the future, the Dash-8 will have to stand up to a whole phalanx of new similarly sized jet commuters including the Canadair Regional Jet. Although the Dash-8 appears to be a fairly basic design, it has many hidden features that enhance its saleability. For example, a movable rear

de Havilland Canada DHC-8 Dash-8 (continued)

fuselage bulkhead enables mixed passenger/cargo operations to be flown, and the Dash-8 can be operated in the all-cargo mode, in which case the payload is 4268kg (9409lb). Normal fuel capacity is 3160 litres (695 Imp gal) contained in integral tanks outboard of the engines. Auxiliary long-range tanks can be provided, and the Corporate model (marketed in North America by Innotech of Montreal) has centre-section integral tanks raising capacity to 5742 litres (1265 Imp Gal), sufficient for a range of 3706km (2300 miles). De Havilland Canada's greatest market for the Dash-8 has been in North America, where it has proved to be a reliable workhorse for feeder carriers.

ABOVE: *A DHC Dash-8 in the livery of Air Nova, an Eastern Canadian subsidiary of Air Canada.*

MAJOR VARIANTS
Dash-8 Series 100: initial production version
Dash-8 Series 200A: increased payload and speed; upgraded engines
Dash-8 Series 300: fuselage stretched by 3.40m (11ft 3in) to raise seating capacity to 56

RECOGNITION FEATURES
High-mounted straight wing; twin turboprops; swept-back tailfin with fairing to upper fuselage; T-type tailplane

Dornier Do 228

ABOVE: *A Dornier Do 228 of the German Navy, which operates the type on oil pollution patrol duty.*

Specification

Crew: *2* **Powerplant:** *two 578kW (775hp) Garrett TPE 331-5 turboprops* **Max speed:** *428km/h (266mph)* **Service ceiling:** *9020m (29,585ft)* **Max range:** *1130km (700 miles)* **Wing span:** *17.00m (55ft 8in)* **Length:** *15.00m (49ft 4in)* **Height:** *4.80m (15ft 11in)* **Weight:** *5700kg (12,562lb) loaded* **Payload:** *19 passengers*

First flown in 1981, the Dornier Do 228 short-haul commuter aircraft is now produced exclusively by Hindustan Aeronautics Ltd. Civil specialist versions include pollution surveillance and geophysical survey. HAL is offering military versions of the Do 228 for anti-ship and anti-submarine duties, while the German Navy operates several examples on oil pollution patrol. These are based with Marineflieger 3 at Nordholz in northern Germany.

> **MAJOR VARIANTS**
> Several sub-variants, all basically similar in configuration.

> **RECOGNITION FEATURES**
> High-mounted wing with distinctive swept wingtips; twin turboprops; long fuselage, square in section; undercarriage bulges under fuselage; fairing from fin to upper rear fuselage

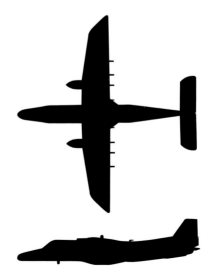

Dornier Do 328

The Dornier (or more correctly Fairchild Dornier, as the American concern took over 80 per cent of Dornier in the 1990s) 328 short-haul commuter first flew in 1991 and was originally equipped with two turbo-props, but Fairchild assessed the type's suitability for turbofan engines and produced the Do 328JET, which flew for the first time in February 1998. Flight testing proceeded well and several benefits came to light. For example, the original 328's propeller wash used to have an adverse effect on the airframe especially noticeable during power adjustments. This effect was completely eliminated in the jet-powered version. Also, the noise level in the cabin decreased considerably.

ABOVE: *A Dornier Do 328 of the US regional airline Horizon Air.*

Specification (Do 328JET)

Crew: *2* **Powerplant:** *two 5484kg (12,086lb) thrust Pratt & Whitney Canada PW 306 B turbofans* **Max speed:** *740km/h (459 mph)* **Service ceiling:** *9450m (31,000ft)* **Max range:** *3700km (2298 miles)* **Wing span:** *21.00m (68ft 10in)* **Length:** *21.30m (69ft 9in)* **Height:** *7.30m (23ft 9in)* **Weight:** *15,200kg (33,516lb) loaded* **Payload:** *33 passengers*

> ### MAJOR VARIANTS
> **328-100:** initial production version
> **328-110:** standard production version
> **328JET:** turbofan-powered version

> ### RECOGNITION FEATURES
> High-mounted straight wing with swept tips; T-type tail, two turbofan or turboprop engines, depending on variant

EMBRAER EMB-110 Bandeirante

ABOVE: *EMBRAER (Embresa Brasileira de Aeronautica S.A.) has proved a Brazilian success story.*

Specification (EMB-110)

Crew: 2 **Powerplant:** *two 410kW (550shp) Pratt & Whitney PT6A-20 turboprops* **Max speed:** *430km/h (267mph)* **Service ceiling:** *9000m (29,500ft)* **Max range:** *1850km (1150 miles)* **Wing span:** *15.42m (50ft 7in)* **Length:** *12.74m (41ft 9in)* **Height:** *5.17m (16ft 11in)* **Weight:** *4500kg (9920lb)* **Payload:** *18 passengers*

The EMBRAER Bandeirante has been one of the most successful of the modern light turboprop commuterliners. By the time production ceased in 1989, over 500 had been sold to both civil and military markets. Following the first flight of the prototype on 19 August 1972, the Forca Aerea Brasileira (FAB) confirmed that it was satisfied with the aircraft, allocating the military designation C-95. The EMB-110P1K used by the FAB has the forward entry door of the stretched Bandeirante models and is used for freight transport or for carrying up to 19 paratroops. It is fitted with a large rear cargo hatch with an inset sliding door that allows troops to gain clear exit from the rear of the aircraft.

MAJOR VARIANTS
Embraer EMB-110: standard short-haul commuter aircraft
Embraer EMB-111: maritime patrol version with longer nose section containing search radar

RECOGNITION FEATURES
Low-mounted, straight wing; twin turboprops in slender nacelles; swept vertical tailfin; small ventral tailfin

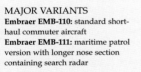

EMBRAER EMB-120 Brasilia

The EMB-120 Brasilia is Embraer's 30-seat twin-turboprop airliner. The EMB-120 first entered service in 1985 with Atlantic Southeast Airlines. In 1991, EMBRAER announced the Improved Brasilia extended-range version – the EMB-120ER – first delivered in 1993. The extended range aircraft includes several features such as an increased take-off weight and improved design of all the leading edges. The ER version has been adopted as the standard production model since 1993. Over 370 aircraft have been delivered and are in service with 32 operators worldwide.

ABOVE: *The prototype Embraer EMB-120 Brasilia.*

Specification (EMB-120ER)

Crew: 2 **Powerplant:** *two 1343kW (1800hp) Pratt & Whitney PW118 turboprops* **Max speed:** *606km/h (376mph)* **Service ceiling:** *9750m (31,980ft)* **Max range:** *3017km (1873 miles)* **Wing span:** *19.80m (64ft 10in)* **Length:** *20.00m (65ft 7in)* **Height:** *6.40m (20ft 10in)* **Weight:** *10,490kg (23,120lb) loaded* **Payload:** *30 passengers/3340kg (7361lb) of cargo*

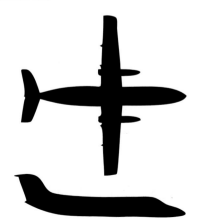

MAJOR VARIANTS
EMB-120RT: initial production version
EMB-120 Cargo: cargo version
EMB-120 Combi: mixed cargo/ passenger configuration
EMB-120ER Advanced: extended range; numerous improvements

RECOGNITION FEATURES
Low-mounted straight wing; twin turboprops; T-type tail; fairing from fin to upper rear fuselage

EMBRAER EMB-121 Xingu

ABOVE: *The Embraer Xingu is a hybrid design, combining components of the Bandeirante and Brasilia.*

Specification (EMB-121A)

Crew: 2 **Powerplant:** *two 552kW (740hp) Pratt & Whitney PT6A-34 turboprops* **Max speed:** *360km/h (224mph)* **Service ceiling:** *8300m (27,231ft)* **Max range:** *2352km (1460 miles)* **Wing span:** *14.10m (46ft 1in)* **Length:** *12.20m (40ft 2in)* **Height:** *4.80m (15ft 10in)* **Weight:** *7000kg (15,435lb) loaded* **Payload:** *9 passengers*

MAJOR VARIANTS
EMB-121A: standard version
EMB-121A-1: re-engined variant and has two small strakes on the tail cone

RECOGNITION FEATURES
Low-mounted straight wing; twin turboprops; T-type tail; swept tailfin, straight tailplane

The EMBRAER EMB-121 Xingu, combining the wing of the AMB-110 Bandeirante and the fuselage of the EMB-120 Brasilia, flew for the first time on 22 October 1976, but technical problems delayed its production. Although designed as a short-range executive turboprop, its main outlet came as a light military transport. An order for six machines by the Brazilian Air Force was quickly followed by one from France, which ordered 50 examples in 1981 for service with the Air Force and the Naval Air Arm.

EMBRAER ERJ-135

The ERJ-135 is one of the EMBRAER Regional Jet Series. The launch of the aircraft was in 1997 and the first flight was made out in 1998. The aircraft entered service with Continental Express and American Eagle in 1999. A total of 132 ERJ-135 regional jets have been ordered for operators including British Midland, Chautauqua Airlines, City Airlines, Flandre Air, Jetmagic, Proteus, Regional Airlines France, Regional Air Lines Morocco and South African Air Link. In December 2002, EMBRAER announced that the company is to set up a production facility for the ERJ-135/140/145 aircraft in China, in a joint venture with Harbin Aircraft.

ABOVE: *The attractive Embraer ERJ-135 is selling well to regional airlines. Production facilities have been set up in China.*

Specification (ERJ-135ER)

Crew: *2* **Powerplant:** *two 3376kg (7441lb) thrust Rolls-Royce A3007 turbofans* **Max speed:** *833km/h (517mph)* **Service ceiling:** *11,275m (36,982ft)* **Max range:** *2463km (1529 miles)* **Wing span:** *20.04m (65ft 9in)* **Length:** *24.39m (80ft)* **Height:** *6.76m (22ft 2in)* **Weight:** *19,000kg (41,876lb)* **Payload:** *37 passengers*

MAJOR VARIANTS
ERJ-135ER (Extended Range)
ERJ-135LR (Long Range)
ERJ-135XR (Extra Long Range)

RECOGNITION FEATURES
Low-mounted swept wing; twin turbojets mounted on rear fuselage; T-type tail; undercarriage bulge under mid-fuselage; **ERJ-135XR** has winglets

EMBRAER ERJ-145

ABOVE: *The ERJ-145 is a stretched version of the -135.*

Specification (ERJ-145ER)

Crew: 2 **Powerplant:** *two 3376kg (7441lb) thrust Rolls-Royce A3007A turbofans* **Max speed:** *833km/h (517mph)* **Service ceiling:** *11,275m (36,982ft)* **Max range:** *2963km (1840 miles)* **Wing span:** *20.04m (65ft 9in)* **Length:** *29.87m (98ft)* **Height:** *6.76m (22ft 2in)* **Weight:** *20,600kg (45,402lb)* **Payload:** *50 passengers*

MAJOR VARIANTS
ERJ-145ER (Extended Range)
ERJ-145LR (Long Range)
ERJ-145XR (Extra Long range)
EMB-145AEW&C: Airborne Early
Warning and Control aircraft

RECOGNITION FEATURES
Low-mounted swept wing; twin turbojets mounted on rear fuselage;
T-type tail; undercarriage bulge
under mid-fuselage

The ERJ-145 is EMBRAER's 50-passenger regional jet airliner. The aircraft first entered service in 1996 and is operational with 27 airlines worldwide. There are three variants of the aircraft: the 50-passenger ERJ-145 launched in 1989; the shorter fuse-lage 37-passenger ERJ-135 launched in 1997; and the medium sized 44-seat ERJ-140 launched in 1999. Some 900 ERJ aircraft (all variants) have been ordered with over 750 delivered and the aircraft is in service world-wide. The EMB-145AEW&C Airborne Early Warning and Control aircraft is a derivative of the ERJ-145 and is equipped with the Ericsson Erieye side-looking airborne radar. It is in service with the Brazilian and Hellenic Air Forces.

Gulfstream American Gulfstream II–V

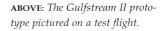

The original Gulfstream executive aircraft, a product of the Grumman Aircraft Corporation, was powered by twin turbo-props, so a jet-powered version seemed a logical development. The outcome was the Gulfstream II, which was a radical and high-ly successful development of the Gulfstream I. The Gulfstream II was succeeded by the III and IV. The most obvious difference between the GIV and preceding aircraft in the Gulfstream series is the GIV's much larger engine nacelles, which house the 1.2m (4ft) Rolls-Royce Tay 610 engines. The Tay enables the GIV to conform to the stringent FAR Pt 36 Stage 3 noise regulations.

ABOVE: *The Gulfstream II proto-type pictured on a test flight.*

Specification (Gulfstream IV)

Crew: *3* **Powerplant:** *two 6260kg (13,820lb) thrust Rolls-Royce Tay Mk 511-8 turbofans* **Max speed:** *936km/h (582mph)* **Service ceiling:** *13,715m (45,000ft)* **Max range:** *6732km (4183 miles)* **Wing span:** *23.27m (77ft 10in)* **Length:** *26.92m (88ft 4in)* **Height:** *7.45m (24ft 5in)* **Weight:** *33,203kg (73,200lb) loaded* **Payload:** *8 passengers*

MAJOR VARIANTS
Gulfstream II: initial production version without winglets
Gulfstream III: later version with winglets
Gulfstream IV: improved Gulfstream III with larger engine nacelles
Gulfstream V: stretched version of Gulfstream IV

RECOGNITION FEATURES
Low-mounted swept wing; T-type tail; twin turbofans mounted on rear fuselage

IAI Arava

ABOVE: *The prototype IAI Arava. The type was used for both civil and military applications.*

Specification (Arava 201)

Crew: 2 **Powerplant:** *two 560kW (750shp) Pratt & Whitney Canada PT6A34 turboprops* **Max speed:** *326km/h (202mph)* **Service ceiling:** *7625m (25,000ft)* **Max range:** *1000km (620 miles)* **Wing span:** *21.60m (70ft 11in)* **Length:** *13.50m (44ft 2in)* **Height:** *5.20m (17ft 1in)* **Weight:** *6804kg (15,000lb)* **Payload:** *up to 24 passengers*

MAJOR VARIANTS
101B: initial production version
102: 20-seat interior
201: military version

RECOGNITION FEATURES
High-mounted straight wing; twin turboprops, twin tail booms, twin tailfins; bulbous fuselage nacelle

---

First flown in November 1969, the Arava STOL utility transport was intended for both military and civil customers, but was built in only small numbers and in fact lent itself more to military than civil use. The initial design, the Arava 101, did not enter production, but formed the basis for the 101B, 102 and 201 production models. The 101B was marketed in the USA as the Cargo Commuterliner and differed from the 101 in having an improved 19-seat interior in passenger configuration and more powerful PT6A36s. The 102 had a 20-seat passenger interior, or alternatively a 12-passenger executive interior or all freight configuration. The Arava 201 is primarily a military version.

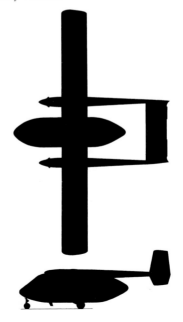

IAI Astra

ABOVE: *The IAI Astra pictured on a test flight in 1984.*

The Israeli Aircraft Industries Model 1125 Astra is a swept-wing development of the Westwind. As well as the swept wing, the aircraft features a much deeper fuselage than its predecessor. Three prototype Astras were built, the first flying on 19 March 1984. In 1989, after 40 Astras had been built, the initial model was superseded by the Astra SP (Special Performance), which featured a new cabin interior design, an updated avionics suite and aerodynamic improvements to the wing resulting in enhanced high-altitude cruise performance and increased range. A larger version, the IAI 1126 Galaxy, was launched in 1993 and the first prototype made its maiden flight on 25 December 1997.

Specification (Model 1125)

Crew: *2* **Powerplant:** *two 1925kg (4250lb) thrust Honeywell TFE731-40R-200G turbofans* **Max speed:** *895km/h (556mph)* **Service ceiling:** *13,725m (45,000ft)* **Max range:** *5211km (3236 miles)* **Wing span:** *16.00m (52ft 8in)* **Length:** *16.90m (55ft 7in)* **Height:** *5.50m (18ft 2in)* **Weight:** *11,181kg (24,650lb)* **Payload:** *8 passengers*

MAJOR VARIANTS
Astra: initial production version
Astra SP: improved version
Astra SPX: more powerful engines; increased weight/payload/range
1126 Galaxy: larger, improved version of SP

RECOGNITION FEATURES
Low-mounted, narrow swept wing; twin turbofans mounted on rear fuselage; mid-mounted tailplane

IAI Westwind

ABOVE: *The Westwind began life as the Rockwell Jet Commander.*

Specification (Westwind)

Crew: *2* **Powerplant:** *two 1680kg (3700lb) thrust Garrett (Allied Signal) TFE731-3 turbofans* **Max speed:** *750km/h (465mph)* **Service ceiling:** *13,715m (45,000ft)* **Max range:** *3985km (2475 miles)* **Wing span:** *13.65m (44ft 10in)* **Length:** *15.95m (52ft 3in)* **Height:** *4.80m (15ft 10in)* **Weight:** *10,600kg (23,50lb)* **Payload:** *12 passengers*

In 1967, Israel Aircraft Industries acquired all production and marketing rights for the North American Rockwell Corporation (formerly Aero Commander) Jet Commander executive jet transport. Initially IAI began manufacture of the Jet Commander 1121A virtually unchanged, but then developed a much improved version called the Commodore Jet, featuring a fuselage lengthened to accommodate 10 passengers. The Model 1123 Commodore Jet was first flown on 28 September 1970 and was later known as the Westwind Eleven-23. Thirty-six Westwind Eleven-23s were built before the Model 1123 was superseded by the Model 1124 Westwind, first flown on 21 July 1975. The Westwind was powered by turbofan engines, giving a greatly enhanced performance, and 53 were built. Adding winglets to the tip tanks and redesigning the aerofoil section produced the Westwind 2.

MAJOR VARIANTS
Westwind Eleven-23: renamed version of Model 1123 Commodore Jet
Model 1124 Westwind: turbofan-powered version
Westwind 2: winglets added to tip tanks; redesigned aerofoil section

---

RECOGNITION FEATURES
Westwind: mid-mounted straight wing with wingtip pods; twin turbofans mounted on rear fuselage; low-mounted tailplane

Learjet Series

The Learjet has been the world's best-selling business jet since the concept was invented. The Model 25C marked Learjet's move into the market for transcontinental long-range jets; it was based on the original stretched Model 25, but the cabin length was reduced to make room for extra fuel in the centre section. As growing sales brought improved financial results, funding became available for the next stage of Learjet development: the provision of a more efficient, quieter engine. Garrett AirResearch had started work on such an engine, designed to replace existing turbojets in this class of aircraft, in the late 1960s, and in May 1971 the new powerplant – the TFE 731-2 turbofan – was flight tested in a Learjet 25. The first production Learjets to use the TFE 731 were unveiled in August 1973. Both were based on the stretched Learjet 25, with increased wing span and a further small fuselage stretch to balance the extra weight of the engines.

The Model 35 was a transcontinental eight-seater, while the Model 36 had an extra fuselage fuel tank and shorter cabin, giving it

ABOVE: *The Learjet 25 was the first of the Learjet series with transcontinental range. Winglets were added retrospectively.*

MAJOR VARIANTS
Learjet 23: initial production version
Learjet 24: improved version; all-metal fuselage
Model 25: stretched version
Model 25C: increased fuel capacity and range
Model 35: transcontinental eight-seater
Model 36: transatlantic capable
Learjet 45: larger fuselage, wing and tail; improved avionics
Learjet 60: new engines; larger dimensions

ABOVE: *Uprated turbofan engines, an enlarged passenger cabin and the introduction of winglets resulted in the Learjet Model 35.*

Specification (Learjet Model 35)

Crew: *2* **Powerplant:** *two 1678kg (3700lb) thrust Garrett AirResearch TF731 turbofans* **Max speed:** *859km/h (534mph)* **Service ceiling:** *13,720m (45,000ft)* **Max range:** *4074km (2532 miles)* **Wing span:** *10.84m (35ft 7in)* **Length:** *13.38m (43ft 3in)* **Height:** *3.84m (12ft 7in)* **Weight:** *6123kg (13,500lb) loaded* **Payload:** *8 passengers*

enough range for transatlantic operations. In mid-1977 Gates Learjet announced the development of a new Learjet family that would be a clean break with the original design philosophy, featuring a much enlarged cabin with standup headroom. Power would be provided by uprated versions of the TFE 731, and lift by a highly modified version of the basic Learjet wing. This was the first on any production aircraft to incorporate the wingtip vertical surfaces known as 'winglets'. Devised by Dr Richard Whitcomb of NASA, winglets are designed to work in the vortex flow which exists at the tip of a wing, turning the flow to provide a small forward thrust, or drag reduction. The new wing, named Longhorn by the company, was tested on a Learjet 25 in August 1977, and a small number of Longhorn 28 and 29 versions of the Learjet were produced. The Learjet 55/60 is a widebody version of the basic Learjet design.

RECOGNITION FEATURES
Learjet Model 35: low-mounted straight wing with wingtip tanks; twin turbofans mounted on rear fuselage; T-type tail

LET L-410 Turbolet

The first of three L-410 light transport aircraft prototypes flew in April 1969, powered by two Canadian PT6A turboprops, and in the following year the type was selected to replace the Lisunov L-2 (DC-3) in service with the Eastern Bloc countries. Large numbers were exported to the Soviet Union. By the late 1990s over 1000 examples had been built and exported to 40 countries. The first L-410 operator was Slov-Air, a newly formed Czech internal airline, which began regular services with four Turbolets in late 1971.

ABOVE: *A LET-410 of Slov-Air, a newly-formed Czech domestic airline that was the first to operate the type.*

Specification

Crew: *2* **Powerplant:** *two 533kW (715hp) Walter Motorlet M601E turboprops* **Max speed:** *311km/h (193mph)* **Service ceiling:** *6320m (20,729ft)* **Max range:** *1380km (857 miles)* **Wing span:** *19.90m (65ft 6in)* **Length:** *14.40m (47ft 4in)* **Height:** *5.80m (19ft 1in)* **Weight:** *6400kg (14,105lb) loaded* **Payload:** *19 passengers*

> **MAJOR VARIANTS**
> A stretched version, the **L-430**, is under development; internal configurations can include commuter, executive, air ambulance and paratroop transport

> **RECOGNITION FEATURES**
> High-mounted straight wing with small tip tanks; deep fuselage with bulged undercarriage fairings amidships; swept tailfin; dihedral tailplane

Pilatus PC-12

ABOVE: *The Pilatus PC-12 commuter aircraft is pitched at markets traditionally served by 'light twins' like the Beech King Air.*

Specification

Crew: *1/2* **Powerplant:** *one 895kW (1200shp) Pratt & Whitney Canada PT6A67B turboprop* **Max speed:** *500km/h (310mph)* **Service ceiling:** *9150m (30,000ft)* **Max range:** *2965km (1841 miles)* **Wing span:** *16.23m (52ft 3in)* **Length:** *14.40m (47ft 3in)* **Height:** *4.27m (14ft)* **Weight:** *4500kg (9920lb) loaded* **Payload:** *9 passengers*

MAJOR VARIANTS
The **PC-12** is offered in standard nine-seat airliner form, in a four-passenger seat/freight combi version and as a six-place corporate transport. A pure freighter model is under consideration.
PC-12 Eagle: military special missions platform, fitted with a ventral reconnaissance pod

---

RECOGNITION FEATURES
Low-mounted straight wing with small winglets; single turboprop engine; T-type tail

---

In October 1989, Pilatus announced that it was developing a new utility, regional feederliner and corporate turboprop in the Beech King Air class, to be called the PC-12. The first of two prototypes flew on 31 May 1991. Most PC-12s built to date have been corporate transport, but recent important regulatory changes in Australia, Brazil, Canada and the USA have cleared single-engined turboprops for airline operations in those countries. This has opened up new potential markets for the PC-12 as a regional airliner, replacing older King Airs and elderly piston twins such as the Navajo Chieftain and Cessna 400 series.

Piper PA-31 Navajo/Chieftain

Since 1964 the Piper PA-31 Navajo Series of light transport aircraft has enjoyed an enviable reputation. At the time of its conception the Navajo was the largest aircraft ever built by Piper into the 'cabin class' market then dominated by Beech and Cessna. The Navajo, powered by twin 224kW (300hp) Lycoming engines, was launched in 1967 and proved less popular than had been anticipated, so in 1969 it was dropped in favour of the PA-31-310, with more powerful engines. This was the first of several versions of the basic airframe, the next being the pressurized six-seat PA-31P Turbo Navajo, which with turbocharged 336kW (450hp) engines was substantially faster than the standard model.

In 1970 Piper converted two standard Navajos into prototypes for the PA-31-310B Navajo B, which featured major avionics and other changes. Deliveries of the Navajo B continued until 1974. Meanwhile, in 1971, Piper had begun development of the Navajo II, which was intended to compete with the Cessna 402 in the commuter airliner market. The Navajo II could accommodate 10 passengers, or six in a luxurious executive layout. Introduction of the new model was delayed

ABOVE: *The Piper Navajo Series of light twin-engined aircraft has proved extremely popular and successful.*

Specification (Turbo Navajo)

Crew: *1* **Powerplant:** *two 231kW (310hp) Lycoming TIO-540-A piston engines* **Max speed:** *418km/h (260mph)* **Service ceiling:** *8000m (26,300ft)* **Max range:** *1800km (1120 miles)* **Wing span:** *12.40m (40ft 8in)* **Length:** *9.94m (32ft 7.5in)* **Height:** *3.96m (13ft)* **Weight:** *2948kg (6500lb)* **Payload:** *6 passengers*

ABOVE: *The Spanish Air Force operates some Navajo aircraft in the communications role.*

when the second prototype and first production aircraft were destroyed in a flood at Lock Haven when the Susquehanna river burst its banks, but the type was eventually launched in September 1972, and was given the name Navajo Chieftain.

In 1982 Piper began development of a successor to the pressurized Navajo. Known as the PA-31P Mojave, it had the fuselage of the PA-31T Cheyenne (itself a turboprop development of the original PA-31P) mated to the wings, engines and tail unit of the PA-31-350 Chieftain. Mojave production ended in 1984 after the 50th aircraft had been built.

MAJOR VARIANTS
PA-31 Navajo: initial production version
PA-31-310: more powerful engines
PA-31P Turbo Navajo: turbocharged engines; pressurized
PA-31-310B: major avionics changes
Navajo Chieftain: new 6–10 passenger model
PA-31P Mojave: new model (see main text)

RECOGNITION FEATURES
Low-mounted straight wing; twin piston engines; swept tailfin; square windows

Raytheon (Beechcraft) 1900

The Beech 1900 traces its ancestry back to the Beech King Air. The most obvious change from the King Air 200 to the 1900C is the substantially lengthened fuselage, more powerful engines, a modified tail with winglets (or taillets), and stabilons on the lower rear fuselage. Development of the 1900 began in 1979, with the 1900C entering into service in 1984. The first ExecLiner corporate transport version was delivered in mid-1985. Military transport, maritime patrol and electronic surveillance versions are also offered.

ABOVE: *A Raytheon 1900 in use with a French commuter airline.*

Specification (Beech 1900D)

Crew: *2* **Powerplant:** *two 955kW (1280shp) P&WC PT6A67D turbo-props* **Max speed:** *533km/h (330mph)* **Service ceiling:** *7625m (25,000ft)* **Max range:** *2778km (1725 miles)* **Wing span:** *17.70m (57ft 11in)* **Length:** *17.60m (57ft 10in)* **Height:** *4.70m (15ft 6in)* **Weight:** *6906kg (15,245lb)* **Payload:** *19 passengers*

MAJOR VARIANTS
Beech 1900C: initial production version
Beech 1900D: substantially deeper fuselage; larger passenger and freight doors and windows; twin ventral strakes and auxiliary horizontal fixed tails (taillets)

RECOGNITION FEATURES
Beech 1900D: low-mounted straight wing; twin turboprops; long fuselage; T-type tail; auxiliary tail surfaces (taillets) on rear fuselage

Raytheon (Beechcraft) King Air

ABOVE: *The Raytheon (Beechcraft) King Air 90 was the first example of this turboprop-powered commuter family.*

Specification (King Air B100)

Crew: *1/2* Powerplant: *two 533kW (715shp) Garrett-AiResearch TPE3231-6-252B turboprops* Max speed: *491km/h (305mph)* Service ceiling: *8870m (29,100ft)* Max range: *2454km (1525 miles)* Wing span: *13.75m (45ft 10.5in)* Length: *11.92m (39ft 11.5in)* Height: *4.60m (15ft 4in)* Weight: *5352kg (11,800lb) loaded* Payload: *8 passengers*

Building on the success of its piston-engined twins, Walter Beech's aircraft company decided in the early 1960s that turboprop powerplants were the way forward. The result was the King Air 90, powered by a pair of PTA-6 turboprops, which resembled the contemporary piston-engined Queen Air except for the engine installation and pressurized cabin. Despite doubts about the marketability of a turboprop business aircraft at that time, the type proved an instant success and customer deliveries began in early 1965. Development of the Series 90 King Air continued with the 1971 Model C90; this in turn was superseded by the Model C90A, which was first flown on 1 September 1983 and became available early in the following year. In May 1969 a stretched version, the King Air 100, made its appearance; this combined the wing, tail unit and engines of the Model 99 airliner with a lengthened Series 90 fuselage. The basic design underwent a major change with the appearance, in 1973, of the Super King Air 200, which featured a T-type tail unit. An improved version, the Super King

Raytheon (Beechcraft) King Air (continued)

Air B200, was introduced in 1981, and the Model 1300 Commuter, announced in January 1988, is a regional airliner version of the B200.

In the face of growing competition from small business jets, Beech has produced what may be the ultimate Super King Air, the Super King Air 350, characterized by its prominent winglets. This variant has

ABOVE: *A Super King Air B200 of the Malaysian Air Force.*

enjoyed phenomenal success, over 300 examples having been sold since it made its first appearance in 1989. The stretched fuselage provides standard seating for eight passengers in a 'double club' cabin arrangement; three more passengers can be accommodated on optional seats at the rear of the cabin.

MAJOR VARIANTS
King Air 90: initial production version
King Air 100: stretched version
King Air 200: T-type tail unit; more powerful engines; increased fuel capacity
Super King Air B200: increased fuel efficiency; increased cabin pressurization
Model 300 Commuter: regional airliner version
Super King Air 350: 8–11 passenger business aircraft; winglets

RECOGNITION FEATURES
Low-mounted straight wing; twin turboprops; five round cabin windows forward of, and one aft of, door on port side of fuselage; **Super King Air 200** has T-type tail

Rockwell Sabreliner

ABOVE: *A Rockwell Sabreliner in service with the US Navy.*

Specification (Series 40)

Crew: *2* **Powerplant:** *two 1495kg (3300lb) Pratt & Whitney JT12A8 turbojets* **Max speed:** *810km/h (503mph)* **Service ceiling:** *13716m (45,000ft)* **Max range:** *3174km (1971 miles)* **Wing span:** *13.61m (44ft 8in)* **Length:** *14.38m (47ft 2in)* **Height:** *5.26m (17ft 3in)* **Weight:** *10,435kg (23,000lb)* **Payload:** *6–10 passengers*

The Sabreliner entered service with the USAF as the T-39A, the first civil aircraft being certificated in April 1963. The Series 40 followed from June 1966 and featured a higher cruising speed and greater internal cabin space. The Series 60 was stretched and is identifiable by its five, rather than three, cabin windows per side. The Series 60A introduced aerodynamic changes over the 60. The Sabreliner 75, meanwhile, is based on the 60 and 60A, but has a deeper fuselage with greater headroom and turbofan engines. The last aircraft was built in 1979, but the aircraft still serves in some numbers.

MAJOR VARIANTS
T-39A: original USAF version
Series 40: increased cruising speed and cabin space
Series 60: stretched and improved version
Sabreliner 75: deeper fuselage; turbofan engines

RECOGNITION FEATURES
Low-mounted swept wing; deep fuselage; twin turbojets mounted on rear fuselage; low-set tailplane

Saab 340

Before 1982, the last airliner built by Saab was the Scandia of 1946, but after nearly 40 years of successful military aircraft design the Swedish company felt that it had a world-beating civil aircraft to offer. The result was the SF (Saab Fairchild) 340A, which first flew on 25 January 1983. Saab saw a considerable market for the 340 in the United States, and they were rewarded with several important sales, including aircraft for the regional networks of American, Eastern, Northwest and Continental. Six leased aircraft served with Bar Harbor Airlines at various locations on the eastern seaboard, but the Saabs were returned when the airline ceased operations in January 1991. The rest of the fleet continued to operate under Continental Express ownership. The Saab 340B (the definitive version) and 340BPlus are operated, or have been operated, by some 40 commuter airlines worldwide.

ABOVE: *The Saab 340 is the first airliner built by the Swedish company for four decades, and has sold well in the US.*

Specification

Crew: *2* **Powerplant:** *two 1395kW (1870shp) General Electric CT7-9B turboprops* **Max speed:** *522km/h (325mph)* **Service ceiling:** *9449m (31,000ft)* **Max range:** *1810km (1125 miles)* **Wing span:** *21.45m (70ft 4in)* **Length:** *19.75m (64ft 8in)* **Height:** *6.89m (22ft 6in)* **Weight:** *12,928kg (28,500lb) loaded* **Payload:** *37 passengers*

MAJOR VARIANTS
340A: initial production version
340B: major production version
340BPlus: cabin and performance improvements

RECOGNITION FEATURES
Low-mounted, straight wing; twin turboprops; swept tailfin with fairing to upper fuselage; dihedral tailplane

Short 330

ABOVE: *A Short 330 of Loganair, Scotland's regional airline.*

Specification

Crew: *2* **Powerplant:** *two Pratt & Whitney Canada PT6A-45R turboprops of 895kW (1200shp) each* **Max speed:** *350km/h (220mph)* **Service ceiling:** *3500m (11,500ft)* **Max range:** *875km (545 miles)* **Wing span:** *22.80m (74ft 9in)* **Length:** *17.7m (58ft)* **Height:** *4.95m (16ft 2in)* **Weight:** *10,400kg (22,930lb) loaded* **Payload:** *30 passengers*

The Short 330 was in the vanguard of the turboprop feederliner revolution, and is still in moderately widespread service as a light freighter in both civil and military use. The Short 330 project was first announced at the September 1974 Farnborough Air Show. The prototype, G-BSBH, had already flown on 22 August under the designation SD3-30, and eight days later had won its first order from Command Airways of Poughkeepsie, New York. The 330 was primarily intended for short-range regional and commuter air routes in the United States, but the aircraft sold well in other countries too.

MAJOR VARIANTS
330-100: initial production version
330-200: increased fuel capacity/range
C-23A Sherpa: military transport version for USAF

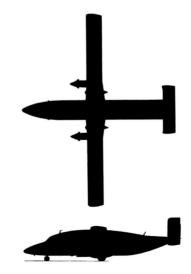

RECOGNITION FEATURES
High-mounted, high aspect ratio, strut-braced straight wing; twin turboprops; twin tailfins; box-like fuselage, tapering upwards towards the tail

Short 360

Developed in the early 1980s by Short Brothers of Belfast, Northern Ireland, the Short 360 owed its existence to the success of the smaller Short 330 and a rising demand from the market, which encouraged the firm to stretch and refine the design in order to produce the even more capable 360. This sturdy design has gained a reputation as a reliable, economical aeroplane which is perfectly suited to short-haul regional operations. The wide, spacious cabin gives the aircraft great passenger appeal, while the square cabin cross-section, large forward door, and low cabin floor height also make it a favourite with freight customers. Since the type's maiden flight in June 1981, the basic 360 design has been improved with the addition of more powerful engines, higher structural weights, and updated cockpit instrumentation. Two Canadian-built PWAC PT6A engines – probably the most successful turboprop engine type in the world – give exceptional reliability and fuel economy.

Just over 160 Short 360s were built, serving with airlines across the globe. The Short 360 can operate comfortably from 1400m (4500ft) long runways, opening up hundreds of European airfields inaccessible by scheduled

ABOVE: The Short 360 is a larger version of the successful 330. Its design has been constantly improved.

Specification

Crew: 2 (plus 1 attendant)
Powerplant: *two 875kW (1173hp) Pratt & Whitney Canada PT6A-67R turboprops* **Max speed:** *393km/h (244mph)* **Service ceiling:** *3048m (10,000ft)* **Max range:** *1697km (1055 miles)* **Wing span:** *22.80m (74ft 9in)* **Length:** *21.60m (70ft 10in)* **Height:** *7.30m (23ft 10in)* **Weight:** *11,793kg (26,000lb) loaded* **Payload:** *32 passengers*

ABOVE: *A Short 360 used by the UK postal services. The aircraft is ideal for point-to-point delivery work.*

flights. Cruise speed is about 370km/h (230 mph), at an altitude of 3048m (10,000ft). The PT6A turboprops are fully ICAO Stage 3 noise compliant, making the 360 one of the quietest turboprop aircraft operating today. The 360 has proved to be a benchmark commuter airliner, and has achieved fair sales outside its primary markets in the United Kingdom and United States. The last Short 360 was built in 1991 and Short Brothers is now a subsidiary of the Canadian Bombardier.

MAJOR VARIANTS
The **Short 360** is available in both passenger and freighter configurations; both are externally similar. The freighter is the **360-300F**.

RECOGNITION FEATURES
Long, narrow, high-mounted, strut-braced wing; two turboprops; upward-curving rear fuselage; swept tailfin. In general configuration the **360** resembles its smaller sibling, the **330**, but the latter is easily distinguished by its twin fins.

Swearingen (Fairchild) Metro

A product of Swearingen Aircraft of San Antonio, Texas – a company well known for its range of Merlin twin-engined executive aircraft – the Metro I prototype made its first flight on 26 August 1969, having been developed originally at the instigation of Fairchild Hiller. Operated by a crew of two, it can be readily converted into a cargo transport, carrying a 2268kg (5000lb) payload. FAA certification for the Metro was granted in June 1970. The first scheduled services using the Metro were begun in 1973 by Commuter Airlines, and by late 1980 nearly 200 had been ordered. Since 1976 the Metro has been one of the major feederliner types in the United States, offering superb safety in a small airliner.

ABOVE: *A Swearingen Metro of Bearskin Airlines, Thunder Bay, Ontario. The Metro first flew in 1969.*

Specification (Metro I)

Crew: *2* **Powerplant:** *two 701kW (940shp) AirResearch TPE 331-3UW-303G turboprops* **Max speed:** *473km/h (294mph)* **Service ceiling:** *8380m (27,500ft)* **Max range:** *805km (500 miles)* **Wingspan:** *14.10m (46ft 3in)* **Length:** *18.09m (59ft 4in)* **Height:** *5.08m (16ft 8in)* **Weight:** *5670kg (12,500lb) loaded* **Payload:** *30 passengers*

MAJOR VARIANTS
Metro II: small portholes replaced by upright rectangular windows
Metro III: increased span and payload

RECOGNITION FEATURES
low-mounted straight wing; twin turboprops; mid-mounted tailplane

Swearingen SJ30

ABOVE: *First flown in 1991, the Swearing SJ30 is now a joint Taiwanese/US operation called Sino Swearingen.*

Specification

Crew: *1* **Powerplant:** *two 860kg (1900lb) William Rolls FJ44-2A turbofans* **Max speed:** *900km/h (560mph)* **Service ceiling:** *14,945m (49,000ft)* **Max range:** *4625km (2875 miles)* **Wing span:** *11.10m (36ft 4in)* **Length:** *12.90m (42ft 7in)* **Height:** *4.20m (13ft 11in)* **Weight:** *5987kg (13,200lb) loaded* **Payload:** *7 passengers*

The SJ30 executive jet was originally developed by Gulfstream as the SA-30 Fanjet Gulfstream, but the company pulled out of the development programme in 1989. The project was rescued by the Jaffe group, and under the designation Swearing/Jaffe SJ30 the aircraft flew for the first time in 1991. The type is now being produced by a joint Taiwanese/US concern, Sino Swearingen, but the programme experienced a setback in April 2003 when an SJ30-2 crashed in rugged terrain north of Del Rio, Texas, during a test flight from San Antonio, killing Sino Swearingen's chief test pilot, Carroll Beeler.

MAJOR VARIANTS
SJ30-2: main production version

RECOGNITION FEATURES
Low-mounted swept wing; twin turbofans mounted on rear fuselage; sharply swept tail surfaces; T-type tail

Yakovlev Yak-40

The Yakovlev Yak-40 (NATO reporting name 'Codling') short-haul commuter airliner was designed from the outset to operate from very rudimentary airstrips and even grass fields. The first production deliveries to Aeroflot began in mid-1968, the 500th example being completed on 15 February 1974. The Yak-40 is still in widespread service, and for many years it was the most widely used airliner on the former Soviet Union's network of internal routes, carrying eight million passengers 173 million kilometres (108 million miles) in its first six years.

ABOVE: *A Yakovlev Yak-40 in the markings of the Serbian Air Force. Six aircraft were delivered to the former Yugoslavia from 1971.*

Specification

Crew: *2* **Powerplant:** *three 1750kg (3858lb) thrust Ivchenko AI-25T turbofans* **Max speed:** *820km/h (510mph)* **Service ceiling:** *11,590m (38,000ft)* **Max range:** *2000km (1242 miles)* **Wing span:** *25.00m (82ft)* **Length:** *20.40m (66ft 9in)* **Height:** *17.00m (55ft 9in)* **Weight:** *10,757kg (35,270lb)* **Payload:** *32 passengers*

MAJOR VARIANTS
Yak-40: main production version
Yak-40D: increased fuel capacity
Yak-40M: stretched version; 40-seat
Yak-40K: cargo-passenger version

RECOGNITION FEATURES
Low-mounted straight wing; three tail-mounted turbofans; swept tailfin with T-type configuration

---

Yakovlev Yak-42

ABOVE: *A Yak-42 in the livery of Aeroflot. The Russian airline no longer operates the type, but it still flies in other parts of the world.*

Specification

Crew: *2/3* **Powerplant:** *three 6400kg (14,110lb) thrust Lotarev D-36 turbofans* **Max speed:** *820km/h (510mph)* **Service ceiling:** *10,000m (32,800ft)* **Max range:** *1850km (1150 miles)* **Wing span:** *34.20m (112ft 2.5in)* **Length:** *36.38m (119ft 4in)* **Height:** *9.83m (32ft 3in)* **Weight:** *52,000kg (114,640lb)* **Payload:** *100–120 passengers*

MAJOR VARIANTS
Yak-42: initial production version
Yak-42B: updated navigation and flight deck
Yak-42D: widely improved version; upgraded avionics; enhanced performance
Yak-42-200: stretched version
Yak-42T: freighter

RECOGNITION FEATURES
Low-mounted swept wing; three tail-mounted turbofans; T-type tail

First flown in 1975, the Yak-42 (NATO reporting name 'Clobber') short-haul airliner entered service with Aeroflot five years later, the intention being that it would replace the Tu-134 on short-haul routes. The Yak-42, like its smaller stablemate the Yak-40, was designed to use restricted airfields with poor surfaces and limited facilities in the remoter areas of the Soviet Union in temperatures ranging from -50°C (-58°F) to +50°C (122°F). It was therefore made independent of airport ground equipment and a heavy-duty undercarriage catered for relatively rough strips. The Yak-42 is no longer used by Aeroflot, but examples are still to be seen flying in Cuba, China and Kazakhstan.

Aermacchi SF-260

First flown in 1964, the Aermacchi (SIAI-Marchetti) SF-260 went on to become one of the world's most successful basic trainers. The initial civil production model was the SF-260A, but in 1974 production switched to the SF-260B with improvements first developed for the military SF-260M, including a stronger undercarriage, a redesigned wing leading edge and a taller fin. A further improved variant was the SF-260C, with increased wing span. The SF-260E and -F are military trainer and light attack variants, while the SF-260TP is a turboprop-powered version for military use.

ABOVE: *An Aermacchi SF-260 of the Alitalia aerobatic team.*

Specification (SF-260E)

Crew: 2 **Powerplant:** *one Textron Lycoming O-540D4A5 piston engine* **Max speed:** *441km/h (274mph)* **Service ceiling:** *5790m (18,996ft)* **Max range:** *1490km (925 miles)* **Wing span:** *8.35m (27ft 4in)* **Length:** *7.10m (23ft 3in)* **Height:** *2.41m (7ft 11in)* **Weight:** *1350kg (2977lb) loaded* **Armament:** *none*

MAJOR VARIANTS
SF-260A: initial production version
SF-260B: strengthened undercarriage; redesigned wing and fin
SF-260M: military version
SF-260C: increased wing span
SF-260E: military trainer
SF-260F: light attack variant
SF-260TP: military version; turboprop powered

RECOGNITION FEATURES
Clean, low-wing monoplane with wingtip tanks; side-by-side cockpit with clear-vision canopy; swept tailfin; long fairing from base of fin to rear of cockpit; retractable undercarriage

Aermacchi (Valmet) M-290TP Redigo

ABOVE: *The Redigo demonstrates its ability to carry a variety of ordnance on its six underwing hardpoints.*

Specification

Crew: *2* **Powerplant:** *one 336kW (450shp) Allison 250B17F turboprop*
Max speed: *352km/h (218mph)*
Service ceiling: *7629m (25,000ft)*
Max range: *1400km (870 miles)*
Wing span: *10.60m (34ft 9in)*
Length: *8.53m (28ft)* **Height:** *3.20m (10ft 6in)* **Weight:** *1350kg (2974lb) loaded* **Armament:** *underwing gun pods, bombs or rockets*

The Aermacchi M.90 is the Italian version of the Finnish Valmet Redigo basic trainer, Aermacchi having bought the production rights in 1996. The type was designed from the outset as a safe and easy platform for primary training, but it can also be used for light attack, having six wing hardpoints for bombs, rockets and machine gun pods. The type is operated by the air arms of Eritrea, Finland and Mexico. A single stretcher or two passengers can be carried in the rear cockpit.

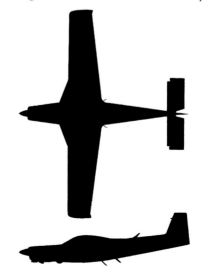

MAJOR VARIANTS
Can be configured as trainer, light transport, coastal patrol, reconnaissance, search-and-rescue and disaster relief.

RECOGNITION FEATURES
Low, straight wing with cranked leading edge at wing root; angular tailfin; side-by-side cockpit; retractable undercarriage

Cessna Model 150/152

Towards the end of World War II, the Cessna Aircraft Company identified a requirement for a reasonably priced two-seat sports and training aircraft and produced the Model 140, a strut-braced high-wing monoplane with a fixed tailwheel landing gear embodying slim main gear legs of spring steel. Powered by a 63kW (85hp) Continental C85-12 engine, the prototype flew on 28 June 1945 and was an immediate success. Together with its economy partner, the Model 120 (which lacked flaps, electric starter and extra side windows) the aircraft sold some 3950 examples in 1946.

In the 1950s, following a slump in the two-seater market, Cessna concentrated on the four-seat single-engined market, but in 1957 the company produced a side-by-side two-seat cabin monoplane with a high wing and fixed tricycle landing gear, the Cessna 142. The designation was soon changed to Model 150, and in 1959, the first year of production,

ABOVE: *Thousands of private pilots the world over have learned to fly in the Cessna 150 since the type was introduced in 1959.*

Specification
(Cessna 152 Aerobat)

Crew: *2* **Powerplant:** *one Avco 82kW (110hp) Lycoming O-235-N2C piston engine* **Max speed:** *200km/h (125mph)* **Service ceiling:** *4480m (14,700ft)* **Max range:** *1160km (720 miles)* **Wing span:** *10.00m (32ft 10in)* **Length:** *7.35m (24ft)* **Height:** *2.60m (8ft 6in)* **Weight:** *726kg (1600lb) loaded*

683 aircraft powered by the 75kW (100hp) Continental O-200A engine were built. By the end of 1963 the company had sold over 2200 Cessna 150s, and the 1964 Model 150D introduced the first major change, namely a cut-down rear fuselage and all-round vision cabin. A swept tail was introduced with the Model 150F and, in 1970, the aerobatic Model 150K Aerobat went into production alongside the standard trainer version. The traditional Cessna spring steel landing gear was replaced by tubular steel on the 1971 Model 150L and then, in 1978, the Continental engine was replaced by the 82kW (110hp) Lycoming O-235-L2C and the aircraft became the Cessna 152, which was also produced in an aerobatic version.

MAJOR VARIANTS
Model 150: redesignated Cessna 142
Model 150D: cut-down rear fuselage; all-round vision cabin
Model 150F: swept tail
Model 150K Aerobat: acrobatic model
Model 150L: modified landing gear
Model 152: new engine

RECOGNITION FEATURES
High wing with square-cut wingtips and bracing struts; swept tailfin; tricycle undercarriage; two-seat cockpit with all-round vision.

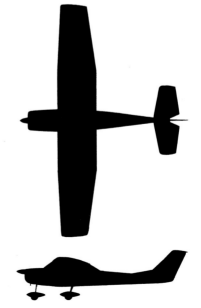

Cessna Model 172

The Cessna Model 172 started life as the Model 170, which first flew in 1947. It featured a larger fuselage than the earlier Model 140 and a more powerful engine, but still employed constant-chord fabric-covered wings. The Model 170A, however, was fitted with a new all-metal wing; this was to become the standard wing design used for virtually all single-engined Cessnas. The Cessna 170B was fitted with large flaps, and in 1956 this variant was fitted with a tricycle undercarriage to become the Cessna 172.

ABOVE: *The four-seat Cessna 172 has become a firm favourite as a touring aircraft.*

Specification

Crew/passengers: *4* **Powerplant:** *one 112kW (150hp) Lycoming O-320-E2D piston engine* **Max speed:** *224km/h (139mph)* **Service ceiling:** *3995m (13,100ft)* **Max range:** *1030km (640 miles)* **Wing span:** *10.90m (35ft 9.5in)* **Length:** *8.20m (26ft 11in)* **Height:** *2.68m (8ft 9.5in)* **Weight:** *1043kg (2300lb)*

MAJOR VARIANTS
Cessna Model 172: standard production model
Cessna F172: aircraft built by Reims Aviation, France
Cessna T-41: military version

RECOGNITION FEATURES
High, strut-braced wing with tapered outer panels; four side windows (two on each side); swept tailfin

Cessna Model 336/337 Skymaster

ABOVE: *The Cessna O-2 was used widely in Vietnam.*

The Cessna Model 336 Skymaster, easily identified by its 'push-pull' engine arrangement, first flew in 1961. Early in 1965, the Model 337 entered production with retractable landing gear. After being equipped with four underwing hardpoints, extra windows for the observer, and military radio, the Model 337 became the Cessna O-2A. A special psychological warfare version, the O-2B, was produced in limited numbers. It used three powerful directional speakers to broadcast messages, and could also perform leaflet drops. The O-2 was retired from USAF service in the 1980s, but a militarized 337, marketed as the Sentry, has been supplied by the CIA to forces in Haiti, Honduras, Nicaragua, and Senegal.

Specification (Model 337)

Crew/passengers: *2 crew; up to 6 passengers* **Powerplant:** *two 157kW (210hp) Continental IO-360-GB piston engines* **Max speed:** *320km/h (199mph)* **Service ceiling:** *8930m (29,300ft)* **Max range:** *2494km (1550 miles)* **Wing span:** *11.63m (38ft 2in)* **Length:** *9.07m (29ft 9in)* **Height:** *2.84m (9ft 4in)* **Weight:** *2013kg (4440lb) loaded* **Armament (O-2A):** *four underwing hardpoints*

MAJOR VARIANTS
Model 336: initial version with fixed landing gear
O-2: military version with fixed landing gear
Model 337: improved version with retractable landing gear
O-2A: military version of Model 337
Cessna O-2B: psychological warfare version

RECOGNITION FEATURES
High wing; twin engines mounted in 'push-pull' configuration in short, deep fuselage nacelle; twin tail booms; twin tailfins; retractable undercarriage

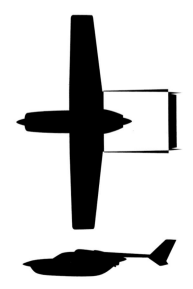

EMBRAER EMB-312 Tucano

ABOVE: *An Embraer Tucano in service with the Brazilian Air Force.*

Development of the high-performance, turboprop EMBRAER EMB-312 Tucano began in 1978, in response to a Brazilian Air Force requirement for a Cessna T-37 replacement. The prototype first flew on 16 August 1980, and deliveries began in September 1983. The Tucano was subsequently licence built in Egypt and the United Kingdom, where it replaced the Jet Provost as the RAF's basic trainer. The British Tucanos are built by Shorts of Belfast, the first Tucano T.Mk 1 for the RAF making its maiden flight on 30 December 1986. The type serves with some 14 air forces.

Specification (EMB-312)

Crew: *2* **Powerplant:** *one 560kW (750hp) Pratt & Whitney PT6A-25C turboprop* **Max speed:** *448km/h (278mph)* **Service ceiling:** *9450m (31,000ft)* **Max range:** *2037km (1265 miles)* **Wing span:** *11.10m (36ft 6in)* **Length:** *9.90m (32ft 4in)* **Height:** *3.40m (11ft 1in)* **Weight:** *2552kg (5625lb)*

MAJOR VARIANTS
S312: version built by Shorts for the RAF
EMB-314 Super Tucano: version with uprated engine
EMB-31M ALX: border patrol and anti-drug-smuggling version with light attack capability

RECOGNITION FEATURES
Low-mounted straight wing, tapered leading and trailing edges; single turboprop; tandem one-piece canopy giving aircraft a hump-backed appearance; low-mounted tailplane

Grob Tutor

ABOVE: *A Grob Tutor operated by Southampton University Air Squadron in the UK.*

Specification

Crew: *2* **Powerplant:** *one 135kW (180hp) Lycoming AE10-360BIF piston engine* **Max speed:** *280km/h (175mph)* **Service ceiling:** *4875m (15,990ft)* **Max range:** *963km (598 miles)* **Wing span:** *10.00m (32ft 8in)* **Length:** *7.59m (24ft 9in)* **Height:** *2.40m (7ft 10in)* **Weight:** *990kg (2182lb) loaded*

Recently introduced into RAF service, the Grob Tutor T1 has replaced the Royal Air Force's ageing fleet of Bulldog primary training aircraft. Ninety of the new aircraft have been supplied for use by University Air Squadrons and Air Experience Flights at 14 locations around the country. Unusually, the aircraft are not owned and maintained by the RAF, but carry civilian registrations and are owned and serviced by private firms. Vosper-Thorneycroft owns and maintains the T1s.

MAJOR VARIANTS
Grob Tutor T1: two-seat trainer; original production version

RECOGNITION FEATURES
Single-engined low-wing monoplane; fixed tricycle undercarriage with small fairing covering the wheels; short nose; large glazed area cabin with two windows each side; tapered wings with square tips; large fin and rudder with oblong tailplane with square tips set at base of fin

---

HAL HPT-32 Deepak

The HAL HPT-32 side-by-side two-seat primary/basic flying trainer aircraft is intended to provide grading and primary instruction, after which pupils switch to the HAL HJT-16 Kiran jet trainer. It has provision for one or two additional seats at the rear of the cabin and also baggage space for secondary liaison and communications roles. The HPT-32 flew for the first time in 1977 and was in production for 10 years, replacing the Indian Air Force's HT-2 basic trainers. The HPT-32 had to be modified considerably before it was finally accepted by the Indian Air Force.

ABOVE: *The HPT-32 Deepak is the Indian Air Force's two-seat primary trainer, with room for one or two additional seats.*

Specification

Crew: *2* **Powerplant:** *one 194kW (260hp) Lycoming AEO-540-D4B5 piston engine* **Max speed:** *281km/h (175mph)* **Service ceiling:** *4270m (14,000ft)* **Max range:** *1400km (869 miles)* **Wing span:** *9.50m (31ft 2in)* **Length:** *7.70m (25ft 4in)* **Height:** *2.90m (9ft 7in)* **Weight:** *1322kg (2915lb) loaded* **Armament:** *up to 255kg (562lb) of light weapons on underwing hardpoints*

MAJOR VARIANTS
HPT-32: main production version

RECOGNITION FEATURES
Straight wing with tapered trailing edge; single engine; fixed tricycle undercarriage; broad tailfin with swept leading edge; side-by-side cockpit

NAMC CJ-6A

ABOVE: *The NAMC CJ-6A, derived from the Yak-18, has appeared in many films pretending to be the World War II Nakajima B6N torpedo-bomber.*

Specification

Crew: *2* **Powerplant:** *one 213kW (285hp) Huosai-6JIA 9-cylinder radial* **Max speed:** *370km/h (230mph)* **Service ceiling:** *5185m (17,000ft)* **Max range:** *724km (450 miles)* **Wing span:** *10.18m (33ft 5in)* **Length:** *8.50m (27ft 10in)* **Height:** *3.20m (10ft 6in)* **Weight:** *1398kg (3086lb) loaded*

MAJOR VARIANTS
CJ-6A: initial production version; unarmed
CJ-6B: armed variant

RECOGNITION FEATURES
Low-mounted straight wing with square-cut tips; radial engine; long tandem cockpit; tailfin raked forward

The NAMC CJ-6A primary trainer is a derivative of the Yakovlev Yak-18. Around 1700 were built, and in recent years many examples have found their way on to the western aviation market. The aircraft is highly prized by private owners as it can be painted to resemble the wartime Japanese Nakajima B6N 'Kate' torpedo-bomber. From the recognition point of view, the CJ-6A differs from the Yak-18 in its redesigned tail-fin, which is raked forward and square cut, whereas the Yak's is rounded.

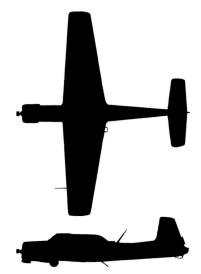

Pilatus PC-7

The Pilatus PC-7 two-seat trainer is based on a 1960s design, the PC-3B, which was powered by a piston engine. In 1967 the P-3B was fitted with a turboprop engine and offered as a military trainer. Orders were slow to materialize, and it was not until 1978 that series production started. After that sales rocketed, and the aircraft was eventually supplied to the air forces of some 20 countries, including Switzerland. Over 500 examples of the PC-7 had been produced by 1998. A modified version, the PC-7 Mk II, was developed for South Africa.

ABOVE: *A Pilatus PC-7 in the insignia of the Guatemala Air Force.*

Specification

Crew: *2* **Powerplant:** *one Pratt & Whitney (Canada) PT6A-25A turboprop* **Max speed:** *412km/h (255mph)* **Service ceiling:** *9755m (31,996ft)* **Max range:** *2260km (1403 miles)* **Wing span:** *10.40m (34ft 1in)* **Length:** *9.80m (32ft 1in)* **Height:** *3.20m (10ft 6in)* **Weight:** *1330kg (2931lb)* **Armament:** *light stores may be carried*

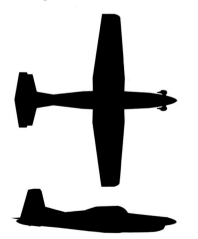

MAJOR VARIANTS
PC-7: initial production version
PC-7 Mk IIM: generally improved variant

RECOGNITION FEATURES
Low-mounted straight wing; tandem cockpit; angular tailfin with fairing to upper fuselage; **Mk II** cockpit is single piece

Pilatus PC-9/AT-6A

ABOVE: *A Pilatus PC-9 of the Royal Australian Air Force.*

Specification (AT-6A)

Crew: 2 **Powerplant:** *one 820kW (1100hp) Pratt & Whitney (Canada) PTA-68 turboprop* **Max speed:** *518km/h (320mph)* **Service ceiling:** *9448m (31,000ft)* **Max range:** *1667km (1035 miles)* **Wing span:** *10.19m (33ft 6in)* **Length:** *10.16m (33ft 5in)* **Height:** *3.23m (10ft 3in)* **Weight:** *2995kg (6500lb) empty*

MAJOR VARIANTS
PC-9: initial production version
PC-9M: major upgrade; improved performance
AT-6A Texan II: USAF trainer licence built by Raytheon

RECOGNITION FEATURES
Similar to **PC-7**, but distinguished by longer tailfin and central cockpit canopy bar

---

A straightforward development of the Pilatus PC-7 Mk II, the PC-9 flew for the first time on 7 May 1984 and has since become one of the world's premier turboprop-powered trainers, being supplied to 12 air forces. The PC-9 is built under licence in Australia by Hawker de Havilland for the RAAF. It is also produced under licence in the USA as the Raytheon AT-6A Texan II and is used to train Joint Primary Pilot Training (JPPT) students, providing the basic skills necessary to progress to one of four training tracks: the Air Force bomber-fighter or the Navy strike track, the Air Force airlift-tanker or Navy maritime track, the Air Force or Navy turboprop track and the Air Force/Navy helicopter track. Instructor pilot training in the T-6A began in 2000, followed by JPPT in October 2001.

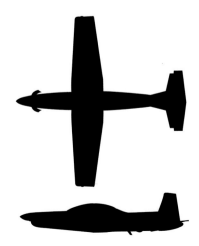

Piper PA-28 Cherokee

The Piper Aircraft Corporation, which had produced the successful Piper Cub Series and the PA-22 TriPacer, saw a window of opportunity in the mid-1950s for a simple all-metal aircraft which would be affordable by thousands of potential customers. The result was the PA-28 Cherokee, which first flew in January 1960 and which was subsequently produced in several different versions, culminating in the Turbo Arrow IV of 1979, featuring a T-type tail.

ABOVE: *The Piper Cherokee has been a firm favourite with flying clubs and private owners for many years.*

Specification (PA-28-161)

Crew: *1* **Powerplant:** *one 119kW (160hp) Lycoming 0-320-A2B piston engine* **Max speed:** *235km/h (146mph)* **Service ceiling:** *3355m (11,000ft)* **Max range:** *1185km (736 miles)* **Wing span:** *10.67m (35ft)* **Length:** *7.25m (23ft 10in)* **Height:** *2.22m (7ft 4in)* **Weight:** *1105kg (2440lb)* **Payload:** *3 passengers*

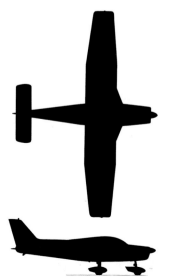

MAJOR VARIANTS
Numerous, some having a retractable undercarriage like the **Cherokee Arrow**, but all basically similar in configuration.

RECOGNITION FEATURES
Low-mounted straight wing; four-seat cabin; single piston engine; fixed landing gear

Piper PA-30 Twin Comanche

ABOVE: *A UK-registered Piper Twin Comanche.*

.

First flown in 1962, the Piper Twin Comanche was developed from the earlier single-engined Comanche, and was the first aircraft of its class to be marketed. The type was a huge success, 2150 examples being built over a nine-year period from 1964. The Twin Comanche has an excellent performance, and during its career it has established a number of speed records over a recognized course. Improvements to the PA-30 resulted in the introduction of the Twin Comanche B in 1965, which featured a stretched fuselage allowing comfortable seating for six. The Turbo Twin Comanche B features turbocharged engines and wingtip tanks. From 1970 onwards the Twin Comanche C featured a slightly higher cruising speed and interior improvements.

Specification

Crew: *1* **Powerplant:** *two 119kW (160hp) Lycoming 10-320B piston engines* **Max speed:** *330km/h (205mph)* **Service ceiling:** *5185m (17,000ft)* **Max range:** *1930km (1200 miles)* **Wing span:** *10.90m (35ft 11in)* **Service ceiling:** *5185m (17,000ft)* **Weight:** *1690kg (3600lb)* **Payload:** *8 passengers*

MAJOR VARIANTS
PA-30: initial production version
Twin Comanche B: stretched fuselage
Twin Comanche C: improved interior and performance

RECOGNITION FEATURES
Low straight wing, cranked inboard of the engines; twin piston engines; low-mounted tailplane; single fin; wingtip tanks (removable)

Raytheon (Beechcraft) Baron

The Beechcraft Baron is one of the most successful twin-piston general aviation families of all time, and is still in great demand today. The original Beech Model 95-55 Baron, first flown in 1960, was a development of the Model 95 Travel Air light twin. In 1964 Beech introduced the B55 Baron, with an extended nose providing 50 per cent more baggage space or room for avionics. It remained in production until 1982. The Baron was procured by various military forces, and in 1965 it was selected as an instrument trainer by the US Army.

ABOVE: *The Beechcraft Baron is one of the most successful of all 'light twins'.*

Specification (Model 58)

Crew: *1* **Powerplant:** *two 224kW (300hp) Teledyne Continental IO-550C piston engines* **Max speed:** *380km/h (236mph)* **Service ceiling:** *6000m (19,685ft)* **Max range:** *2917km (1575 miles)* **Wing span:** *11.50m (37ft 10in)* **Length:** *9.10m (29ft 10in)* **Height:** *3.00m (9ft 9in)* **Weight:** *2313kg (5100lb)* **Payload:** *6 passengers*

> MAJOR VARIANTS
> **Model B55:** major production version
> **Model 56TC Turbo Baron:** turbocharged engines
> **Model 58:** current production version; stretched version of Model 55

> RECOGNITION FEATURES
> Low-mounted straight dihedral wing with leading edge 'kink' between engines and wing root; two piston engines; retractable landing gear; swept tailfin

Raytheon (Beechcraft) Sierra

ABOVE: *The Raytheon (Beechcraft) Sierra incorporates many refinements, including a retractable undercarriage.*

Specification

Crew: *1* **Powerplant:** *one 149kW (200hp) Lycoming IO-360-A2B piston engine* **Max speed:** *274km/h (170mph)* **Service ceiling:** *4572m (15,000ft)* **Max range:** *1271km (789 miles)* **Wing span:** *9.90m (32ft 9in)* **Length:** *7.80m (25ft 9in)* **Height:** *2.50m (8ft 1in)* **Weight:** *1247kg (2750lb)* **Payload:** *4 passengers*

The Beechcraft Sierra was first flown in 1969 as the Musketeer Super R. It differed from its predecessors in that it had a constant-speed propeller as standard and a retractable tricycle-type landing gear. Other refinements included an electrically actuated hydraulic system based on a self-contained unit in the rear fuselage. An emergency valve, sited adjacent to the pilot's feet, allowed selection of the landing gear to free-fall within three seconds. The Sierra's main wheels retract outwards into the wings, and the nosewheel turns through 90 degrees as it retracts rearwards.

MAJOR VARIANTS
Sierra: basic production version

RECOGNITION FEATURES
Low-mounted straight wing; single piston engine; retractable landing gear; four windows on either side of cabin

Raytheon (Beechcraft) T-34 Mentor

First flown in December 1948, the Beechcraft T-34 Mentor was developed from the civilian Beechcraft Bonanza and was built in large numbers, serving with the US services and with many other countries. Variants were the T-34A for the USAF (450), T-34B for the USN and T-34C, which had a PTRA turboprop in place of the earlier Continental piston engine (300 built). Export T-34C-1s could be equipped to carry out light attack missions. This variant was exported to Morocco, Peru, Argentina, Indonesia and Ecuador, all as counter-insurgency aircraft.

ABOVE: *A Raytheon (Beechcraft) T-34B Mentor in service with the US Navy. The type was widely exported.*

Specification (T-34C)

Crew: *2* **Powerplant:** *one 298kW (400hp) Pratt & Whitney PT6A-25 turboprop* **Max speed:** *464km/h (288mph)* **Service ceiling:** *9145m (30,000ft)* **Max range:** *1205km (748 miles)* **Wing span:** *10.16m (33ft 3in)* **Length:** *8.75m (28ft 8in)* **Height:** *3.02m (9ft 7in)* **Weight:** *1978kg (4360lb) loaded*

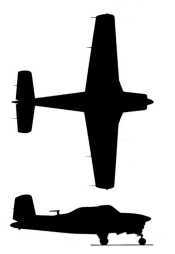

MAJOR VARIANTS
T-354A: USAF version
T-34B: US Navy version
T-34C: engine upgrade

RECOGNITION FEATURES
Low-mounted straight wing, leading edge cranked at wing root; single engine; large tandem cockpit; tall tailfin; small strake on fuselage underside beneath tail

Raytheon (Beechcraft) V35 Bonanza

ABOVE: *Early models of the Beechcraft Bonanza are easily identifiable by their butterfly tail.*

Specification (V35B)

Crew: *1* **Powerplant:** *one 153kW (205hp) Continental E18511 piston engine* **Max speed:** *306km/h (190mph)* **Service ceiling:** *4575m (15,000ft)* **Max range:** *1955km (1214 miles)* **Wing span:** *10.20m (33ft 6in)* **Length:** *8.10m (26ft 5in)* **Height:** *2.30m (7ft 7in)* **Weight:** *1236kg (2725lb) loaded* **Payload:** *4 passengers*

Beech's Model 35 Bonanza was destined to remain in production for 37 years, by which time 10,403 aircraft had been built before production switched to the Model 36 Bonanza and Model 33 Debonair/Bonanza, which had a conventional tail. The definitive V35 was introduced in 1970 as the V-35B, also available in turbocharged form as the V35B-TC. A number of companies have offered conversions of standard Bonanzas, such as Colemill's Starfire Bonanza with a 224kW (300hp) engine, and the radical Fleet Super-V incorporating twin wing-mounted engines.

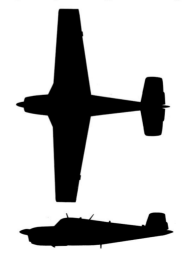

MAJOR VARIANTS
Numerous variants, most externally similar although often re-engined
V-35B: major production version
V-35BTC: turbocharged version
S-35: six seats; redesigned cabin

RECOGNITION FEATURES
Low-mounted straight wing; single piston engine; butterfly tail; large cabin; retractable undercarriage

Robin DR400

First flown in 1972, the Robin DR400 has been constantly developed since its conception. The first variants were designed as family tourers, seating two adults and two children, but later versions were capable of seating up to five adults. One variant, the DR400 Remo is used as a glider tug; the name 'Remo' is an abbreviation of 'Remorquer' which is French for 'tug'.

ABOVE: *Two very neat French examples of the Robin DR400.*

Specification (DR400 Standard)

Crew: 1 **Powerplant:** *one 133kW (178hp) Avco Lycoming O-360A piston engine* **Max speed:** *429km/h (267mph)* **Service ceiling:** *4270m (14,000ft)* **Max range:** *1450km (900 miles)* **Wing span:** *8.70m (29ft 7in)* **Length:** *6.90m (22ft 10in)* **Height:** *2.20m (7ft 3in)* **Weight:** *1100kg (2425lb)* **Payload:** *4 passengers*

MAJOR VARIANTS
DR400: standard production version
DR400 Cadet: light trainer
DR400 Remo: glider tug variant

RECOGNITION FEATURES
Low-mounted straight wing with dihedral outer wing panels; spatted tricycle undercarriage; single piston engine

Robin HR100

ABOVE: *The Robin HR100 in French Navy use as a trainer.*

Specification (HR100)

Crew: *1* **Powerplant:** *one 134kW (180hp) Lycoming IO-540-D4A5 piston engine* **Max speed:** *288km/h (186mph)* **Service ceiling:** *3965m (13,000ft)* **Max range:** *2011km (1250 miles)* **Wing span:** *10.00m (32ft 10in)* **Length:** *7.39m (24ft 3in)* **Height:** *2.28m (7ft 6.5in)* **Weight:** *1398kg (3086lb)* **Payload:** *3 passengers*

First flown in 1971, the Robin HR100 is a five-seat all-metal touring aircraft, and was the first all-metal type to be developed by Avions Pierre Robin (the former Centre Est Aéronautique). The first of five prototypes flew on 3 April 1969 and series production began in 1971.

> MAJOR VARIANTS
> Re-engined variants:
> **HR100-200B Royal; HR100-210 Safari; HR100-250TR President; HR100-285TR Tiara; R1180T Aiglon**

> RECOGNITION FEATURES
> **HR100-250:** low-mounted, broad, straight wing with no aper; single piston engine; spatted tricycle under-carriage; slight sweep on tailfin

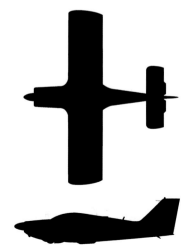

Robin HR200

First flown in 1971, the Robin HR200 two-seat light training aircraft was not particularly successful to begin with. It first flew in 1971 and was taken out of production only five years later. In 1992, however, the production line was re-opened and the type has since shown a healthy sales record, many being exported to the United States, Canada and Australia.

ABOVE: Sales of the HR200 have improved in recent years.

Specification (HR200 Acrobin)

Crew: *2* **Powerplant:** *one 119kW (160hp) Lycoming O-320D piston engine* **Max speed:** *177km/h (110mph)* **Service ceiling:** *3965m (13,000ft)* **Max range:** *1050km (685 miles)* **Wing span:** *8.30m (27ft 4in)* **Length:** *6.60m (21ft 9in)* **Height:** *1.90m (6ft 4in)* **Weight:** *725kg (1600lb) loaded*

MAJOR VARIANTS
HR200-120: major early production version
R2100 and 2100A: larger tail
R2160: modified aerobatic aircraft
R2160M: militarized version

RECOGNITION FEATURES
Low-mounted, straight, broad wing with no taper; single engine; large bubble canopy; tricycle undercarriage; swept tailfin

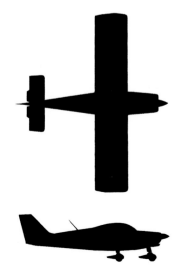

Slingsby T-67/T-3

ABOVE: *Two Slingsby T67 Firefly aircraft of the Royal Hong Kong Auxiliary Air Force, which disbanded in 1993.*

Specification (T-3A)

Crew: *2* **Powerplant:** *one 194kW (260hp) Textron Lycoming Ltd AEIO-540-D4A5 engine* **Max speed:** *249km/h (155mph)* **Service ceiling:** *5790m (19,000ft)* **Max range:** *566km (352 miles)* **Wing span:** *10.60m (34ft 9in)* **Length:** *7.50m (24ft 9in)* **Height:** *2.30m (7ft 9in)* **Weight:** *1159kg (2550lb)*

MAJOR VARIANTS
T-67C: basic production version
T-67M: military variant
T-3A: updated USAF version

RECOGNITION FEATURES
Low-mounted, long straight wing; single piston engine; side-by-side cockpit; slim rear fuselage

The T-3A is the newest version of Slingsby Aviation's T-67 Firefly line of military training aircraft. The prototype began flying in the summer of 1991, and the US Air Force accepted delivery in February 1994. Of the total fleet of 110 T-3s which originally cost $32 million, 57 were stationed with the Air Force Academy's 557th Flying Training Squadron in Colorado Springs, with another 53 with the 3rd Flying Training Squadron in Hondo, Texas. Final assembly of the British-made T-3 was done in Hondo by Northrop Grumman. The USAF's T-3 fleet was grounded in the late 1990s following constant technical trouble, but the T-67 is operated as a primary trainer by a number of other air forces.

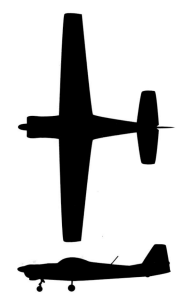

Socata TB-30 Epsilon

The Socata TB-30 Epsilon two-seat trainer flew for the first time on 22 December 1979. It was designed from the outset to create a cost-effective training process for French Air Force student pilots and navigators. The French air force took delivery of most of the 174 examples produced, but the type also serves with the air forces of Portugal and Togo. Production ceased in 1989. The Togolese Air Force operates its aircraft in the counter-insurgency role.

ABOVE: *The Socata Epsilon was designed with economy in mind.*

Specification

Crew: *2* **Powerplant:** *one 246kW (330hp) Textron Lycoming AEIO-54L1B5D piston engine* **Max speed:** *530km/h (236mph)* **Service ceiling:** *6710m (22,000ft)* **Endurance:** *3 hrs 45 mins* **Wing span:** *7.90m (25ft 11in)* **Length:** *7.60m (24ft 10in)* **Height:** *2.7m (8ft 8in)* **Weight:** *1250kg (2755lb)* **Armament:** *480kg (1056lb) of offensive stores on underwing hardpoints*

MAJOR VARIANTS
TB-30: basic production version; armed and unarmed configurations

---

RECOGNITION FEATURES
Low-mounted, straight wing; long fuselage, tapering sharply towards tail; swept tailfin; strake under rear fuselage; large tandem cockpit

Sukhoi Su-26

ABOVE: *The Sukhoi Su-26 has become one of the world's premier aerobatic aircraft, and is widely used for competition flying.*

Specification (Su-26)

Crew: *1* **Powerplant:** *one Vedeneyev M-14P piston engine* **Max speed:** *450km/h (279mph)* **Service ceiling:** *not applicable* **Range:** *800km (500 miles)* **Wing span:** *7.80m (25ft 7in)* **Length:** *6.80m (22ft 5in)* **Height:** *2.80m (9ft 1in)* **Weight:** *835kg (1840lb)*

A product of the famous Pavel Sukhoi design bureau, the Su-26 was intended to be a breakthrough in the design of aerobatic light aircraft, as it was constructed of composite materials. The prototype flew on 30 June 1984. It is widely used by aerobatic exponents throughout the world. The Su-29 is a two-seat version, distinguished from the Su-26 by its larger cockpit and by the fact that it has a greater wing span and length. The pilot's seat in the Su-26 is inclined at 45 degrees to counter the effects of the 'g' forces.

MAJOR VARIANTS
Su-26: basic production version
Su-29: two-seat version

RECOGNITION FEATURES
Mid-mounted straight wing with tapered trailing edge; large radial engine; fixed tailwheel undercarriage with distinctive curved mainwheel struts; bubble canopy

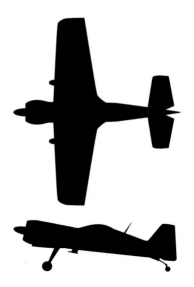

Index

Index

PICTURE CREDITS
All images courtesy of Aerospace/Art-tech except for the following:
Cody Images: 7, 247, 262, 263, 277
Austin J. Brown/aviationpictures.com: 72, 134, 192, 218, 269, 275, 282
Patrick Laureau: 111
aviation-images.com: 110